ADAM SMITH AND THE CHARACTER OF VIRTUE

Recent years have witnessed a renewed debate over the costs at which the benefits of free markets have been bought. This book revisits the moral and political philosophy of Adam Smith, capitalism's founding father, to recover his understanding of the morals of the market age. In so doing it illuminates a crucial albeit overlooked side of Smith's project: his diagnosis of the ethical ills of commercial societies and the remedy he advanced to cure them. Focusing on Smith's analysis of the psychological and social ills endemic to commercial society – anxiety and restlessness, inauthenticity and mediocrity, alienation and individualism – it argues that Smith sought to combat corruption by cultivating the virtues of prudence, magnanimity, and beneficence. The result constitutes a new morality for modernity, at once a synthesis of commercial, classical, and Christian virtues and a normative response to one of the most pressing political problems of Smith's day and ours.

Ryan Patrick Hanley is Assistant Professor of Political Science at Marquette University. His research in the history of political philosophy has appeared in the *American Political Science Review*, the *American Journal of Political Science*, the *Review of Politics*, *History of Political Thought*, the *European Journal of Political Theory*, and other academic journals and edited volumes. He is also the editor of the forthcoming Penguin Classics edition of Adam Smith's *Theory of Moral Sentiments*, featuring an introduction by Amartya Sen, and a co-editor, with Darrin McMahon, of *The Enlightenment: Critical Concepts in History*.

ADAM SMITH AND THE CHARACTER OF VIRTUE

RYAN PATRICK HANLEY

Marquette University

 CAMBRIDGE
UNIVERSITY PRESS

CAMBRIDGE UNIVERSITY PRESS
Cambridge, New York, Melbourne, Madrid, Cape Town, Singapore, São Paulo, Delhi

Cambridge University Press
32 Avenue of the Americas, New York, NY 10013-2473, USA

www.cambridge.org
Information on this title: www.cambridge.org/9780521449298

First published 2009

Printed in the United States of America

A catalog record for this publication is available from the British Library.

Library of Congress Cataloging in Publication data
Hanley, Ryan Patrick, 1974–
Adam Smith and the character of virtue / Ryan Patrick Hanley.
p.   cm.
Includes bibliographical references and index.
ISBN 978-0-521-44929-8 (hardback : alk. paper)
1. Smith, Adam, 1723–1790.   2. Virtue.
3. Ethics, Modern – 18th century.   I. Title.
B1545.Z7H36   2009
179′.9–dc22   2009006836

ISBN   978-0-521-44929-8 hardback

for Ralph Lerner

Il est nécessaire que tous ceux qui s'intéressent à l'avenir des sociétés démocratiques s'unissent, et que tous, de concert, fassent de continuels efforts pour répandre dans le sein de ces sociétés le goût de l'infini, le sentiment du grand et l'amour des plaisirs immatériels.

— Alexis de Tocqueville

CONTENTS

PREFACE

This book addresses three questions. One question is scholarly: namely, how ought we to account for the revisions that Smith made to the sixth edition of *The Theory of Moral Sentiments*? This scholarly question is itself animated by a political question: namely, what role should virtue play in modern commercial societies, and specifically, can virtue, properly conceived, enable us to enjoy the material advantages of commerce while minimizing commerce's most deleterious potential consequences? Finally, this political question, in turn, is motivated by a personal question: namely, what insight might Smith's account of virtue provide to citizens of commercial societies concerned with living the best life possible? In addressing these three questions, this book aspires to speak to three audiences: first, historians of eighteenth-century political thought interested in Smith's self-conception as a moral philosopher–turned-economist-turned-moralist again; second, social and political theorists engaged in the debate over the virtues requisite for the sustenance of commercial societies and the management of globalizing capitalism; and third, philosophers and psychologists and others both inside and outside the academy interested in the question of the happiest and best individual life and its role in promoting the continued happiness and flourishing of communities and social orders.

Readers – Smith specialists or otherwise – who find themselves following such or similar paths are always very welcome to write me directly if they would like to pursue further any of the positions taken or themes discussed in this book: ryan.hanley@marquette.edu.

ACKNOWLEDGMENTS

Writing this book (my first) taught me at least three Smithean lessons. The first is that I too stand "at all times in need of the cooperation and assistance of great multitudes" (WN I.ii.2). I owe my education to the labors of many excellent teachers, especially Alan Kors and Will Harris, who introduced me to the Enlightenment as an undergraduate, and Leon Kass and Pierre Manent, whose generous contributions as readers of my dissertation helped to lay the foundations of the present work. Graduate study in the University of Chicago's Committee on Social Thought was a great privilege, and at Chicago I was very fortunate to have been able to study Smith alongside several friends from whom I then learned and still now learn a great deal, including Fredrik Albritton-Jonsson, Lauren Brubaker, Chad Flanders, Fonna Forman-Barzilai, and Eric Schliesser. A postdoctoral fellowship at Yale's Whitney Humanities Center allowed me to continue my research, and at Yale I benefited greatly from the company and counsel of Mark Jurdjevic, Norma Thompson, and the late Robert Wokler. I also owe much to two other institutions. The Liberty Fund has enabled me to continue my study of Smith in various colloquia, and the International Adam Smith Society, during my tenure as its secretary-treasurer, afforded me a window into the world of Smith scholarship. I am extremely grateful to its organizers, including Viv Brown, Hank Clark, Doug Den Uyl, Sam Fleischacker, Charles Griswold, Knud Haakonssen, and Jim Otteson, for extending that opportunity to me and for supporting my work with IASS – and for teaching me so much about Smith through their own writings. I'm also deeply indebted to many friends and colleagues for generously sharing with me their insights on the themes at the heart of this work, as well as, in many instances, sharing their thoughts on my treatments of them. None of them deserve to be implicated in this work's faults, but I would be remiss were I not to thank especially Chris Berry, Richard Boyd, John Danford, Patrick Deneen, Darrell Dobbs, Michael Frazer, Louis Hunt,

Pam Jensen, Chris Kelly, Fr. Tim Kitzke, Peter McNamara, Fred Miller, Leon Montes, Jerry Muller, Patricia Nordeen, Clifford Orwin, Maria Paganelli, Nick Phillipson, Jennifer Pitts, Dennis Rasmussen, Diana Schaub, Claudia Schmidt, John Scott, Rick Sher, Steven Smith, Eduardo Velásquez, and Chris Wolfe. I'm also indebted to Lew Bateman and Eric Crahan at Cambridge University Press for bringing this ship to port, and to the Press's two reviewers, whose generous and extensive reports were model pieces of academic criticism.

A second lesson concerns the "duties of gratitude" that Smith reminds us are at all times due to our benefactors (TMS III.6.9). I am very grateful to the Institute for Humane Studies and the Mellon, Earhart, Bradley, and Olin Foundations for grants that supported my graduate education. I owe particularly great debts to the Mellon Foundation for the postdoctoral fellowship that enabled me to begin this book in earnest, and to the National Endowment for the Humanities for a fellowship instrumental to my completing it. In a related vein I am grateful to my university and department for five outstanding assistants – John LeJeune, Mark O'Brien, Christy Lennon, Adrian Zink, and Patty Rodda – whose efforts were invaluable. I am grateful also to the publishers who have allowed work first appearing in their pages to reappear here. Earlier versions of parts of Chapters 1, 3, 4, and 5 first appeared as "Commerce and Corruption: Rousseau's Diagnosis and Adam Smith's Cure," *European Journal of Political Theory* 7 (2008): 137–58 (Sage Publications); and earlier versions of portions of Chapters 2, 3, 4, and 6 first appeared in "Adam Smith, Aristotle and Virtue Ethics," in *New Voices on Adam Smith*, ed. Leonidas Montes and Eric Schliesser (London: Routledge, 2006), 17–39. (It perhaps bears mentioning that the process of redistributing a single article across four chapters on two distinct occasions did much to further my sympathetic identification with Smith's lament that he was "a slow a very slow workman, who do and undo everything I write at least half a dozen of times before I can be tolerably pleased with it" (CAS 276)). And the epigraph, drawn from II.ii.15 of Tocqueville's *De la démocratie en Amérique* (copyright Librairie Philosophique J. Vrin, 1990), appears here by kind permission of the publisher.

Finally, I owe debts of a much different and deeper sort to my family. The labors of my mother and father made my education possible, their example led me to love virtue in the first place, and their love and support sustained me in my execution of this project. The tremendous gifts they have given me inspire me to strive to do the same for the only people who have lived with this project as much as or more than they: my sister, my daughter, and my wife. Their love continually reaffirms how great indeed is the happiness that such a love brings, and my love for them compels me to hope these years spent in Smith's company have made me a better brother and father and husband (TMS III.2.1).

The greatest blessing of my academic life is to have been a student of Ralph Lerner. My gratitude to him is eclipsed only by my regret that I have nothing better than this book to give him in return. A student of the character of virtue could have wished for no better teacher.

ABBREVIATIONS

Citations to Smith's works are to the Glasgow edition published in hardcover by Oxford and paperback by the Liberty Fund. Passages are referenced using the Glasgow edition's standard system of paragraph numbering (with the exception of references to the correspondence; these are indicated by letter number) and take the following abbreviations. Spelling and capitalization (but not punctuation) have been modernized throughout.

CAS   *Correspondence of Adam Smith*, ed. E. C. Mossner and I. S. Ross (Indianapolis: Liberty Fund, 1987).

ED   "Early Draft of Part of *The Wealth of Nations*," in LJ [written c. 1763].

EPS   *Essays on Philosophical Subjects*, ed. W. P. D. Wightman and J. C. Bryce (Indianapolis: Liberty Fund, 1982) [first edition published 1795].

HA   "The Principles Which Lead and Direct Philosophical Enquiries; Illustrated by the History of Astronomy," in *EPS* [written c. 1752–1758].

HALM   "The Principles Which Lead and Direct Philosophical Enquiries; Illustrated by the History of the Ancient Logic and Metaphysics," in *EPS* [date unknown].

HAP   "The Principles Which Lead and Direct Philosophical Enquiries; Illustrated by the History of the Ancient Physics," in *EPS* [date unknown].

LER   "A Letter to the Authors of the *Edinburgh Review*," in *EPS* [published 1756].

LJ   *Lectures on Jurisprudence*, ed. R. L. Meek, D. D. Raphael, and P. G. Stein (Indianapolis: Liberty Fund, 1982) [delivered c. 1762–1764; LJA = "Report of 1762–1763" and LJB = "Report dated 1766"].

LRBL   *Lectures on Rhetoric and Belles Lettres*, ed. J. C. Bryce (Indianapolis: Liberty Fund, 1985) [delivered c. 1762–1763].

Senses   "Of the External Senses," in *EPS* [date unknown].

TMS   *The Theory of Moral Sentiments*, ed. D. D. Raphael and A. L. Macfie (Indianapolis: Liberty Fund, 1982) [first edition published 1759; sixth edition published 1790].

WN   *An Inquiry into the Nature and Causes of the Wealth of Nations*, ed. R. H. Campbell, A. S. Skinner, and W. B. Todd (Indianapolis: Liberty Fund, 1981) [first edition published 1776].

INTRODUCTION

We live in strange times. Depending on where one looks, the student of capitalist society can discover good reasons for either hope or despair. Even before the most recent global financial crisis, partisans of the latter view were particularly vocal. The titles of two recent books in economics tell much of the contemporary story: warning us of "the moral consequences of economic growth," they caution us that we stand in the midst of a "battle for the soul of capitalism."[1] Part of this concern emerges from an ever-growing awareness that our capitalist culture has recently entered a new stage. This "new capitalism," as it has come to be called, has been criticized on a number of fronts, including its effects on labor, on the corporation, and on political identity.[2] But its most powerful critics have focused on the effects of consumerism and materialism on human well-being. It is a concern that has united a strange set of allies, from postmodernists to paleo-conservatives, from Pope Benedict to Baudrillard, from Lyotard to Leo Strauss.[3] Indeed across the political and the philosophical spectra, an unexpected consensus has

---

[1] Benjamin Friedman, *The Moral Consequences of Economic Growth* (New York: Knopf, 2005); John C. Bogle, *The Battle for the Soul of Capitalism* (New Haven, CT: Yale University Press, 2005).

[2] On labor, see Richard Sennett, *The Corrosion of Character: The Personal Consequences of Work in the New Capitalism* (New York: Norton, 1998) and *The Culture of the New Capitalism* (New Haven, CT: Yale University Press, 2006); on the corporation, see Daniel Yankelovich, *Profit with Honor: The New Stage of Market Capitalism* (New Haven, CT: Yale University Press, 2006); on the corporation and identity, see Luc Boltanski and Eve Chiapello, *The New Spirit of Capitalism*, tr. Gregory Elliot (London: Verso, 2005); and on religion, see William E. Connolly's opening chapter, "The Spirit of Capitalism," in his *Capitalism and Christianity, American Style* (Durham, NC: Duke University Press, 2008), 1–16.

[3] For the postmodern critique, see especially Jean Baudrillard, *The Consumer Society: Myths and Structures* (Thousand Oaks, CA: Sage, 1998); Jean Lyotard, *The Postmodern Condition* (Minneapolis, MN: University of Minnesota Press, 1984); and Fredric Jameson, *Postmodernism, Or, The Cultural Logic of Late Capitalism* (Durham, NC: Duke University Press, 1991). For critiques from another side of the spectrum, see Leo Strauss, *Natural Right and*

emerged over the fact that the moral psychologies and political orders to which consumerism and materialism have given rise have eviscerated the human psyche. And this is hardly a concern limited to "humanists"; social scientists – from psychologists to sociologists to political scientists – have all attested to these dangers as well.[4] But what should we make of this strange consensus? At the very least, we can provisionally conclude that a strikingly widespread conception exists today that capitalism has been detrimental to the human person and that the status of human life in the new capitalism is (to mix metaphors) fit only for last men trapped in iron cages.

But one wonders: are things really as bad as all that? However widespread, the view just described is only one of at least two. Alongside that pessimistic view, a more hopeful perspective is also now emerging. Its most prominent manifestation is the recent boom in popular studies of happiness. A cynic might write this explosion off as merely a consequence of the crisis in capitalism itself; the product of that crisis is, after all, those who claim to have "invented happiness," and one might uncharitably – but perhaps not unfairly – be tempted to dismiss their rediscovery of their invention as little more than a resuscitation of the narcissism and navel-gazing that distinguish the last men.[5] But doing so would miss the forest for the trees. Many of these happiness studies take as their departure point the well-known gap between happiness and wealth accumulation, and in so doing they reflect a familiar but now urgent longing for a happiness more substantial than that afforded by capitalist success. Other recent studies look even further and seek to

History (Chicago: University of Chicago Press, 1953), 248–51; Irving Kristol, "Capitalism, Socialism, and Nihilism," in *Neoconservatism: The Autobiography of an Idea* (New York: Free Press, 1995); Alasdair MacIntyre, *After Virtue*, 2nd ed. (Notre Dame: University of Notre Dame Press, 1984); cf. Pope Benedict XVI's Angelus delivered at Castel Gandolfo, 23 September 2007; and as Joseph Cardinal Ratzinger, "Church and Economy: Responsibility for the Future of the World Economy," *Communio* 13 (1986): 199–204.

[4] In psychology, see Tim Kasser, "Materialism and Its Alternatives," in *A Life Worth Living: Contributions to Positive Psychology*, ed. Mihaly Csikszentmihalyi and Isabella Selega Csikszentmihalyi (Oxford: Oxford University Press, 2006), 200–14; in political science, see Robert E. Lane, *The Loss of Happiness in Market Democracies* (New Haven, CT: Yale University Press, 2000); in social and political theory, see William A. Galston, "The Effect of Modern Markets on Civic Life," in *The Practice of Liberal Pluralism* (Cambridge: Cambridge University Press, 2005), 128–47; and Benjamin R. Barber, *Consumed: How Markets Corrupt Children, Infantilize Adults, and Swallow Citizens Whole* (New York: Norton, 2007). Jerry Z. Muller provides an excellent introduction to and overview of the intellectual history of anticapitalist debates in *The Mind and the Market: Capitalism in Modern European Thought* (New York: Knopf, 2002), 3–19.

[5] Nietzsche, *Thus Spoke Zarathustra* ("Zarathustra's Prologue," sec. 5).

defend and indeed revivify a reverence and longing for even more elevated states of human flourishing, whether understood as "nobility of spirit" or "greatness."[6] All such studies reflect the influence of a growing academic inquiry into the proper understanding of human flourishing, or virtue – an inquiry as diverse as that of the pessimists profiled earlier. Uniting many of these inquiries is the conscious and hopeful attempt to remedy capitalism's iniquities. In my field, the history of political philosophy, this turn was largely inspired by scholars who sought to recover a "republican" or "civic humanist" virtue-centered tradition of political thought as an alternative to procedural liberalism.[7] Yet these concerns were hardly limited to liberalism's critics, for in time the recovery of virtue became a primary interest of political theorists within the liberal tradition as well.[8] And these debates are no longer internal to political theory, as an interest in the necessary conditions and nature of human flourishing is now the focus of philosophers who propose "virtue ethics" or "ethics of care" as alternatives to utilitarian and deontological ethics.[9] So too psychology has a vibrant interest now in both "emotional intelligence," focusing on the role of sentiments in shaping cognitive states, and "positive psychology," which focuses on the place of

---

[6] See, e.g., Rob Rieman, *Nobility of Spirit: A Forgotten Ideal*, trans. Marjolijn de Jager (New Haven, CT: Yale University Press, 2008); Robert Faulkner, *The Case for Greatness: Honorable Ambition and Its Critics* (New Haven, CT: Yale University Press, 2007).

[7] This literature is well known; important contributions in political theory include Michael J. Sandel, *Democracy's Discontent: America in Search of a Public Philosophy* (Cambridge, MA: Belknap Press, 1996), and Philip Pettit, *Republicanism: A Theory of Freedom and Government* (Oxford: Clarendon Press, 1997); important contributions in the history of ideas include Quentin Skinner, *Liberty Before Liberalism* (Cambridge: Cambridge University Press, 1998), and J. G. A. Pocock, *Virtue, Commerce, and History: Essays on Political Thought and History, Chiefly in the Eighteenth Century* (Cambridge: Cambridge University Press, 1985).

[8] See especially Galston, "Liberal Virtues and the Formation of Civic Character," in *Seedbeds of Virtue*, ed. Mary Ann Glendon and David Blankenhorn (Lanham, MD: Madison, 1995), 35–60; Stephen Macedo, *Liberal Virtues* (Oxford: Clarendon Press, 1990); Peter Berkowitz, *Virtue and the Making of Modern Liberalism* (Princeton: Princeton University Press, 1999); and the essays in John W. Chapman and Galston, eds., *NOMOS XXXIV: Virtue* (New York: New York University Press, 1992). An excellent guide to these debates which helpfully brings out the tension between the liberal commitment to justice and the love of the noble or good is provided in Susan D. Collins, *Aristotle and the Rediscovery of Citizenship* (Cambridge: Cambridge University Press, 2006), 6–41.

[9] I deal extensively with virtue ethics in Chapter 2. For an important overview of virtue ethics, see especially Roger Crisp and Michael Slote, eds., *Virtue Ethics* (Oxford: Oxford University Press, 1997). On the ethics of care, see especially Virginia Held, "The Ethics of Care," in *The Oxford Handbook of Ethical Theory*, ed. David Copp (Oxford: Oxford University Press, 2006).

"character strengths and virtues" in the good life, as alternatives to the traditional focus on diagnosing and treating psychopathology.[10]

An explanation of why both capitalism's critics and virtue's champions have grown so rapidly over the past two decades lies beyond the scope of this book. It might be best to limit ourselves to the conjecture that the optimism of the latter camp is perhaps best understood as a response to the pessimism of the former; a renewed interest in our capacity to maximize subjective happiness would hardly be an unexpected consequence of a sense of anomie, isolation, and impotence in the face of seemingly inexorable forces. But leaving to sociologists of knowledge the question of why these two literatures have emerged in tandem, my aim in this book is to explain how their substances are mutually illuminative. In particular, my goal is to explain how a particular understanding of virtue might offer a remedy for specific ills diagnosed by capitalism's critics past and present.

The subject for my development of this claim is the moral philosophy of Adam Smith. For many years, rightly or wrongly, Smith has been famous as a founding father of capitalism. In recent decades, at least in academic circles, he has also emerged as one of capitalism's earliest and most trenchant critics; as several recent works have noted, Smith himself anticipated several of the ills that capitalism's critics continue to insist upon today.[11] But what has not yet been sufficiently emphasized is that Smith in his own name set forth a sustained and developed remedy for the ills he diagnosed.[12] The

---

[10] On emotional intelligence, see especially Daisy D. Grewal and Peter Salovey, "Benefits of Emotional Intelligence," in *Life Worth Living*, ed. Csikszentmihalyi and Csikszentmihalyi, 104–19. On positive psychology and the virtues, see especially Christopher Peterson and Martin E. P. Seligman, *Character Strengths and Virtues: A Handbook and Classification* (Oxford: Oxford University Press, 2004).

[11] Important recent contributions to the debate over Smith's awareness of commerce's deleterious effects and how this awareness inclined him toward either pessimism or optimism include James E. Alvey, *Adam Smith: Optimist or Pessimist? A New Problem Concerning the Basis of Commercial Society* (Aldershot: Ashgate, 2003); Jerry Evensky, *Adam Smith's Moral Philosophy: A Historical and Contemporary Perspective on Markets, Law, Ethics, and Culture* (Cambridge: Cambridge University Press, 2005); Lisa Hill, "Adam Smith and the Theme of Corruption," *Review of Politics* 68 (2006): 636–62; and Dennis Rasmussen, *The Problems and Promise of Commercial Society: Adam Smith's Response to Rousseau* (University Park, PA: Penn State University Press, 2008). I engage each of these at greater length in what follows. My understanding of optimism has also been helpfully shaped by engagement with Joshua Foa Dienstag, *Pessimism: Philosophy, Ethic, Spirit* (Princeton: Princeton University Press, 2006).

[12] Within the Smith literature, the most important exception to this rule is Charles L. Griswold, Jr., *Adam Smith and the Virtues of Enlightenment* (Cambridge: Cambridge University Press, 1999). Griswold's book presents itself, like the present work, as in part a study of "Smith's diagnosis of and therapy for the modern age" (20) and, like the present work, it opens with the claim that "[w]e find ourselves in a curious situation," caught between

articulation of this remedy, I want to argue, in fact constitutes the principal intent of one of the most disputed aspects of Smith's corpus, namely the revisions to the sixth (1790) edition of *The Theory of Moral Sentiments*. In particular I want to suggest that the sixth edition's entirely new Part VI, "Of the Character of Virtue," was intended by Smith as a remedy for the challenges that he identified with the advent and progress of commercial society and indeed contains Smith's most direct effort to fulfill the mandate implicit in his own insistence that the amelioration of commercial society's moral defects is indeed "an object worthy of serious attention" (LJB 333). Smith's study of virtue in Part VI thus represents at once his mature answer to what he considered the primary question in moral philosophy – "wherein does virtue consist?" (TMS VII.i.2) – as well as his considered response to the ills of commercial corruption that he himself so powerfully articulated.

Smith's study of the character of virtue can thus on some level be understood as an effort to demonstrate how "corruption" can be ameliorated by "virtue." At the same time, these all-too-familiar categories have to be handled with great care by students of Smith. In the first place, Smith's conception of corruption is itself quite subtle. A great deal of excellent commentary has illuminated the ways in which various aspects of his conception resonate with the expositions of the deleterious effects of commerce to be found in either republican or Marxist critiques. Yet Smith's own position, I argue, is less concerned with the political effects of commercialization on which republican and Marxist critiques focus than with commercialization's psychological effects. So too his conception of virtue. While Smith's theory of virtue bears some broad similarities to the conceptions of "civic virtue" familiar from republican accounts, the horizon of Smith's vision goes well beyond the virtues conventionally associated with the good republican citizen – and indeed well beyond the virtues conventionally associated with the good bourgeois of whom Smith is also often considered a champion. Smith's vision of virtue encompasses these perspectives but also speaks to the aspirations of those seeking a less qualified excellence. In so doing he

reasons for optimism and pessimism (1ff). Yet despite our similar departure points, our differences, I hope, will become clear in what follows. Provisionally, Griswold begins with optimism and thoroughly presents the tragic side of commercial society ("tragedy" is his last word; 376n13); I begin with pessimism but argue that Smith provides good reasons to hope and believe that specific aspects of this tragedy can be transcended. I also add at the outset that while I have sought in every instance to register, as fully and specifically as I possibly can, both my debts to and disagreements with their works, no footnote that I am capable of writing could express the entire degree of influence that engagement with the seminal books of Griswold, Haakonssen, Fleischacker, Otteson, and Cropsey have had on my understanding of Smith, as readers, I hope, will recognize throughout.

speaks to the longings for transcendence and nobility and greatness that he presumes to persist in his readers' hearts – categories impossible to subsume under the republican or Marxist or bourgeois perspectives yet central to Smith's account. Smith's theory is also many-layered as a consequence of its intent; rather than offering a stock "civic virtue" to remedy corruption, it offers instead a synthesis of multiple visions of virtue, each element of which forms an integral response to a specific type of corruption. As a result, this theory, seen from a distance, may appear a hodgepodge of commercial, classical, and Christian virtues. His synthesis of elements of these traditions is, however, as unified as his conception of corruption. The thread that unites the various strains in his vision of virtue is moreover precisely the same thread that connects the various elements of his conception of corruption: namely, self-love. Indeed just as Smith's differential diagnosis of several discrete effects of commercialization can be traced to his conception of the way in which commerce corrupts self-love, so too his remedy is founded on the rehabilitation of self-love through its education, elevation, and ennoblement.

Smith's understanding of virtue's normative role in ameliorating the challenges of commercial modernity in turn compels us to reconsider a familiar characterization of his broader commitments. In particular, it compels us to reconsider the propensity to regard Smith as principally or exclusively committed to a conception of inquiry that privileges descriptive or phenomenological analysis – broadly speaking, "scientific" analysis – over normative or prescriptive analysis. This position, common among both his supporters and his detractors, minimizes Smith's normative concerns in favor of a vision of Smith as an objective and detached student of economic and ethical phenomena. But this view not only obscures Smith's commitment to normativity; it also has given rise to the assumption prevalent among specialists and generalists alike that Smith, intentionally or otherwise, deflected, displaced, or deflated the traditional questions of how human beings might best live and best live together to a new question of how they might maximize profits, thereby substituting economics for politics as the central human concern.[13]

---

[13] Among Smith scholars, see especially Joseph Cropsey, *Polity and Economy: An Interpretation of the Principles of Adam Smith* (South Bend: St. Augustine's Press, 2001 [1957]), 119–20, cf. 38, 115; Peter Minowitz, *Profits, Priests, and Princes: Adam Smith's Emancipation of Economics from Politics and Religion* (Stanford, CA: Stanford University Press, 1993), 12, 97–98; Susan E. Gallagher, *The Rule of the Rich? Adam Smith's Argument Against Political Power* (University Park, PA: Penn State University Press, 1998), 98; Richard F. Teichgraeber III, *"Free Trade" and Moral Philosophy: Rethinking the Sources of Adam Smith's Wealth of Nations* (Durham, NC: Duke University Press, 1986), 9–10, 20; Vivienne Brown, *Adam Smith's Discourse: Canonicity, Commerce and Conscience* (London: Routledge, 1994), 139, 210; Brian C. J. Singer, "Montesquieu, Adam Smith and the Discovery of the Social," *Journal of*

This view has been recently restated by Pierre Rosanvallon. Arguing that Smith's faith in the benefits of well-regulated self-interest is the seed of a "utopian capitalism" destined to culminate in the "withering away of politics," he points to the most destructive aspect of this doctrine:

The essential consequence of such a conception consisted in a global refusal of the political. It is no longer politics that should govern society but the market instead. The latter is thus not the limited technical instrument that organizes economic activity, but has a much more radical sociological and political meaning. Reread from this perspective, Adam Smith is not so much the founding father of modern economics as the theorist of the withering away of politics. He is not an economist who does philosophy, but a philosopher who becomes an economist as a continuation of his philosophy. For this reason, Smith is the anti-Rousseau *par excellence*.[14]

This view, I want to suggest, is misguided – not least for the perhaps pedantic reason that it minimizes Smith's debts to and agreements with Rousseau, some of which are documented in Chapter One. The more important reason is that this common view can only be defended at the expense of excising those aspects of Smith's corpus that reveal both his awareness of the limits of the economic conception of man and his commitment to providing a normative resolution to commercial society's moral challenges. These reveal that Smith is neither a participant in nor an advocate of what has been called modernity's "great disembedding," the process by which impersonal markets governed by the logic of "the order of mutual benefit" replaced the legitimating and order-inducing bonds afforded by the reciprocal ideals of Christian charity, premodern aristocratic social hierarchies, or shared commitments to teleological orders in biology and cosmology.[15] Smith may

---

Classical Sociology 4 (2004): esp. 31, 36. Among political theorists more generally, see Sheldon Wolin, *Politics and Vision: Continuity and Innovation in Western Political Thought* (Princeton: Princeton University Press, 2004 [1960]), 269–71; Pierre Manent, *The City of Man*, trans. Marc A. LePain (Princeton: Princeton University Press, 1998), 107–8. For an important early response, see Donald Winch, *Adam Smith's Politics* (Cambridge: Cambridge University Press, 1978), 16–23.

[14] Rosanvallon, "The Market, Liberalism, and Anti-Liberalism," in *Democracy Past and Future*, ed. Samuel Moyn (New York: Columbia University Press, 2006), 149–52.

[15] On the "great disembedding" and its effects on morality, see esp. MacIntyre, *A Short History of Ethics: A History of Moral Philosophy from the Homeric Age to the Twentieth Century*, 2nd ed. (Notre Dame: University of Notre Dame Press, 1998 [1966]), 166–67; MacIntyre, *After Virtue*, 1–5, 33–34, 62, 77, 126, 174, 204–5, 225; Charles Taylor, *Modern Social Imaginaries* (Durham, NC: Duke University Press, 2004), 18, 21, 49–67, 145–48, 186–87 (in which the term itself is to be found); Taylor, *A Catholic Modernity?* (Oxford: Oxford University Press, 1999), 14–18, 35; cf. Michael Stocker, "The Schizophrenia of Modern Ethical Theories," in *Virtue Ethics*, ed. Crisp and Slote, 68. The same point also constitutes a main theme of Sennett, *Corrosion of Character*.

not have chosen to wave the flag for any one of these particular commitments, but advocating their subversion through the great disembedding was neither his implicit nor his explicit aim. His interest – and his interest to us today – lies in his effort to chart a course whereby we might best navigate the challenges of a world in which freedom and subjectivity have displaced the order and security afforded by certain traditional institutions and beliefs.

Taken together, this work's principal claims, in the order in which they appear in the text, are the following:

1. Smith is first and foremost a champion of commercial society on the grounds of its capacity to maximize opulence and freedom and especially its capacity to maximize the opulence and freedom available to the poorest and weakest (Chapter 1, section one).
2. Smith's enthusiasm for commercial society hardly blinds him to its faults, and chief among the faults he identifies is the propensity of commercial society to induce and exacerbate such psychological ills as restlessness, anxiety, inauthenticity, duplicity, mediocrity, alienation, and indifference to others (Chapter 1, sections two and three).
3. In forthrightly addressing himself to the amelioration of these ills, Smith reveals himself to be a true friend of commercial society, and his commitment to remedying them reveals his conviction that ethics is a normative enterprise that supplements the empirical social science and purely descriptive ethics with which he is often associated (Chapter 2, sections one and two).
4. Smith's normative approach is best understood as a virtue ethics rather than a deontological or utilitarian ethics – a virtue ethics that aims to harmonize the longing for individual perfection with the conditions of liberal commercial society (Chapter 2, sections three, four, and five).
5. Smith's normative virtue ethics receives its fullest expression in the new Part VI of the sixth edition of TMS, in which Smith consciously set forth "a practical system of morality" (Chapter 3, section one), dedicated to the articulation of a moral education that uses a specific rhetoric and ascending dialectic to improve and ennoble our self-love in three discrete stages (Chapter 3, sections two and three).
6. The first stage of this education lies in Smith's effort to inculcate the virtue of prudence to ameliorate the anxiety, restlessness, and deceit to which he thought commercial civilization susceptible (Chapter 4, sections one, two, and three) – a remedy that itself exacerbated the

propensities to mediocrity and individualism to which he also thought commercial civilization prone (Chapter 4, section four).

7. The amelioration of mediocrity and individualism was the aim of the second stage of Smith's moral education, which took the form of an effort to recover the virtue of magnanimity, the peak ethical virtue of the ancients (Chapter 5, sections one, two, and three) – a remedy that in its turn exacerbated commercial society's encouragement of excessive self-preference and indifference to others (Chapter 5, section four).

8. The remedy for such excessive self-preference and indifference is to be found in the third stage of Smith's moral education, dedicated to recovering the Christian virtue of beneficence, a demanding active virtue that transcends sentimentalism (Chapter 6, sections one and two).

9. Smith's account of beneficence culminates in his portrait of the wise and virtuous man, at once the embodiment of his vision of human perfection (Chapter 6, section three), as well as Smith's apologia for his own life and the key to his decision to turn from the study of moral philosophy to the study of political economy (Chapter 6, section four).

My development of these claims in turn rests on several interpretive assumptions that readers similarly deserve to have made fully explicit at the outset. First, this book is written from the perspective of a student of political philosophy principally concerned to "get right" Smith's conception of virtue and thereby illuminate a crucial but understudied aspect of his thought which offers an important response to a central political problem of both his day and ours. As such, in what follows I aim to provide a reconstruction of the motivations for and the coherence of one of his core philosophical claims rather than an illumination of its intellectual antecedents or contexts. These are themselves projects of great import; in the future I hope to execute a study of Smith's sources in this vein.[16] But that project is not this one, and although I have not avoided referring to contexts that demonstrably bear on aspects of Smith's thought examined here, the present work privileges theoretical over contextual analysis.

Second, my efforts to reconstruct Smith's theory of virtue have led me to take recourse to his unpublished drafts and lectures and correspondence to present his theory as accurately as possible. As Smith specialists know too

---

[16] I take some steps in this direction in "Social Science and Human Flourishing: The Scottish Enlightenment and Today," *Journal of Scottish Philosophy* 7 (2009): 29–46, and in my annotations to the forthcoming Penguin Classics edition of The Theory of Moral Sentiments.

well, this hermeneutical approach has certain risks, not least of which is that it challenges Smith's own solicitude for his published work – a solicitude famously evident in both his constant revising of his published corpus and his insistence that his unpublished manuscripts be destroyed on his death. But on the whole the risks involved in interpreting Smith's published work alongside the drafts and lecture transcripts available seem less great than the risks involved in ignoring them. These writings do not always show Smith at his best, and they certainly show us a Smith sensitive to the duty to accommodate his presentations to the needs of varying audiences, but they also offer glimpses into the development of his thought.[17] I have, in any case, in all instances attempted to minimize these risks to the greatest extent possible by drawing on only those aspects of the unpublished corpus that speak directly and demonstrably to themes treated explicitly in his published writings, and by marking where and how Smith revised his presentations of these ideas. Relatedly, throughout my analysis I have been guided by the assumption that Smith is a sophisticated and deliberate writer whose arguments need to be reconstructed with care – though never a deceptive or secretive writer, and merely one who consistently strove to say what he meant and indeed who became better at so doing over time.[18]

Third, as the present work is squarely focused on Smith's answer to his question concerning the nature of virtue, it gives considerably less attention to his second question at TMS VII.1.2, which concerns the nature and sources of moral judgment. As a consequence, the mechanisms of sympathy and spectatorship central to this theory of judgment are not nearly so thoroughly examined in the present work as they have been in most other

---

[17] In so doing I follow the precedent set by Knud Haakonssen, *The Science of a Legislator: The Natural Jurisprudence of David Hume and Adam Smith* (Cambridge: Cambridge University Press, 1981), 2–3. Other interpreters have taken different approaches; for important statements of the various hermeneutical positions available to Smith interpreters, see especially Griswold's account of "the principle of charity" in *Smith and the Virtues of Enlightenment*, 26–28; Brown's account of "dialogism" in *Smith's Discourse*, esp. 1–5, 19–21; and Montes' defense of contextualism in his *Adam Smith in Context: A Critical Reassessment of Some Central Components of His Thought* (London: Palgrave MacMillan, 2004), 1–8.

[18] In interpreting Smith I have thus sought merely to be guided by the same hermeneutical canons he encourages us to apply to others: to read him as an author whose "meaning is not to be discovered without great attention and being altogether awake" (LRBL i.v.10), but at the same time never to presume him to have subscribed to that "strange fancy" of a "double doctrine" in writings that "were intended to seem to mean one thing, while at bottom they meant a very different, which the writings of no man in his senses ever were, or ever could be intended to do" (HALM 3n). Samuel Fleischacker provides a helpful guide to Smith's cautious literary style in *On Adam Smith's Wealth of Nations: A Philosophical Companion* (Princeton: Princeton University Press, 2004), 3–11.

recent studies of Smith's moral philosophy. It would be folly to neglect the impartial spectator or sympathy altogether, but I have limited my treatments of these to those aspects that bear directly on Smith's understanding of virtue, on the grounds that his virtue theory is both important and understudied, and in light of my recognition that anything I might say on spectatorship and sympathy would be superfluous in light of the excellent treatments these concepts have already received in studies by others.[19]

By developing these claims in these manners, I hope this work will help promote clarity in discussions of capitalism's corruptions or "moral consequences" – to use the language of the titles mentioned at the outset – as well as present Smith's answer to how capitalism's "crisis" or "battle" might be resolved. But it is not only a substantive conception of virtue that renders Smith of continued interest today; the very spirit of his philosophical engagement with practical political problems is perhaps his greatest legacy. Smith's uniqueness is largely captured by his capacity to appreciate the benefits as well as the challenges of commercial society. As a consequence, he occupies a unique place on the spectrum: rather than degenerating into partisanship or detraction, his attitude toward commercial society is rather one of guarded optimism informed by a sense of pragmatic realism. A similar attitude may prove useful to us. If indeed we are today, for better or worse, "stuck" with commercial liberalism,[20] our challenge is to demonstrate how it can be improved so that its best effects are maximized and its worst ameliorated, rather than to demonstrate either how it might be replaced, on the one hand, or why it should be complacently accepted, warts and all, on the other. What is needed – and what Smith provides – is an opportunity to transcend the all-too-common propensity to side "for" or "against" the

---

[19] Helpful recent overviews of both concepts include Alexander Broadie, "Sympathy and the Impartial Spectator," in *The Cambridge Companion to Adam Smith*, ed. Knud Haakonssen (Cambridge: Cambridge University Press, 2006), 158–88; and D. D. Raphael, *The Impartial Spectator: Adam Smith's Moral Philosophy* (Oxford: Oxford University Press, 2007), 12–20 and 32–42. My understandings of sympathy and spectatorship have particularly benefited from the excellent extended treatments in James Otteson, *Adam Smith's Marketplace of Life* (Cambridge: Cambridge University Press, 2002), 13–64; Griswold, *Smith and the Virtues of Enlightenment*, 76–146; Fonna Forman-Barzilai, "Sympathy in Space(s): Adam Smith on Proximity," *Political Theory* 33 (2005): 189–217; and Karen Valihora, "The Judgement of Judgement: Adam Smith's *Theory of Moral Sentiments*," *British Journal of Aesthetics* 41 (2001): 138–61.

[20] See, e.g., Raymond Geuss, "Liberalism and Its Discontents," in *Outside Ethics* (Princeton: Princeton University Press, 2005), 11–28; see esp. 12 for both the quote and for its description of Freud's position with regard to civilization: "it is strictly impossible to do away with it altogether; the best we can do is try to mitigate some of its worst effects."

project of commercial modernity or liberal Enlightenment more generally.[21] In this sense his aim is comparable to that of Charles Taylor. Commenting on the futility of the struggle between the Enlightenment's "boosters" and its "knockers," Taylor suggests the real challenge "is to see that the issue is not how much of a price in bad consequences you have to pay for the positive fruits, but rather how to steer these developments towards their greatest promise and avoid the slide into the debased forms."[22] Without offering false consolation in the face of the magnitude of the problems we face, Smith, like Taylor, offers us reason for hope on precisely this front.

This intention itself challenges a final view of his project. It has, for some time, been fashionable to regard Smith's conception of commercial society as tragic. On the grounds of his recognition of the place of "illusions" in epistemology and of "deceptions" in ethics (TMS I.i.1.13; TMS IV.1.10), in conjunction with his tough-minded claims that the world prefers "wealth and greatness" to "merit and virtue" (TMS I.iii.3.2–4), Smith's attitude toward commercial modernity has often been taken to be one of resignation to its ills and evils. Hence a variety of similar observations, from the claim that "Smith thinks the advancement of society is well worth the corruption of the individual," to the claim that, in Smith, "social cohesion is achieved at the price of social compassion," to the claim that Smith seems to argue that "the conditions of our material prosperity are tied to those of our spiritual poverty."[23] Remarkably little has been done to meet these challenges. Even the most well-intentioned efforts in this vein seem resigned to the concession that his defense of commercial society is founded on little more than

---

[21] In so doing I also hope to move beyond the political reading of Smith. Recent years have witnessed a scholarly reaction to an earlier "laissez-faire" appropriation of Smith, much of which either distances him from such positions or emphasizes the confluence of his political economy with contemporary welfare state or "social-democratic" policies; in this vein, see esp. Iain McLean, *Adam Smith, Radical and Egalitarian: An Interpretation for the Twenty-First Century* (London: Palgrave MacMillan, 2007), 120, 138–42; Gavin Kennedy, *Adam Smith's Lost Legacy* (London: Palgrave MacMillan, 2005), 96–100, 235–40; Fleischacker, *Smith's Wealth of Nations*, 273–81; and Gordon Brown, remarks delivered at the University of Edinburgh, 25 April 2002, with video available at http://www.ed.ac.uk/explore/av/enlightenment2002/adamsmith/html; and also Brown's preface to McLean's book (viii–ix).

[22] Taylor, *The Ethics of Authenticity* (Cambridge, MA: Harvard University Press, 1991), 11–12, 72–3.

[23] Stewart Justman, *The Autonomous Male of Adam Smith* (Norman: University of Oklahoma Press, 1993), 97; Robert Heilbroner, "The Socialization of the Individual in Adam Smith," *History of Political Economy* 14 (1982): 427–39, as reprinted in J. C. Wood, ed., *Adam Smith: Critical Assessments* (New York: Routledge, 1994), vol. 5, p. 132; Griswold, *Smith and the Virtues of Enlightenment*, 16.

the belief that its benefits are worth its costs; commercial society is to be welcomed for the freedom and order it brings, even if our attachment to such freedom and order fails to encourage or directly inhibits our pursuit of genuine happiness and our realization of genuine excellence.[24] Yet Smith's

---

[24] This view received its clearest expression a half-century ago in Cropsey's study, which concludes that it is "not to be questioned" that Smith "advocated commercialism and did so seriously." That he did so in spite of his explicit recognition of its "gross moral shortcomings" is in fact "of the essence of his teaching," for commercial society "is vindicated by some end which it is meant to procure to mankind." Cropsey identifies this end clearly: "commerce generates freedom and civilization" by overcoming barbarism and premodern authoritarianism, as argued at WN III.iv.4; in this light, Smith's "reprobation of the moral and intellectual defects of commercial society" are only "the tokens of his regret over the price that must be paid for humane, civilized life as he understood it" (Cropsey, *Polity and Economy*, 108–12). A similar view has now been well developed by Rasmussen. His focus is commercial society's moral ills, and, like Cropsey, he identifies as the "central puzzle" of Smith's thought the question of "why he advocates commercial society despite these problems" (Rasmussen, *Problems and Promise*, 7; cf. 11–12, 89–90, 158–59). Rasmussen answers that commercial society has "positive *political* effects" (136), and "*the* most important benefit" is that "it helps provide people with a greater degree of liberty and security" as compared to previous social orders (13; cf. 9, 91–92, 101, 131–2, 140, 145, 153, 157, 159, 165). Smith's defense of commercial society is thus presented as justified on "overall economic and moral balance sheets" or "a kind of cost-benefit analysis" (13; cf. 91, 114, 123–24, 162, 164); Smith "acknowledges" and "accepts" that commercial society has an inherent "moral shortcoming," yet "its advantages ultimately far outweigh its disadvantages" (113–14, 128–29). But the cost on other side of the ledger is equally clear: namely the impossibility of "complete" or "unalloyed happiness" in commercial society (13, 89, 131, 138–39, 158). Rasmussen does an excellent job of reviewing Smith's arguments for commercial society as well as Smith's orientation toward Rousseau; my agreement with his thorough expositions on each front will be evident in my notes that follow. But this larger argument fails on two fronts. First, it fails to capture Smith's commitment to ameliorating these ills through practical normative intervention; the balance sheet image suggests a level of complacency belied by Smith's engagement with these issues from his first publication to his last. Thus while Rasmussen rightly claims that we need to "ameliorate the problems of commercial society" (175; cf. 109, 173) and that "counterarguments and countermeasures" are needed (9, 71, 90–91, 159), beyond calling attention to Smith's well-known educational proposals, he gives little indication how this might be done or how Smith might serve as a guide for such. Among my principal aims is to remedy this omission. Second, Rasmussen minimizes Smith's commitment to happiness understood as human flourishing. He seeks to go beyond Cropsey in explicating the relationship of liberty and security to happiness (137). But ultimately he claims merely that Smith sought to overcome unhappiness by overcoming the "obstacles" of "dependence and insecurity" (13; cf. 131, 139, 144, 150, 169–70). He concedes that the alleviation of misery "might not seem to be a terribly lofty goal" (141). More importantly, his conception of Smith's defense is predicated on a shift from achieving happiness to avoiding misery – from achieving a *summum bonum* to avoiding a *summum malum*, to use Shklar's familiar Hobbesian distinction. But this, I think, fails to capture the whole of Smith's concerns – concerns which prompted from him a rather different sort of inquiry in *The Theory of Moral Sentiments*, and especially its

13

own position is, I think, quite different: happiness, conceived as individual and social flourishing, remains a possibility for modern men, even in our modern world. In setting forth his proposals on this front Smith eschews the pleasures afforded by other familiar positions, from the euphoric joy of the reformer who optimistically hopes and believes our most fundamental problems can be transcended, to the melancholy realism of the hard-nosed pessimist resolved to the ostensible inescapability of our tragic condition. Adam Smith, even in preparing for his death, seems to have discovered a very different sort of solace – an optimism that is guarded, perhaps, yet genuine. In so doing, he gives us reasons for hope, too.

sixth edition, than mere balance sheet tallying. As described by another subtle philosopher: "Material comforts are all very well, but, if the *summum bonum* is to be achieved, the Soul also demands a look in" (P.G. Wodehouse, *The Clicking of Cuthbert* (Woodstock: Overlook Press, 2002 [1922]), 3).

I

THE PROBLEM: COMMERCE
AND CORRUPTION

SMITH'S DEFENSE OF COMMERCIAL SOCIETY

The following study focuses on Smith's understanding of the ills of commercial society and the response to these ills he set forth in order to maximize commercial society's benefits. Yet the very fact that Smith spent such effort on this problem suggests the depth of two convictions on his part (and perhaps suspicions on ours): first, that commercial society is too entrenched to be readily removed and replaced; and second, that commercial society, for all its possible shortcomings, remains very much worth saving given the magnitude of its benefits. So as not to lose sight of his steadfast and indeed unambivalent dedication to commercial society we would thus do well to begin by restating the specific benefits that prompted such dedication from Smith. They are two: first, commercial society's relief of poverty through the increases it makes possible in the material welfare of all; and second, commercial society's promotion of freedom by substituting interdependence for the direct dependence characteristic of social relations in earlier political and economic orders.

With respect to the first point, an ever-growing consensus has emerged among recent scholars that Smith was dedicated to the alleviation of poverty.[1]

---

[1] Among the most important contributions to this diverse synthesis is Istvan Hont and Michael Ignatieff, "Needs and Justice in the *Wealth of Nations*: An Introductory Essay," in *Wealth and Virtue: The Shaping of Political Economy in the Scottish Enlightenment*, ed. Hont and Ignatieff (Cambridge: Cambridge University Press, 1983), 1–44. This essay particularly reveals how Smith reconciled "the paradox of commercial society" in demonstrating how the existence of pervasive material inequalities was not inconsistent with sufficient provision for the poor (see esp. 2–8, 41–43); see also Winch, *Adam Smith's Politics*, 88–90. Also crucial to this consensus are Gertrude Himmelfarb, *The Idea of Poverty: England in the Early Industrial Age* (New York: Knopf, 1984), 42–63; Jerry Z. Muller, *Adam Smith In His Time and Ours: Designing the Decent Society* (Princeton: Princeton University Press, 1993), esp. 8, 58, 72–73; Emma Rothschild, *Economic Sentiments: Adam Smith, Condorcet, and the Enlightenment* (Cambridge, MA: Harvard University Press, 2001), 62–71; Samuel Fleischacker, *A Third*

I want to restate and extend this claim by calling particular attention to a less-emphasized but central element of this concern: namely, the confluence of Smith's emphasis on the vulgarity of the selfishness of the rich and his emphasis on its material benefits for the innocent poor. This confluence perhaps is most directly and famously evident in his first account of the invisible hand in an economic context. Here Smith unsparingly explains that the rich are driven by little more than "their natural selfishness and rapacity" and seek in all things only "the gratification of their own vain and insatiable desires." Yet paradoxically the unintentional effect of the rapacity of the rich is to "divide with the poor the produce of all their improvements," enabling the poor to "derive from his luxury and caprice, that share of the necessaries of life, which they would in vain have expected from his humanity or his justice" (TMS IV.1.10). This theme is further developed in Smith's subsequent writings. ED presents itself as an attempt to explain a paradox "not perhaps so easily understood," namely how the poor benefit from a system seemingly built on "oppressive inequality." Smith takes every opportunity he can to call attention to the vulgarity of the dispositions characteristic of the superiors in this system. In describing the "enormous luxury" of the rich that is always supported by the labor of the poor, he consistently disparages the "slothful and oppressive profusion of the great" (ED 4–5, 10). He further heightens our disapprobation by repeatedly calling attention to the challenges such inequality poses to our understanding of desert and reward, reminding us that "the rent which goes to support the vanity of the slothful landlord is all earned by the industry of the peasant," that the lender who "indulges himself in every sort of ignoble and sordid sensuality" does so at the expense of his borrowers, and that the "indolent and frivolous retainers upon a court" are supported at taxpayer expense – a line of argument culminating in the claim that the "opulent merchant, who spends a great part of his time in luxury and entertainments" will always enjoy more than the "poor labourer," who "while he affords the materials for supplying the luxury

Concept of Liberty: Judgment and Freedom in Kant and Adam Smith (Princeton: Princeton University Press, 1999), 161–83; Rothschild and Amartya Sen, "Adam Smith's Economics," in *Cambridge Companion*, 319–65; and Evensky, *Smith's Moral Philosophy*, esp. 12–16 (as well as the several pieces cited at 13n21). In various ways each of these provides further evidence for Peter Gay's claim that Smith "is on the side of the men, who are less powerful and far more desperate than their masters" (*The Enlightenment: An Interpretation, vol. 2: The Science of Freedom* (New York: Norton, 1996), 365); cf. Spencer Pack, *Capitalism as a Moral System: Adam Smith's Critique of the Free Market Economy* (London: Edward Elgar, 1991), 4, 140–42. Rasmussen's excellent account of Smith's conception of how commercial society can relieve poverty synthesizes several of these perspectives and anticipates my own treatment of several passages here; see *Problems and Promise*, esp. 9, 12, 92, 101–8, 129.

of all the other members of the common wealth, and bears, as it were, upon his shoulders the whole fabric of human society, seems himself to be pressed down below ground by the weight, and to be buried out of sight in the lowest foundations of the building." All this Smith takes as evidence of commercial society's seeming truth: "those who labour most get least" (ED 4–5).

Yet even here Smith insists that the material benefits of commercial society are sufficient to outweigh these real dangers, and hence his central claim that its main engine, the division of labor, "notwithstanding the great inequalities of property, occasions in all civilized societies that universal opulence which extends itself to the lowest ranks of the people," indeed "to the lowest member of the community" (ED 10, 6). The same motif is to be found in the jurisprudence lectures. Here again the rich man first seems "a monster who destroys what might afford subsistence for a vast number of the human species" – "a pest to society, as a monster, a great fish who devours up all the lesser ones." He merely "consumes on himself" and "gives nothing away and has no generosity." With this, Smith presents the paradox: even as the rich man "appears to be the most destructive member of society we can possibly conceive," the limits of his capacity for personal consumption, in conjunction with the stimulus his desires give to production, render him advantageous to society. Thus his well-known conclusion that it would be harmful to the interests of the poor to inhibit the acquisitive efforts of the rich; to "render all on an equality" has "indeed something very agreeable in it, yet a people who are all on an equality will necessarily be very poor" (LJA iii.134–39; LJB 139). As has been noted, herein lies the fundamental distinction between Smith's vision of modernity and the defenses of premodern society set forth by Rousseau among others. Smith and Rousseau alike despise the "immoderate consumption of the wealthy" (LJA vi.137). Yet critics of commercial modernity either misunderstand or underestimate the profound cost of premodern equality in their failure to appreciate that what "establishes there universal equality" is only "universal poverty" (WN V.i.b.7; cf. WN Intro.4; WN I.i.11; WN II.Intro.1–2; ED 5–6). Smith sides with commercial society on the grounds that poverty is a problem both more pressing and more capable of human alleviation than inequality; inequality with general opulence is vastly preferable to "egalitarian barbarism."[2]

---

[2] The phrase belongs to Hont and Ignatieff, "Needs and Justice," 10. On Smith's dedication to the alleviation of poverty rather than inequality, see, e.g., Muller, "The Portrait and the Painter," *Adam Smith Review* 2 (2006): 229–30; and Rasmussen, *Problems and Promise*, 103. For the "Introduction" to WN as a response to Rousseau, see Hont, *Jealousy of Trade: International Competition and the Nation-State in Historical Perspective* (Cambridge, MA: Harvard University Press, 2005), 91–99, which restates and extends his earlier analysis of

Smith's defense of commercial society on the grounds of its material benefits to the poor culminates in his portrait in the *Wealth of Nations* of the rich man whose desire for food is limited by his belly's capacity, but whose appetite for luxury "seems to have no limit or certain boundary," and "cannot be satisfied, but seem[s] to be altogether endless" (WN I.xi.c.7). Smith himself can imagine a different form of consumption that "betokens a more liberal or generous spirit," yet it remains the case that it is precisely the rich man's "trifling" and "base and selfish disposition" that is "more favourable to private frugality, and, consequently, to the increase of the public capital" (WN II.iii.42). Smith, we might say, justifies commercial society by its public effects. But we might push this claim even further, as he not only justifies but defines opulence by its public effects, and particularly by its effects on the least and lowest. This is the idea that underlies his insistence on "comeatibleness" as the essential measure of opulence – thus his claim that "the wealth of a state consists in the cheapness of provisions and all other necessaries and conveniences of life," whereas poverty consists "in the uncomeatibleness or difficulty with which the several necessaries of life are procured" (LJA ii.33; cf. LJA vi.33; LJA vi.129; LJB 175, 230, 245, 247; ED 12; WN I.v.1; WN V.ii.k.3). Indeed, across Smith's corpus one finds a consistent preference for the interests of consumers over producers (see LJA vi.161; WN I.viii.35), an idea especially prominent in both his antimercantilist argument (see WN IV.viii.4) and his solicitude for the capacities of the poor to maintain a living standard sufficient to preclude infanticide and keep infant mortality rates low (WN I.viii.15; WN I.viii.24; WN I.viii.38; LJA iii.133; TMS V.2.15). Taken together, it seems fair to say that the fundamental departure point for Smith's defense of commercial society is its capacity to provide for the poor. His conviction ran deep that "no society can surely be flourishing and happy, of which the far greater part of the members are poor and miserable" (WN I.viii.36), and his concern to avoid this latter state largely explains his enthusiasm for the division of labor, which for all its inconveniences yet "occasions, in a well-governed society, that universal opulence which extends itself to the lowest ranks of the people" and establishes a system in

the "paradox of commercial society"; and Ignatieff, "Smith, Rousseau, and the Republic of Needs," in *Scotland and Europe 1200–1850*, ed. T. C. Smout (Edinburgh: John Donald, 1986), 192. Smith's own conception of the capacity of commercial society to ameliorate inequality evolved over time, from an early emphasis on the "nearly" equal distribution of necessities afforded by the invisible hand (TMS IV.1.10), to a more moderate recognition that "with regard to the produce of the labour of a great society there is never any such thing as a fair and equal division" (ED 4–5), to his ultimate claim that "wherever there is great property, there is great inequality," as "the affluence of the few supposes the indigence of the many" (WN V.i.b.2).

which "a general plenty diffuses itself through all the different ranks of the society" (WN I.i.10).

Smith's pronounced emphasis in four separate works on the selfishness of the rich leads us to posit a provisional conclusion. Even in calling attention to the material utility of selfishness, Smith hardly excuses (much less celebrates) it; his condemnation of its vulgarity is sincere. Yet the unintended consequence of this vulgar disposition he regards as a matter of great beauty. Smith's attachment to the beauty of this unintended beneficial consequence emerges not simply from a love of spontaneous orders, but rather from his natural love of justice, and particularly the unexpected justice that is unwittingly and paradoxically promoted by the most unjust dispositions. In time I hope to show that this fascination with and gratitude for the harnessing of the powers of the strong for the relief of the weak is the fundamental fact uniting Smith's seemingly separate defenses of both commercial society and his specific vision of virtue.

Smith's first defense of commercial society might be said to rest on the paradox of inequality as a contributor to the amelioration of poverty. His second defense shares two fundamental similarities with his first defense: first, it is launched from the perspective of the benefits of commercial society for the poor; and second, it rests on the resolution of a second paradox – in this case, the demonstration of how social interdependence promotes individual independence by severing direct dependence. Put differently, the mechanisms of commercial society promote not only universal opulence but also a universal freedom of which the weak are the principal beneficiaries. Smith develops the fundamental idea that underlies this defense of commercial society in the course of his contribution to the contemporary debate over the best means of managing urban criminality, a topic that had engaged Montesquieu, Defoe, and Fielding, among others. Smith's claim is that the best defense against criminality is neither good police nor good laws, but independence itself: "Nothing tends so much to corrupt and enervate and debase the mind as dependency, and nothing gives such noble and generous notions of probity as freedom and independency," a concept he elsewhere further develops, observing that "the establishment of commerce and manufactures, which brings about this independency, is the best police for preventing crimes" (LJA vi.6; LJB 205).[3] This is one of the fundamental

---

[3] On Smith's conception of the dangers of dependence and the benefits of independence, see esp. Winch, *Adam Smith's Politics*, 77–80; Hont and Ignatieff, "Needs and Justice," in *Wealth and Virtue*, ed. Hont and Ignatieff, 13; Nicholas Phillipson, "Adam Smith as Civic Moralist," in *Wealth and Virtue*, 188, 194, 200–201; Rothschild, *Economic Sentiments*, 10; Fleischacker, *Third Concept of Liberty*, 151, 158; and Friedman, *Moral Consequences of Growth*, 54–56.

claims of Smith's defense of commercial society: that commerce substitutes interdependence for direct dependence and makes possible the freedom of the previously oppressed.[4] Indeed across his analyses of various social institutions we see this process at work – from his descriptions of the injustice and irrationality of primogeniture, which necessarily promotes discord and dependence (see LJA i.115–16; LJA ii.1; cf. LJB 168), to his castigation of the ancient conception of marriage for rendering wives entirely dependent upon (indeed enslaved to) their husbands as a consequence of their being regarded as property (LJA iii.49).[5] Both institutions promote a disposition Smith finds vulgar and destructive: "obsequiousness" to the will of one's "superiors" (WN V.i.f.9). Yet Smith's most sustained and trenchant critique of dependence comes in the course of his analysis of feudalism.

The feudal system afforded Smith a clear and dramatic illustration of the dire moral and political effects of systems that require or promote dependence. His portrait of feudalism consistently emphasizes as its defining element the absolute dependence of laborers and retainers on feudal lords, which rendered it tantamount to slavery (WN II.iii.9; WN III.ii.9; WN III.iv.6). Smith illustrates the effects of such dependence in describing Europe's progress in the wake of Rome's fall at the hands of the barbarians, after which "property came to be very unequally divided." His claim here is that the inequality of precommercial societies such as this is infinitely more pernicious than the inequality to be found in commercial society, and the link between property and power far more direct in the former than in the latter (LJA i.116). Smith's explanation of why this is so affords him another opportunity to expose a paradox. His aim is to show how the conditions that afford the powerful with maximal opportunities to gratify their selfishness are at once the conditions that afford the weak with maximal freedom. In rude ages that afford minimal opportunities for indulgence, it is impossible

---

[4] Smith's account of how interdependence overcomes direct dependence is helpfully treated in Christopher Berry, "Adam Smith: Commerce, Liberty and Modernity," in *Philosophers of the Enlightenment*, ed. Peter Gilmour (Edinburgh: Edinburgh University Press, 1989), 114–18; and more recently in Eric Schliesser, "Adam Smith's Benevolent and Self-Interested Conception of Philosophy," in *New Voices on Adam Smith*, ed. Montes and Schliesser (London: Routledge, 2006), 346–47, 351; Hill, "Adam Smith, Adam Ferguson and Karl Marx on the Division of Labour," *Journal of Classical Sociology* 7 (2007): 346–47; and Rasmussen, *Problems and Promise*, 123–25, 129, 142–50, which again anticipate my treatment here.

[5] Smith's critique of ancient marriage should not be taken as an endorsement of modern marriage practice; see his warnings regarding the moral effects of divorce (LJA iii.10–11) and his conclusion that "it is always better that the marriage tie should be too straight, than that it should be too loose" (LJB 118).

for even the most selfish and unjust man "to lay out his whole fortune on himself; the only way he had to dispose of it was to give it out to others." But such gifts came with strings attached, as they had the devastating consequence of having "rendered the whole of these people dependent on him," which gave the lords "vast authority" and enabled them to "attain such influence" over their dependents as to "make them in a manner their slaves" (LJA i.118–19; LJB 21; cf. WN V.i.b.12). This in turn launched a vicious cycle in which rent came to signify not the value of land but the "acknowledgment of their dependence" (LJA i.119). Rent itself, largely paid in food, was then consumed by the rent-payers, leading to a dependence on the landowner "for maintenance and every thing they enjoyed," with the natural effect of leading to the system of vassalage in war (LJA i.121).

The conditions of commercial society of course present a much different picture. Smith never suggests that modern men are more generous than their predecessors; even today "men are so selfish that when they have an opportunity of laying out on their own persons what they possess, though on things of no value, they will never think of giving it to be bestowed on the best purposes by those who stand in need of it" (LJA i.117). Yet while selfishness may be constant, by bringing more opportunities for the gratification of such selfishness, commercial society renders selfishness advantageous. Smith's claim is that, in commercial society, "the arts which are now cultivated give him an opportunity of expending his whole stock on himself," in turn stimulating the many tradesmen dedicated to the gratification of such desires – tradesmen he calls the "ministers of luxury" (LJA i.117; cf. LJB 36, 59). Herein of course lies the heart of his famous claim in the *Wealth of Nations* that it was the vain desire for "trinkets and baubles," coupled with a technological boom that eliminated "bounds to his vanity, or to his affection for his own person," which led the rich to barter away their authority and effect a "revolution of the greatest importance to the public happiness" (WN III.iv.15–17; cf. LJA iv.159). On such grounds he claims not only that commerce promotes a more equal distribution of power (see LRBL i.144; LRBL ii.143), but also that the attempt to gratify vanity, coupled with the growth in opportunities for such gratifications, promotes a more general distribution of power in the political and ecclesiastical spheres (see WN V.iii.3; WN V.i.g.25). Smith further develops this argument in several discussions of the wealthy man who, in a precommercial state, could directly support one thousand dependants alone. In one instance he explains interdependence by arguing that, in commercial society, production of even mundane commodities requires "the assistance and cooperation of many thousands," and thus "to supply this poor labourer about 1000 have given their joint assistance"

(WN I.i.11; WN I.ii.2; LJA vi.22–23). Where in precommercial society one thousand directly depend on one, one indirectly depends on one thousand in commercial society; by maintaining the ratio, Smith dramatizes the magnitude of the shift from direct to indirect dependence. The same ratio shift figures in a second illustration. Here Smith explains that the same fortune of ten thousand pounds that previously guaranteed the direct dependence of one thousand families is in commercial society barely sufficient to maintain ten footmen directly. Yet this same fortune now "indirectly" contributes to vast numbers by providing a dispersed support, contributing "to very few perhaps a tenth, to many not a hundredth, and to some not a thousandth, nor even a ten thousandth part of their whole annual maintenance." As a result, "though he contributes, therefore, to the maintenance of them all, they are all more or less independent of him, because generally they can all be maintained without him" – here again interdependence overcomes dependence (WN III.iv.11; cf. WN V.iii.1; WN V.i.b.7).

The substance and nature of Smith's two main arguments for commercial society – its capacity to increase and disperse opulence and its capacity to increase and disperse freedom – are crucial to the argument that follows with regard to Smith's conception of virtue. With regard to their substance, we reiterate that Smith launches each defense of commercial society from the perspective of the worst off. It would be wrong to say that Smith frames his arguments as appeals to "just results" or "social justice."[6] Yet, at the same time, Smith's arguments frequently work toward ends that could be identified with the ends promoted by such appeals, and particularly the end that best meets the needs of the least. But herein also lies the import of the nature and methods of the arguments examined earlier. As we have seen, in making these arguments Smith tends to proceed by providing counterintuitive resolutions to dilemmas that seem paradoxical when viewed from the perspective of common sense. In the first argument, the paradox involved the coexistence of inequalities of wealth with the amelioration of poverty; in the second, the instrumental role of interdependence in the obviation of dependence. Indeed the crucial aspect of Smith's argument concerning the birth of freedom "in our present sense of the word" (WN III.iii.5) is the fact that it reveals the shortcomings of the equation of wealth with power that Smith identifies with Hobbes (WN I.v.3; cf. WN V.i.6.7). The benefit of modern commercial society lies in its subversion of this commonsense

---

[6] On the unavailability of our contemporary conceptions of distributive justice in eighteenth-century debates prior to Smith, see esp. Fleischacker, *A Short History of Distributive Justice* (Cambridge, MA: Harvard University Press, 2004), esp. 4, 12–13, 17–19, 37–40, 62–68.

assumption; hence Smith's claim that today "the person who either acquires, or succeeds to a great fortune, does not necessarily acquire or succeed to any political power, either civil or military" (WN I.v.3).[7] In this sense, the subversion of commonsense assumptions may well be the fundamental motif of Smith's defenses of commercial society, consistently dedicated to demonstrating how "two events, which vulgar prejudices and superficial reflection are apt to consider as altogether incompatible" are, in practice, in fact "perfectly consistent" (ED 11).[8] His resolutions of the two aforementioned paradoxes each begin with appeals to the common indignation that decent men naturally feel at the prospect of a society in which those earn least who work most and those enjoy most who work least. Such an appeal would seem, on its face, to work against Smith's goals and prejudice decent men against commercial society. But by demonstrating that commercial society in fact promotes precisely the more just result that its opponents wish to realize, Smith transforms the decent man's indignation at its seeming result into an attachment to its actual result. Smith's own love of justice manifests itself in this resolution of indignation in a manner both conceptually and ethically

---

[7] Of course even in defending the partial utility of the existence of individuals of great wealth, Smith never supposes that if some inequality is good, more must be better. In this regard see his caution against plutocracy and his insistence on the need to maintain a "gradual descent of fortunes betwixt these great ones and others of the least and lowest fortune" and the need for "a gradual declension and subordinate degrees of wealth" for the sake of political stability (LJA iii.139; LJA iv.161). On Smith's subversion of Hobbes' equation see Winch, *Adam Smith's Politics*, 91 and n.

[8] Smith has been described as a "'common sense' philosopher" on the grounds of his methodology in WN and his propensity to appeal to familiar moral categories; see esp. Fleischacker, *Smith's Wealth of Nations*, xv and 22–26; and the discussions in Griswold and Brubaker cited in Chapter 4, Note 26 (this volume). While often true, also important are Smith's many attempts to overcome all-too-familiar prejudices and instantiate unfamiliar and counterintuitive conclusions. This suggests an important difference between Smith's and Hume's epistemologies and methods. On this crucial but largely understudied difference, see the excellent essay by Eric Schliesser, "Wonder in the Face of Scientific Revolutions: Adam Smith on Newton's 'Proof' of Copernicanism," *British Journal for the History of Philosophy* 13 (2005): 697–732; particularly helpful is its suggestion that Smith breaks from Humean common sense in welcoming "strangeness" to "perhaps spur on the development of new theories" (709–10). These differences are further developed with reference to the differences in Hume's and Smith's conceptions of moral psychology (esp. envy and resentment) and political theory (esp. justice and property rights) in Pack and Schliesser, "Smith's Humean Criticism of Hume's Account of the Origin of Justice," *Journal of the History of Philosophy* 44 (2006): 47–63. Schliesser explicitly addresses how his account of philosophy's relationship to common life differs from Fleischacker's – and also helpfully discriminates between the differing orientations of natural and moral philosophy to common life – in "Smith's Conception of Philosophy," in *New Voices*, ed. Montes and Schliesser, 330–31, 338–41.

satisfying to a decent and inquisitive reader. It is a method that animates not only his arguments for commerce, but also his arguments for virtue.

WHAT IS CORRUPTION? POLITICAL AND PSYCHOLOGICAL PERSPECTIVES

Smith's defense of commercial society's tremendous advantages hardly blinded him to its potential ills. As has long been recognized, Smith is not only a founding father of commercial society, but also a father of the critique of it that would come to dominate European political thought in the next two centuries. Yet his exposition of this critique is unique insofar as it presents itself not as an effort to provide reasons to reject commercial society, but as an effort to inspire its defenders to mitigate its ills so that its gains might be preserved. So far from revealing ambivalence toward commercial society, Smith's exposition of its deficiencies is thus perhaps better understood as an attempt to fulfill the obligations of its true friend: namely to describe, as fully as possible, the nature of these deficiencies in order to stimulate the development of a solution.[9]

What then are these detriments? Smith's own conception partakes of the popular conception that commercial society, and particularly the love of pleasure and gain that it liberates, is detrimental both to the soul of the individual and to the bonds of civic life. One of capitalism's greatest friends, Ludwig von Mises, captured this lament in his account of the "grumblers" over capitalism's "mean materialism": "They cannot help admitting that capitalism has the tendency to improve the material conditions of mankind. But, they say, it has diverted men from the higher and nobler pursuits. It feeds the bodies, but it starves the souls and the minds."[10] Yet this, of course, is vague and lacks precision with regard to the specific ills that capitalism poses. Smith's critique has the advantage of developing this general lament through a sustained and specific inquiry. This inquiry rests on a distinction between two types of corruption: corruption understood as a political problem and corruption understood as a psychological problem.

---

[9] Put differently, my study seeks to separate itself from those that have suggested that Smith's critique reveals an ambivalence toward or argument "against" free market practices; see, e.g., Pack, *Capitalism as a Moral System*, esp. 166–75. My conception of Smith as a true friend of commercial society is shaped by Strauss's claim that "the friend of liberal democracy is not its flatterer"; see his "Social Science and Humanism," in *The Rebirth of Classical Political Rationalism* (Chicago: University of Chicago Press, 1989), 6.

[10] Ludwig von Mises, *The Anti-capitalistic Mentality* (Indianapolis: Liberty Fund, 2006 [1956]), 45; cf. 5.

Smith, that is, distinguishes the understanding of corruption that focuses on its effects on citizens from the understanding of corruption that focuses on its effects on the soul or psyche of the human being seen in his or her totality.

Smith's own conception of corruption is shaped by the latter perspective rather than the former. Thus, although his analysis often employs the same terms and categories of "virtue" and "corruption" endemic to the political perspective, the meanings he gives to these terms and categories are subtly, yet decisively, different. The most comprehensive understanding of the political perspective has been set forth by those thinkers associated with what has come to be known as the "republican" or "civic humanist" tradition of neo-Aristotelian political thought, extending from the Renaissance's "Machiavellian moment" through the revival of humanist virtue-centered discourse in certain anti-commercial arguments found in eighteenth-century British political thought. In its Enlightenment form, its central concern was that commerce liberates self-interest and, in so doing, expands the sphere of negative liberty and weakens the attachment of citizens to the common good, ultimately rendering them effeminate and incapable of the martial virtues necessary for civil defense.[11] Yet this political perspective, although influential during the period in which Smith wrote, unnecessarily restricts the problem at issue. More recent students of virtue have noted this problem, from MacIntyre's reminder that to Plato areté belongs "not to a man's specific social function, but to his function as a man," to Peter Berkowitz's critique of Sandel on the grounds that Sandel reduces "the whole of virtue" to "civic virtue, or the virtues that govern participation in political life." Giving precedence to political virtues threatens to overlook the fact that the activities of commercial society threaten not merely our civic capacities, but the very health of the soul of the human being.[12]

---

[11] See, e.g., Pocock, The Machiavellian Moment: Florentine Political Thought and the Atlantic Republican Tradition (Princeton: Princeton University Press, 1975). An overview of the eighteenth-century corruption debate is offered in Malcolm Jack, Corruption and Progress: The Eighteenth-Century Debate (New York: AMS Press, 1989); an excellent guide to eighteenth-century debates over luxury prior to Smith is offered in Istvan Hont, "The Early Enlightenment Debate on Commerce and Luxury," in The Cambridge History of Eighteenth-Century Political Thought, ed. Mark Goldie and Robert Wokler (Cambridge: Cambridge University Press, 2006), 379–418.

[12] MacIntyre, Short History, 35; cf. MacIntyre, After Virtue, 228; Berkowitz, Virtue and Modern Liberalism, 195n21; cf. Thomas Pangle, "The Retrieval of Civic Virtue: A Critical Appreciation of Sandel's Democracy's Discontent," in Debating Democracy's Discontent, ed. Anita L. Allen and Milton C. Regan, Jr. (Oxford: Oxford University Press, 1998), 17–31. Pocock in contrast limits republican virtue "not simply to morally desirable practices or the inner disposition of the self towards them, but to the practice of citizenship in the classical or Graeco-Roman sense of that term" ("Cambridge Paradigms and Scotch Philosophers:

Such a conception of human excellence may in fact be said to constitute its own tradition in late-modern European political thought, a tradition that transcends familiar divisions of proliberal and antiliberal. Within this tradition one might class thinkers as diverse as Rousseau and Ferguson in the eighteenth century, Tocqueville and Mill in the nineteenth, and Nietzsche in the twentieth.[13] It is to this tradition that Smith belongs. To demonstrate, we might begin by comparing his conception of commercial corruption to the well-known conception of his contemporary, Rousseau.[14] Comparison of Smith to Rousseau not only has the advantage of avoiding the potentially anachronistic dangers of identifying Smith with successors alongside whom he has rarely been studied, but also provides us with a chance to revisit the question of his oft-studied relationship with Rousseau. For some time it has been thought that Rousseau served as "an important if unavowed interlocutor" in TMS given Smith's well-known and demonstrable engagement with the *Discourse on the Origins of Inequality* (or *Second Discourse*) immediately prior to the publication of the first edition of TMS.[15] Our central evidence for his engagement with Rousseau – three passages from the *Second Discourse* that Smith translated and appended to his 1756 *Edinburgh Review* article – has recently and repeatedly been mined for what it reveals of his debts to Rousseau on the question of whether commercial society ameliorates or

A Study of the Relations Between the Civic Humanist and the Civil Jurisprudential Interpretation of Eighteenth-Century Social Thought," in *Wealth and Virtue*, ed. Hont and Ignatieff, 235). Elsewhere Pocock interestingly identifies Smith with a conception of virtue as "unity of personality," yet the horizon of this conception remains political insofar as such virtue can only be realized "in political action" (Pocock, *Virtue, Commerce, and History*, 121–23; see also Pocock, *Barbarism and Religion* (Cambridge: Cambridge University Press, 1999), vol. 3, p. 375).

[13] See Ferguson, *Essay on the History of Civil Society*, I.6; Mill, *On Liberty*, III; Tocqueville, *Democracy in America*, II.iii.19, II.iv.6–8; Nietzsche, *Beyond Good and Evil*, X.

[14] With the exception of those readings comparing him to Rousseau that are noted later, there have been few attempts to understand Smith from the context of this trajectory. For brief but suggestive comparisons of his project to Tocqueville's, see Rothschild, *Economic Sentiments*, 25; Ralph Lerner, "Commerce and Character: The Anglo-American as New-Model Man," *William and Mary Quarterly* (1979); reprinted in Lerner, *The Thinking Revolutionary: Principle and Practice in the New Republic* (Ithaca: Cornell University Press, 1987), 195, 202; Taylor, *Modern Social Imaginaries*, 81–82 and 180–81; Friedman, *Moral Consequences of Growth*, 50; Brian Smith, "Adam Smith, the Concept of Leisure, and the Division of Labor," *Interpretation* 34 (2006): 44; and John Danford, "Adam Smith, Equality, and the Wealth of Sympathy," *American Journal of Political Science* 24 (1980): 688–89.

[15] Hont and Ignatieff, "Needs and Justice," in *Wealth and Virtue*, ed. Hont and Ignatieff, 10; see also Jacob Viner, *Guide to John Rae's 'Life of Adam Smith'* (New York: Augustus Kelley, 1965), 35–36; Raphael, *Adam Smith* (Oxford: Oxford University Press, 1985), 71–72, 80; Wokler, *Rousseau* (Oxford: Oxford University Press, 2001), 44.

exacerbates poverty and inequality.[16] But less emphasized has been the fact that at least two of the passages are centrally concerned not with distributive justice but with commercial society's effects on moral psychology. In particular these two passages present the core of Rousseau's most sweeping indictment of the psychological effects of commercial modernity: namely that it has given rise to the form of life that we have come to know as the bourgeois.

[16] Smith's letter is reprinted in EPS, pp. 242–54; on the significance of its introductory part, see esp. Jeffrey Lomonaco, "Adam Smith's 'Letter to the Authors of the *Edinburgh Review*'," *Journal of the History of Ideas* 63 (2002): 659–76. On how it illuminates Smith's debate with Rousseau over commercialization and inequality, see esp. Lucio Colletti, *From Rousseau to Lenin* (New York: New Left Books, 1972), 155–63, 195–215; Michael Ignatieff, *The Needs of Strangers* (London: Picador, 1984), 107–31; Ignatieff, "Smith, Rousseau, and the Republic of Needs"; R. A. Leigh, "Rousseau and the Scottish Enlightenment," *Contributions to Political Economy* 5 (1986): 1–21; Donald Winch, *Riches and Poverty: An Intellectual History of Political Economy in Britain, 1750–1834* (Cambridge: Cambridge University Press, 1996), esp. 60, 66–75; Pierre Force, *Self-Interest Before Adam Smith: A Genealogy of Economic Science* (Cambridge: Cambridge University Press, 2003), 20–47, 121–25, and 154–68; and Schliesser, "Smith's Conception of Philosophy," 343–51. I treat additional aspects of Smith's extended engagement with Rousseau elsewhere; see my "From Geneva to Glasgow: Rousseau and Adam Smith on the Theater and Commercial Society," *Studies in Eighteenth-Century Culture* 35 (2006): 183–211; "Commerce and Corruption: Rousseau's Diagnosis and Adam Smith's Cure," *European Journal of Political Theory* 7 (2008): 137–58 (from which the following two paragraphs are adapted); and "Enlightened Nation Building: The 'Science of the Legislator' in Adam Smith and Rousseau," *American Journal of Political Science* 52 (2008): 219–34. The longest and latest treatment of this engagement is Rasmussen, *Problems and Promise*. Rasmussen reads Smith's engagement with Rousseau through the lens of the three translated passages in LER, each of which he connects to one of three separate critiques of commercial society to be found in each thinker: the "division of laborers" (25–30, 71–76), the "empire of opinion" (30–35, 76–82), and the "pursuit of unhappiness" (35–40, 82–89) (the labels are his). The first emphasizes that the division of labor "can make people weak and ignorant and thereby undermine citizenship" (76); the second that the love of opinion encourages "role playing, ostentation, deception, and immorality" (16, 25, 34, 40); and the third that a desire for "ever more wealth" leads to "nearly endless toil and anxiety" in its pursuit (86). In brief, my own account of restlessness substantially agrees with this third critique, and my account of inauthenticity partly agrees with this second critique (Rasmussen tends to see these as much less significant problems for Smith than I do; see his 77, 82, 114) but rejects the first critique as political and insufficiently psychological (for reasons detailed later). Furthermore, Rasmussen's account stops here and thus largely fails to attend to several other central elements of Smith's conception of commercial corruption, including vanity and excessive self-estimation, indifference to nobility and acceptance of mediocrity, and the subversion of sympathy and indifference to others. As a consequence, he also devalues Smith's attachment to "superior virtues" and suggests "Smith does not seem to be too concerned about ensuring that people will possess these virtues in commercial society" (120n56) – a reading that differs substantially from the one I develop later.

Rousseau is today credited as the father of the critique of commercial society that takes the problem of the bourgeois as its starting point, a critique that receives its fullest expression in Nietzsche's account of the last man.[17] The critique is founded on the claim that commerce stimulates the desire for esteem to the degree that men can live only in the opinions of others.[18] Plagued by solicitude for recognition, they no longer have access to the simple goodness natural to their uncorrupted, self-sufficient state. The transformation has two effects. First, such men are no longer whole, because their inauthenticity renders them duplicitous with others and divided within themselves. Second, in coming to love the easy and moderate pleasures afforded by commercial society, they are rendered incapable of conceiving or achieving genuine excellence. The bourgeois – the characteristic man of commercial society – is thus an artificial man in a middle state: his inauthenticity inhibits his wholeness, and his love of convenient pleasures inhibits his greatness.

The development of these themes is the main purpose of the latter two of the three passages that Smith translated in the *Edinburgh Review*. The first passage describes the transition from the life of the self-sufficient savage concerned with the satisfaction of his natural needs to the interdependent, specialized lives characteristic of societies dedicated to the production of surplus. Smith, as is well known, directly appropriated the language of his translation of this passage in providing his defense of commerce against Rousseau (TMS IV.1.10). Less well known are the equally significant influences of the other two passages on Smith's thought. The second passage describes the psychological effects of "attracting consideration," the characteristic moral disposition of modern society. This disposition, Rousseau insists, promotes corruption of a specific type. Realizing that only certain qualities are capable of attracting attention, civilized man concludes "he must either have them or affect them: he must for his advantage show himself to be one thing, while in reality he is another. To be and to appear to be, became two things entirely different; and from this distinction arose imposing ostentation,

---

[17] See Karl Löwith, *From Hegel to Nietzsche: The Revolution in Nineteenth-Century Thought*, trans. David E. Green (New York: Holt, Rinehart and Winston, 1964), 235–40, 260–62.

[18] The following description of the problem of the bourgeois is drawn from Arthur M. Melzer, "Rousseau and the Problem of Bourgeois Society," *American Political Science Review* 74 (1980): 1018–33; Melzer, *The Natural Goodness of Man* (Chicago: University of Chicago Press, 1990), 63–68; Allan Bloom, *Giants and Dwarfs: Essays, 1960–1990* (New York: Simon and Schuster, 1990), 179–81 and 211–13; Werner Dannhauser, "The Problem of the Bourgeois," in *The Legacy of Rousseau*, ed. Clifford Orwin and Nathan Tarcov (Chicago: University of Chicago Press, 1997); and Laurence D. Cooper, *Rousseau, Nature, and the Problem of the Good Life* (University Park, PA: Pennsylvania State University Press, 1999), 117–18.

deceitful guile, and all the vices which attend them." Rousseau's claim is that the emergence of this new artificial need transformed the relationship of the human being with himself, leading him to value his appearance over his substance on the grounds that such appearances are more valued by those whose attention he seeks. In continuing he makes clear that this revaluation of value necessarily corrupts social relationships:

Thus man, from being free and independent, became by a multitude of new necessities subjected in a manner, to all nature, and above all to his fellow creatures, whose slave he is in one sense even while he becomes their master; rich, he has occasion for their services; poor, he stands in need of their assistance; and even mediocrity does not enable him to live without them. He is obliged therefore to endeavour to interest them in his situation, and to make them find, either in reality or in appearance, their advantage in labouring for his. It is this which renders him false and artificial with some, imperious and unfeeling with others, and lays him under a necessity of deceiving all those for whom he has occasion, when he cannot terrify them, and does not find it for his interest to serve them in reality. To conclude, an insatiable ambition, an ardor to raise his relative fortune, not so much from any real necessity, as to set himself above others, inspires all men with a direful propensity to hurt one another; with a secret jealousy, so much the more dangerous, as to strike its blow more surely, it often assumes the mask of good will; in short, with concurrence and rivalship on one side; on the other, with opposition of interest; and always with the concealed desire of making profit at the expense of some other person: All these evils are the first effects of property, and the inseparable attendants of beginning inequality.[19] (LER 14)

This claim is pregnant with significance – not least because it contains what has been called "Rousseau's fundamental principle – that society based on personal dependence and mutual self-interest is the source of all human evil."[20] Concomitantly one might also note that Smith's recognition of the human propensity to persuade others to contribute to the active satisfaction of our interests in commercial society (see TMS VII.iv.25 and WN I.ii.1–2) constitutes not only the seed of his argument for interdependent commercial society's superiority to the forcible struggles of precommercial society, but also his indictment of Rousseau's misunderstanding of the nature of persuasion itself. But we must take care not to overstate the differences, for the deep concerns with regard to deceit, duplicity, and dependence that

[19] Rousseau, "Discourse on the Origin of Inequality," in *The Discourses and Other Early Political Writings*, trans. Victor Gourevitch (Cambridge: Cambridge University Press, 1997), 170–71.
[20] Melzer, *Natural Goodness of Man*, 108; cf. 75–81, 290; see also Force, *Self-Interest Before Smith*, 220.

Rousseau here sets forward would in time prove central to Smith's own conception of commercial corruption.

These concerns are further developed in the third translated passage of the essay. Here Rousseau turns from the effect of the love of consideration on social relations to its effect on the individual and his pursuit of happiness. He presents this effect in comparing savage to civilized man. The latter fares poorly, as he "toils, bestirs and torments himself without end, to obtain employments which are still more laborious; he labours on till his death, he even hastens it, in order to put himself in a condition to live, or renounces life to acquire immortality." In valuing "the looks of the rest of the universe" and finding that a dependence on esteem compels them to be "happy and contented with themselves upon the testimony of another, rather than upon their own," civilized man dooms himself to a life of futility and pathos and dependency insofar as he lives "always out of himself" and "cannot live but in the opinion of others" – a dependence that culminates in the fact that it is "from their judgment alone that he derives the sentiment of his own existence."[21] Hence Rousseau's perplexity that even in civilization there could be

so much real indifference for good and evil, with so many fine discourses of morality; how every thing being reduced to appearances, every thing becomes factitious and acted; honour, friendship, virtue, and often even vice itself, of which we have at last found out the secret of being vain; how in one word always demanding of others what we are, and never daring to ask ourselves the question, in the midst of so much philosophy, so much humanity, so much politeness, and so many sublime maxims we have nothing but a deceitful and frivolous exterior; honour without virtue, reason without wisdom, and pleasure without happiness.[22] (LER 15)

So concludes Rousseau's breathless critique. A number of discrete elements can now be identified, including a psychological solicitude for attention, a dependence on others for the gratification of this desire for recognition, an increasing propensity toward duplicity and deceit with others to better achieve such gratification, and an increasing propensity to personal misery as a result of such enslavement to this particular vision of gratification. What unites these discrete elements is the fact that commercial modernity has given rise not merely to a new disposition or set of dispositions, but to a new

---

[21] For helpful explications of Rousseau's indictment of commercial society for inhibiting self-sufficiency and the consciousness of the sentiment of existence, see especially Melzer, *Natural Goodness of Man*, 68; and Cooper, *Rousseau, Nature, and the Good Life*, 20–29.

[22] Rousseau, *Discourse on Inequality*, in *Discourses*, trans. Gourevitch, 187.

comprehensive vision of what has been called a "new-model man."[23] In this sense Rousseau takes a dramatic step beyond the republican conception of corruption, for what he identifies is not simply the degeneration of a disposition but a thoroughgoing transformation or reinvention of the human being. It is on this same foundation that Smith builds his own understanding of the broad and sweeping effects of commercial corruption, and his specific conception of virtue is proposed precisely in an effort to prevent the realization of this total and sweeping transformation of the human person.

The context of his theory of corruption is thus psychological rather than political. Students of Smith have long recognized that his assessments of commercial society have a "dark side" and, taken cumulatively, his studies of this dark side are sufficient to reveal that he cannot be simply dismissed as a subscriber to a caricature of naïve Enlightenment optimism; Smith, quite simply, is no "Pollyanna."[24] Yet it is less clear how we ought to regard his assessment of this dark side. Till now, interpretations of Smith's understanding of the deleterious effects of commercialization have tended to fall into two camps. The first follows a line of thought developed by Marx. In *Capital*, Marx recounted Smith's grim portrait of the effects of the division of labor on the moral and mental capacities of laborers.[25] Following Marx, several important studies have found, in Smith's scathing analysis of the propensity of specialized labor to encourage "stupidity" (WN V.i.f.51; cf. LJB 329) and "mental mutilation" (WN V.i.f.60–61; cf. LJA iv.82), evidence of a critique of free markets that potentially undermines his defense of

---

[23] As described in Lerner, "Commerce and Character," esp. 218–21. Specific aspects of Smith's treatment of this new-model man – and especially the turn from glory to gain – are well developed in Danford, "Smith, Equality, and the Wealth of Sympathy," esp. 690–95.

[24] Smith's "darker side" and his "profound pessimism" are explicitly invoked in Heilbroner's account of the "dilemma of economic progress accompanied by moral decay" in "The Paradox of Progress: Decline and Decay in *The Wealth of Nations*," in *Essays on Adam Smith*, ed. Andrew S. Skinner and Thomas Wilson (Oxford: Clarendon Press, 1975), esp. 524, 528–32; a helpful review is also provided in Patricia H. Werhane, *Adam Smith and His Legacy for Modern Capitalism* (Oxford: Oxford University Press, 1991), 168–73. Sankar Muthu has recently and compellingly shed new light on Smith's "dark and pessimistic commercial narrative" in his study of Smith's assessment of international corporations; see his "Adam Smith's Critique of International Trading Companies: Theorizing 'Globalization' in the Age of Enlightenment," *Political Theory* 36 (2008): 185–212; quote at 193. For an explicit counter to the view of Smith as "Pollyanna," see Evensky, *Smith's Moral Philosophy*, 164.

[25] Marx, *Capital*, in *The Marx-Engels Reader*, ed. Robert C. Tucker, 2nd ed. (New York: Norton, 1978), I.xiv.4–5, pp. 394, 399–400. See also the selections from the *Grundrisse* in *Karl Marx: Selected Writings*, ed. David McLellan, 2nd ed. (Oxford: Oxford University Press, 2000), 402–5.

commercialization.[26] Another line of critique developed a separate focus. Smith's comments on the tendency of market orders to encourage the enervation or degeneration of the martial virtues has given rise to a number of important studies that emphasize the tensions in his seeming attachment to both commercial liberalism and to classical republicanism, particularly emphasizing his recognition that the passions and interests that drive the former would seem to undermine the civic virtues necessary for the latter.[27] Textual support can certainly be marshaled for this interpretation; Smith himself forthrightly insists that commerce "sinks the courage of mankind, and tends to extinguish martial spirit" (LJB 331), that luxury leads men to be reticent "to leave their business and engage in war as a common soldier" (LJA iv.84–85; cf. LJA iv.99; LJB 39–40, 47), and that wealth leads to a "diminution of strength" (LJA iv.93; LJB 37) – points all the more important given his striking claim that the art of war "is certainly the noblest of all arts" (WN V.i.a.14).

Yet the republican and the Marxist analyses focus on the corruption of specific types of individuals. The former focuses on the degeneration of the citizen-soldier and the latter on the degeneration of the laborer; in so doing, they each present a version of the political perspective on corruption. By focusing exclusively on these specific types, however, each unnecessarily restricts the sphere of Smith's consciously broader study of the effect

---

[26] Classic readings in this vein include Nathan Rosenberg, "Adam Smith on the Division of Labour: Two Views or One?" *Economica* (new ser.) 32 (1965): 127–39; Robert Lamb, "Adam Smith's Concept of Alienation," *Oxford Economic Papers* 25 (1973): 275–85; and Pack, *Capitalism as a Moral System*, esp. 138–65. Helpful and careful guides to Smith's specific anticipations of and divergences from Marx can be found in Ronald L. Meek, "Smith and Marx," in *Smith, Marx, and After* (London: Chapman and Hall, 1977), 3–17; and now Hill, "Smith, Ferguson and Marx," 339–66.

[27] Important statements of Smith's debts to republican ideas include Albert O. Hirschman, *The Passions and the Interests: Political Arguments for Capitalism Before Its Triumph* (Princeton: Princeton University Press, 1997 [1977]), 100–13, esp. 105–6; Winch, *Adam Smith's Politics*, 86–87, 103–20, 174–75, esp. its claim that Smith's discussions of corruption and education are delivered with "political or civic purposes" in mind (119); Ignatieff, "Smith, Rousseau and the Republic of Needs," in *Scotland and Europe*, ed. Smout, esp. 188, 197; Justman, *Autonomous Male*, 13, but cf. 85; Force, *Self-Interest Before Smith*, esp. 3, 159, 225–28, and 236; Montes, *Smith in Context*, esp. 57–69; Taylor, *Modern Social Imaginaries*, see again 81–82 and 180–81; and John Dwyer, "Ethics and Economics: Bridging Adam Smith's *Theory of Moral Sentiments* and *Wealth of Nations*," *Journal of British Studies* 44 (2005): 674. For important responses, see Hont and Ignatieff, "Needs and Justice," in *Wealth and Virtue*, ed. Hont and Ignatieff, 6–8, 43–44; Phillipson, "Smith as Civic Moralist," in *Wealth and Virtue*, esp. 179–81; and Berry, "Adam Smith and the Virtues of Commerce," in *NOMOS XXXIV: Virtue*, 75, 82–84.

of commerce on the soul or psyche of the human being.[28] Some sense of the breadth of his concern can be seen in the sweeping generalizations he occasionally makes regarding "the present effeminate and puny set of mortals" (LJA vi.22; cf. ED 3), "the present misery and depravity of the world, so justly lamented" (TMS I.iii.1.7), and "the present depraved state of mankind" (TMS II.i.5.8). What unites these ubiquitous, if hyperbolic, laments is a pervasive sense of the degeneration not merely of a class or type, but of "mankind" or the "world" as a whole. Smith brings this same holistic perspective to his account of the effects of commerce on the individual, which similarly emphasizes the fact that commercial corruption is not limited to a particular part of the psyche but to the psyche's capacities or integration as a whole. This point is made with direct reference to the republican perspective in *The Wealth of Nations*. In a discussion of the dangers of cowardice, Smith explicitly claims that even if "the martial spirit of the people were of no use towards the defence of the society," combating cowardice "would still deserve the most serious attention of government" because the coward "wants one of the most essential parts of the character of a man." One who lacks this essential part is deprived of the very possibility

[28] On the scope of Smith's corruption conception, see also Hill, "Smith and Corruption," 636–62; and Edward J. Harpham, "Liberalism, Civic Humanism, and the Case of Adam Smith," *American Political Science Review* 78 (1984): 764–74. Hill likewise argues that Smith does not fit into existing corruption traditions, and that he rather "forges one all his own" (636), one which is "eccentric" and constitutes a "hybrid conception" (646). Her distinction of Smith from republican and proto-Marxist conceptions is especially helpful (656), but the emphasis on Smith's concern with the "moral health of the body politic" (636) and the "norms of the elite classes" (651) privileges the political at the expense of the psychological. Elsewhere Hill more explicitly distances Smith's conception of corruption from the psychological, arguing that, contra Ferguson, Smith understood corruption as a challenge to "public *order* rather than as a total social and individuo-psychic pathology" or as a challenge to "martial or political virtues"; see Hill, "Smith, Ferguson and Marx," 347, 353, 356–57 (italics original). Harpham, who also distinguishes Smith from the civic humanist tradition, does, however, emphasize the psychological side, noting that Smith's concern "is not to create better citizens who can participate in the political life of the community" but "emerges out of his concern for the psychological attachments which tie men in different social orders together into a common political community" (770–71) – a crucial observation lost in the debate over the relative degrees of Smith's commitments to liberalism and republicanism. For a useful admonishment that calls for "rejecting the simple binary choice" between the two with regard to Smith, see Winch, "Adam Smith and the Liberal Tradition," in *Traditions of Liberalism: Essays on John Locke, Adam Smith and John Stuart Mill*, ed. Knud Haakonssen (St. Leonards, New South Wales: Centre for Independent Studies, 1988), 89; see also Winch, "Commercial Realities, Republican Principles," in *Republicanism: A Shared European Heritage*, ed. Quentin Skinner and Martin van Gelderen (Cambridge: Cambridge University Press, 2002), vol. 2, pp. 294–96.

of happiness, as "happiness and misery, which reside altogether in the mind, must necessarily depend more upon the healthful or unhealthful, the mutilated or entire state of the mind, than upon that of the body" (WN V.i.f.60). Put differently, the enervation of martial courage is not a political but a psychological problem; what is to be feared in the loss of courage is not simply the instability or vulnerability of the republic, but the instability and vulnerability of the mutilated and fragmented psyche.

The import of psychic integration is further developed in Smith's most direct treatment of corruption, TMS I.iii.3, itself new to the sixth edition. The title of this added section suggests the breadth of its inquiry: "Of the corruption of our moral sentiments, which is occasioned by this disposition to admire the rich and the great, and to despise or neglect persons of poor and mean condition." By invoking in the title of this chapter the fundamental category of the title of the work as a whole, Smith suggests the extent of the problem; if commerce corrupts "moral sentiments," then the effects of corruption extend to the whole range of subjects to be treated in a theory of moral sentiments. Now, Smith of course grants that there is a certain social utility to the disposition that engenders such corruption; anticipating Burke and Tocqueville, he notes that the propensity to idolize the rich and powerful is "necessary both to establish and to maintain the distinction of ranks and the order of society" (TMS I.iii.3.1; TMS I.iii.2.3; TMS VI.ii.1.20; TMS VI.iii.30), at the same time that he calls it "the great and most universal cause of the corruption of our moral sentiments" (TMS I.iii.3.1).[29] But his main interest, here and elsewhere, is to show that the type of corruption that commerce encourages threatens precisely those aspects of the soul and mind that distinguish human beings as human, aspects which include not only sentiments but also the capacity for the cultivation of intellectual virtues. This concern is especially evident in Smith's indictment

---

[29] Cf. Burke, *Reflections on the Revolution in France* (esp. pp. 169–75 in the O'Brien Penguin edition); Tocqueville, *Democracy in America*, II.iii.5. Smith's locution admits the possibility of other sources of corruption beyond those specifically endemic to commercialization. In light of comments made elsewhere, foremost among these in Smith's mind would seem to be religious enthusiasm and party animosity; indeed elsewhere in TMS it is explicitly claimed that "faction and fanaticism" have "always been by far the greatest" corruptors of sentiments (TMS III.3.43). Yet these claims may be less irreconcilable than they initially appear. Smith's most direct account of the political dangers of religious enthusiasm (WN V.i.f.40ff.) emphasizes that it is not enthusiasm per se but enthusiasm unleashed on a people rendered stupid by commercially induced mental mutilation that is the real problem, which suggests that commercial corruption remains the "universal cause" that drives and exacerbates the efficient causes of corruption suggested by faction and enthusiasm. For further elaboration of the trajectory of Smith's argument in WN V.i.f–g, see my "From Geneva to Glasgow," 194–96.

of the "inconveniences" of commerce set forth at LJB 326–33. Readings of this passage have tended to note its emphasis on how commerce affects the martial virtues, but alongside this concern is a pronounced concern over commerce's effects on healthy cognitive functioning. The question of intellectual capabilities, rather than the martial virtues, is itself the passage's point of departure: hence its insistence that labor specialization cultivates "few ideas" (LJB 328), with the consequence that "in every commercial nation the low people are exceedingly stupid" (LJB 329). Such concerns are themselves emblematic of his conviction that specialization promotes mental mutilation and his claim in WN that, by confining activities to a few simple operations, laborers are led into "drowsy stupidity" or "gross ignorance and stupidity," which finally leaves their minds "mutilated and deformed" and the worker "as stupid and ignorant as it is possible for a human creature to become" (WN V.i.f.51; WN V.i.f.61; WN V.i.f.50). Yet the LJ passages particularly reveal the depth of Smith's concerns with regard to specialization's effects on cognitive functioning and intellectual capacities; hence his interest in the self-sufficient, unspecialized country worker who serves as a model of the sort of intellectual development possible "when the mind is employed about a variety of objects" which leads to the mind being "expanded and enlarged" and to have at its disposal a broad "range of thoughts" (LJB 328–29; WN V.i.f.51; cf. ED 25–26). In this same context Smith also recommends religion on the grounds that it provides raw material for "thought and speculation" and thereby preempts a propensity to debauchery and drunkenness characteristic of men of "no ideas" (LJB 330; cf. ED 30). Smith concludes the passage with a litany of commerce's cognitive effects, noting that in systems of specialized labor "every ones thoughts are employed about one particular thing," that a man is "in a great measure unacquainted with the business of his neighbour," that men have time to "study" only one particular field and no time to "learn" others, and that "their minds constantly employed" solely in the arts of luxury, and, hence, they are inferior to those brave ancestors whose "minds were not enervated" (LJB 331–32). The cumulative effect of such repeated variations on this theme is to impress on auditors and readers the fact that commerce affects the person as a whole, inhibiting not simply martial virtue, but "social" and "intellectual" virtues as well (WN V.i.f.50).

Smith introduces his discussion of commercial corruption in LJB as a discussion of both "the effects of a commercial spirit on the government, temper, and manners of a people, whether good or bad" and the "proper remedies" for such (LJB 224). He concludes it with a remarkable summary: "These are the disadvantages of a commercial spirit. The minds of men are contracted and rendered incapable of elevation, education is despised or at least neglected, and heroic spirit is almost utterly extinguished. To remedy these defects would be an object worthy of serious attention" (LJB 333). Such a claim is striking not only for its concerns with the elevation of the mind and the preservation of heroic spirit – goals atypical of the liberalism with which Smith is typically associated – but also for its anticipations of his ensuing project. In what follows I argue that Smith's account of the character of virtue is itself an exercise in giving "serious attention" to the problem described here and developing a remedy capable of ameliorating the "disadvantages" alluded to herein. At the same time, it is not yet clear precisely what these disadvantages are, and particularly what Smith might mean in claiming that commerce contracts minds or extinguishes heroic spirit. This now deserves our attention in order to see the degree to which Smith's critique of commerce extends beyond Marxist concerns with the mental mutilation of laborers and republican concerns with the enervation of citizen-soldiers – as well as beyond contemporary concerns with consumerism and materialism – even as it incorporates elements of each of these perspectives.

SMITH ON CORRUPTION: FROM THE CITIZEN TO THE HUMAN BEING

The departure point for Smith's study of these specific elements of corruption is his observation that the desire for esteem and recognition is at once the animating passion of commerce as well as the origin of commercial corruption. As has been well established, Smith's conception of the role of vanity in stimulating commercial ambition is indebted to Rousseau's discussions of *amour-propre*.[30] Rousseau particularly speaks for Smith in insisting on the centrality of "the love of distinction" to the pursuit of wealth:

One does everything to grow rich, but it is in order to be regarded (*considéré*) that one wants to be rich. This is evident in that instead of being content with that middle state which constitutes well-being, each wants to attain to that degree of riches which rivets all eyes, but which increases cares and pains and becomes almost as

---

[30] See especially Force, *Self-Interest Before Smith*, 31, 42–47, 243–46, 262 (though see also the important replies to Force in Berry, "Smith Under Strain," *European Journal of Political Theory* 3 (2004): 455; and John Robertson, *The Case for the Enlightenment: Scotland and Naples 1680–1760* (Cambridge: Cambridge University Press, 2005), 394–96, which also calls helpful attention to Smith's engagement with Rousseau's critique of commercial "inequality and hypocrisy" (395)).

burdensome as poverty itself. . . It is wholly evident that the desire of distinguishing one's self is the sole origin of the luxury of magnificence.[31]

Smith agrees. Whether he is regarded as having followed Rousseau's conception of distinction or having anticipated Veblen's emphasis on conspicuous consumption, the result is the same: Smith's most direct formulations in *The Theory of Moral Sentiments* of the psychological motives for commercial activity emphasize not love of ease or pleasure but love of recognition.[32] As a phenomenologist, Smith marvels at the ubiquity of this solicitude: "Of such mighty importance does it appear to be, in the imaginations of men, to stand in that situation which sets them most in the view of general sympathy and attention" (TMS I.iii.2.8). This claim is so ubiquitous in Part I of *The Theory of Moral Sentiments* that solicitude for esteem is akin to those "connecting principles" described in the *History of Astronomy* that "became the great hinge upon which every thing turned" (HA II.12). Smith indeed uses this observation to explain a wide range of psychological reactions to external phenomena, ranging from the fear of death (which he attributes to man's horror at the prospect that he will be "no more thought of in this world," that he will be "forgot by every body," and that he will be soon "obliterated" from the affections and memory of both friends and family (TMS I.i.1.13)), to the fear of public humiliation (on the grounds that recognition is the greatest good and shame "the greatest of all evils" (TMS I.iii.2.9)).[33] As Smith repeatedly makes clear in Part I, in commercial society even infamy is preferable to anonymity, and the blessings of tranquility pale in comparison to the ignominy suffered by those the world has forgotten. And it is precisely within the context of the question of how best to gratify this psychological need that Smith turns to commerce. Like Rousseau, he claims that modern man's quest to "better his condition" through wealth pursuit has its roots in a psychological need for recognition from others rather than physical needs: "it is chiefly from this regard to the sentiments of

---

[31] Rousseau, "Fragments politiques," in *Œuvres complètes*, ed. Bernard Gagnebin and Marcel Raymond (Paris: Gallimard, Bibliothèque de la Pléiade, 1959–95), vol. 3, p. 502.

[32] For comparisons of Smith and Veblen, see Arthur O. Lovejoy, *Reflections on Human Nature* (Baltimore: Johns Hopkins University Press, 1961), 208–15; cf. 150, 190–91; and Edwin G. West, "Adam Smith and Rousseau's *Discourse on Inequality*: Inspiration or Provocation?" *Journal of Economic Issues* 5 (1971): 64. For helpful treatments of the role of recognition in TMS I.iii and its Rousseauan resonances, see Force, "Self-Love, Identification, and the Origin of Political Economy," *Yale French Studies* 92 (1997): 57–58; and Tzvetan Todorov, "Living Alone Together," *New Literary History* 27 (1996): 6.

[33] The latter point is especially important insofar as Smith's explicit insistence on the centrality of the love of recognition to the aristocracy (see TMS I.iii.3.6) suggests that the problem of the bourgeois is not limited to the middle class.

mankind, that we pursue riches and avoid poverty." Indeed the emulation that drives "that great purpose of human life which we call bettering our condition" is animated by the desire "to be observed, to be attended to, to be taken notice of with sympathy, complacency, and approbation" – that is, by "vanity" or the desire "of our being the object of attention and approbation" (TMS I.iii.2.1). In his awareness of the strength of the modern solicitude for recognition indeed lies Smith's Rousseauan account of why we continue to pursue "wealth and greatness" despite their high psychic costs: their "sole advantage" is that "they more effectually gratify that love of distinction so natural to man," and draw upon him "the attention of the world" (TMS IV.1.8; TMS I.iii.2.1).

It is thus that Smith in his own name advances the claim originally set forth in his translations from the *Second Discourse*: namely that markets are driven by the solicitude for recognition characteristic of the modern self.[34] Yet this only marks the beginning of Smith's debts to Rousseau. Smith also follows Rousseau in two further respects. First, he explicitly identifies several of the specific ill effects of *amour-propre* also noted by Rousseau. Second, so far from complacently thinking that commerce's benefits outweigh the moral ills consequent to the encouragement of the love of esteem, Smith too develops a normative moral remedy to offset these effects, one different in substance but worthy of comparison in intention to the famously disparate (and perhaps even mutually exclusive) remedies set forth in the *Social Contract*, *Emile*, and the *Reveries*.[35]

The first and most obvious ill effect that Smith traces to commercial vanity is an increase in restlessness and anxiety. His analysis on this front aligns him with a familiar tradition that extends from Pascal through Rousseau to Tocqueville and indeed extends to contemporary analyses of capitalism as inimical to rest and leisure and which identifies capitalist success as more likely to bring anxiety than tranquility.[36] Rousseau's well-known claim that

---

[34] This idea has had an important recent resurgence in contemporary economic and political theory. On the centrality of recognition and esteem as seen from two very different perspectives, compare Nancy Fraser and Axel Honneth, *Redistribution or Recognition? A Political-Philosophical Exchange* (London: Verso, 2003); to Geoffrey Brennan and Philip Pettit, *The Economy of Esteem: An Essay on Civil and Political Society* (Oxford: Oxford University Press, 2004).

[35] On these remedies and their tensions, see Cooper, *Rousseau, Nature, and the Good Life*, 172–81.

[36] See, e.g., Pascal, *Pensées* (esp. 139 in the Brunschvicg edition); Tocqueville, *Democracy in America*, II.ii.13. For a contemporary restatement, see, e.g., Liah Greenfeld, "When the Sky Is the Limit: Busyness in Contemporary American Society," *Social Research* 72 (2005): 315–38.

commerce is born of discontent with the self and the illustrative portrait of the sweating, scurrying modern citizen with which his *Second Discourse* concludes are the foundations of a great deal of subsequent critique of market orders. But this concern is equally present in Smith's work. For all his fame as a champion of spontaneous orders, Smith gives reason to doubt that markets are always well ordered. So far from appearing orderly or tranquil, when seen from the widest view market economies often appear to Smith as scenes of "tumult and bustle" that culminate in "rapine and injustice," and human society as a "great scramble" in which "every one scrambles to get as much as he can and keep what he has got" – indeed as a "general scramble for preeminence" in which "when some get up others must necessarily fall undermost" (TMS I.iii.2.8; LJA iv.163; LJA vi.54; cf. WN V.iii.90; LJB 219).[37] Labor conditions in such a society seem to perpetuate this, as specialization famously renders men more productive precisely by eliminating indolent sauntering, or by removing opportunities for leisure and rendering laborers literally restless (WN I.i.7). Yet Smith's principal concern here is not simply that commercial society appears to be a disordered and chaotic scramble, but more particularly that the soul of a commercial man replicates this chaotic disorder; psychic restlessness obviates tranquility.

This becomes clear in his study of the relationship of commerce to happiness. It is well known that Smith considers tranquility a prerequisite for happiness.[38] Yet he also explicitly and repeatedly notes that commercial passions are more likely to bring misery and anxiety than happiness and tranquility; thus, "the great source of both the misery and disorders of human life, seems to arise from over-rating the difference between one permanent situation and another" – avarice "over-rates the difference between poverty and riches," ambition that between "a private and a public station," and vainglory "that between obscurity and extensive reputation." Acting under any of these passions often leads only to personal and political disorder; renouncing them, in contrast, enables us to open ourselves to the possibility of happiness; for "the pleasures of vanity and superiority are seldom

---

[37] At the same time, seeming disorder on a local or short-term level may not necessarily be incommensurate with the achievement of unintended order on a wider scale over a longer term. For a helpful exposition of this claim, see Otteson, "Unintended Order Explanations in Adam Smith and the Scottish Enlightenment," in *Liberalism, Conservatism, and Hayek's Idea of Spontaneous Order*, ed. Louis Hunt and Peter McNamara (London: Palgrave Macmillan, 2007), esp. pp. 21, 25, 30.

[38] To say that Smith considered tranquility requisite for happiness is different from suggesting that it is happiness's "key component"; Rasmussen, *Problems and Promise*, 83–84, 87, 138. Smith's definition of happiness also embraces the consciousness of being loved and of meriting esteem for one's virtuous activities.

consistent with perfect tranquility, the principle and foundation of all real and satisfactory enjoyment," yet such tranquility, it would seem, is available to even those "in the most humble station, where there is only personal liberty," provided one renounce "the frivolous pleasures of vanity and superiority." Like Rousseau (and Pascal before him), Smith would have students of history's greatest men know that "the misfortunes of by far the greater part of them have arisen from their not knowing when they were well, when it was proper for them to sit still and to be contented." In this way he challenges his auditors to see the genuine pleasures of "our actual, though humble station" and to temper our enthusiasm for the imagined pleasures of lofty stations (TMS III.3.31), as the truth of such stations hardly lives up to the billing given them by our imaginations. Thus, in both the first and the sixth editions he notes that "to those who have been accustomed to the possession, or even to the hope of public admiration, all other pleasures sicken and decay." Smith indeed can think of few greater tragedies than "discarded statesmen" and other castoffs condemned to "the most listless and insipid indolence, chagrined at the thoughts of their own insignificancy, incapable of being interested in the occupations of private life." In the hope of having his auditors avoid such a fate Smith makes perhaps his most pointedly normative claim in *The Theory of Moral Sentiments*: if you hope to live "free, fearless, and independent" and are "in earnest resolved never to barter your liberty for the lordly servitude of a court," then "there seems to be one way to continue in that virtuous resolution; and perhaps but one. Never enter the place from whence so few have been able to return; never come within the circle of ambition; nor ever bring yourself into comparison with those masters of the earth who have already engrossed the attention of half mankind before you" (TMS I.iii.2.7). Too many have been seduced by this false dream already, and "notwithstanding the restraint it imposes, notwithstanding the loss of liberty with which it is attended," it yet "renders greatness the object of envy, and compensates, in the opinion of mankind, all that toil, all that anxiety, all those mortifications which must be undergone in the pursuit of it" – not to mention "what is of yet more consequence, all that leisure, all that ease, all that careless security, which are forfeited for ever by the acquisition" (TMS I.iii.2.1). Smith is clear: contra Machiavelli, he argues that the pursuit and even the attainment of power are inimical to personal liberty. But unlike Machiavelli, Smith sees that it is not only the great objects of human ambition that induce anxiety, but even the most minute appearances of the most common objects of consumption; it is often "frivolous distinctions and preferences in things otherwise equal, which give in the pursuit more distress and uneasiness to mankind" (LJA vi.16; cf. TMS I.iii.2.8).

In emphasizing that commerce transforms our relations with ourselves and leads to restlessness and anxiety, Smith follows Rousseau. But Smith also follows Rousseau in insisting that commerce transforms our relations with others. Earlier we saw that among Rousseau's concerns in the *Second Discourse* was the fear that *amour-propre* privileges a concern for appearances over a concern with the truth of one's character; in Rousseau's terms, *paraître* supplants *être*. His explanation why is simple: a psychology built around the love of recognition in conjunction with a culture that rewards appearances necessarily gives incentives for duplicity, deceit, and dissembling. But Smith himself takes a similar position, evident in his own portrait of "corrupted societies." Taking the court for his example, Smith claims that corrupted societies are precisely those in which advancement and merit have been separated: "success and preferment depend, not upon the esteem of intelligent and well-informed equals, but upon the fanciful and foolish favour of ignorant, presumptuous, and proud superiors," and "external graces, the frivolous accomplishments of that impertinent and foolish thing called a man of fashion, are commonly more admired than the solid and masculine virtues of a warrior, a statesman, a philosopher, or a legislator." In such "quiet and peaceable" societies, "flattery and falsehood too often prevail over merit and abilities" (TMS I.iii.3.6). These strong incentives to duplicity, in turn, cannot but give rise to a profound psychological disjunction, even in the seemingly blithely vain and hypocritical:

Vain men often give themselves airs of a fashionable profligacy, which, in their hearts, they do not approve of, and of which, perhaps, they are really not guilty. They desire to be praised for what they themselves do not think praise-worthy, and are ashamed of unfashionable virtues which they sometimes practise in secret, and for which they have secretly some degree of real veneration. There are hypocrites of wealth and greatness, as well as of religion and virtue; and a vain man is as apt to pretend to be what he is not, in the one way, as a cunning man is in the other. (TMS I.iii.3.7)

Having lost sight of – and almost, but not quite, having grown indifferent to – what is genuinely praiseworthy, such a man becomes dependent on "fraud and falsehood" to gratify his need for recognition, even when that fraud requires concealing his genuine goodness and advertising his vices (TMS I.iii.3.8). The consequences of the separation of *paraître* from *être* are thus every bit as evident to Smith as to Rousseau, and the recovery of the capacity to appreciate merit – in both ourselves and others – is a key element of his normative response to this problem.

To this point we have emphasized Smith's Rousseauan concerns with regard to the stimulus given by commercial society to restlessness and anxiety on the one hand and to deceit and duplicity on the other. In making such claims Smith anticipates a number of the concerns prominent in twentieth-century sociology and twentieth-century social democratic critiques of capitalism. Yet these aspects of Smith's critique hardly exhaust its whole. In developing another side of his critique, Smith shows that his concerns go much further than the concerns of the academic or social-democratic critique and indeed tie him more deeply to that tradition that again begins with Rousseau, but, we might say, culminates not with Marx or Weber but with Nietzsche, insofar as it presents a critique of the bourgeois from above as well as from below. This side of Smith's critique centers on his conviction that commercial man is not simply prone to vanity and anxiety and duplicity, but that his very vanity and anxiety and duplicity inhibit his appreciation and realization of genuine excellence and thereby condemn him to moral mediocrity at best and splendid viciousness at worst. Put differently, Smith's vision of modern commercial man shares with both Rousseau's portrait of the bourgeois and Nietzsche's portrait of the last man a fear of the mediocrity that the pacification of aspirations encourages, as well as a related fear that commercial man has been desensitized to the transcendent as a result of his solicitude for commercial pleasures. This fear, while underemphasized by Smith's readers, yet serves as one of the most important principles uniting his diagnosis of the ills of commercial society to his normative remedy for their alleviation. Whereas commentators indeed have often attended to Smith's interest in alienation and mental mutilation, his no-less-pronounced interest in nobility in precisely this context has been largely overlooked. Smith himself, however, insists that not only does specialized labor render a man stupid and subvert his capacity to form a "just judgment" of ordinary concerns, it renders him incapable "of conceiving any generous, noble, or tender sentiment" (WN V.i.f.50). Here again, the context of Smith's conception of corruption is not merely the subversion of a specific faculty, but rather the very excellence of the human being taken as a whole – a perspective reiterated in Smith's subsequent claim that, as a result of labor specialization, "all the nobler parts of the human character may be, in a great measure, obliterated and extinguished in the great body of the people" (WN V.i.f.51). And this is hardly an idiosyncratic locution limited to a few hyperbolic passages; throughout *The Theory of Moral Sentiments*, as we shall see in greater detail later, Smith repeatedly attests to the centrality of these parts and dispositions, undermining the cynicism that disparages "the love of what is really honourable and noble in human conduct," encouraging our efforts to cultivate "the love of what is honourable and noble" in our own characters, admiring the magnanimous man able to "despise all dangers in the pursuit of what was honourable and noble," invoking the passions that "make us aim at what is noble and honourable," distinguishing "the desire of doing what is honourable and noble" from mere vanity, and praising all those who "aim at really being what is honourable and noble" (TMS III.2.26; TMS III.3.4; TMS VII.ii.1.7; TMS VII.ii.1.5; TMS VII.ii.4.8; TMS VII.ii.4.10). Their simple ubiquity aside, what is striking in these locutions is the dual character of Smith's invocations: in Smith, the "honourable and noble" is a category that refers both to the internal excellence of a certain side of the human psyche and to an external and transcendent excellence beyond ourselves at which some can be said to "aim." Smith's repeated use of the locution in the latter sense is particularly important because it suggests the centrality of his concern for a sort of excellence that extends beyond – literally transcends – the mere social or political excellence characteristic of the polis. This same perspective is crucial to his very understanding of virtue. Smith's most direct definition of virtue is built precisely on this distinction of social and political conventions and standards from transcendent standards for excellence – a point made clear in his explicit insistence that there in fact exists "a considerable difference between virtue and mere propriety." The latter, he claims, "requires no more than that common and ordinary degree of sensibility or self-command which the most worthless of mankind are possessed of" (TMS I.i.5.7). Yet "virtue is excellence, something uncommonly great and beautiful, which rises far above what is vulgar and ordinary" (TMS I.i.5.6).[39]

Smith's distinction between genuine transcendent virtue and mere social propriety is central to his moral philosophy, and particularly central to his diagnosis of and therapy for commercial society. A renewed appreciation of the centrality of this category within his system also compels us to reconsider three common conceptions of his ethical project. The first is the claim that Smith reduces all virtue to mere propriety or social construction – a view popular at least since Victor Cousin's lectures on Scottish

---

[39] Smith's distinction between virtue as excellence and mere propriety has been largely overlooked by those who have regarded his theory of virtue as a propriety theory on the grounds of his self-identification in TMS VII. For an exception, see Raphael, *Impartial Spectator*, 72. See also Smith's explicit claim that while "there is no virtue without propriety," the equation of virtue with propriety is "imperfect" on the grounds that although "propriety is an essential ingredient in every virtuous action, it is not always the sole ingredient" (TMS VII.ii.1.50).

philosophy.[40] Yet this view overlooks Smith's conscious distinction of virtue from propriety, as noted earlier, as well as his sustained campaign to explain how moral agents – and particularly those who live in "corrupt" societies governed by flawed social norms – might develop a capacity to act independently of public opinion. The second is the view that Smith's invocations of a nobility beyond middling commercial virtues is little more than a residual "vestige" of his engagement with premodern ethical categories – categories which his own ethics is said to displace or obviate.[41] On the contrary, in what follows I argue that his engagement with such categories is far from vestigial, or even peripheral, to his political thought, and is in fact central to both his phenomenological account of the moral effects of commerce and his normative ethical remedy for its deficiencies. Attention to this category of the noble also helps to ameliorate a third conception that is at once more accurate and also much more widespread. This is the belief that Smith is best understood as a partisan of "bourgeois virtues" or virtues of men of "middling rank."[42] Smith's sincere endorsement of the genuine benefits of certain of these virtues is of course a distinctive aspect of his ethics and one of the central reasons for its historical significance, and studies that have focused on these have done much to illuminate Smith's contributions. At the same time, focus on the middling virtues has tended to supplant attention to Smith's no-less-sustained interest in a form of human excellence independent of and transcending modern liberal virtues. Smith's interest in combining these sorts of virtues necessarily calls into question the assumption that "virtue" is a zero-sum game in which modernity's founders traded the excellence of antiquity for the "low but solid" virtues of modernity. Smith's own dialectical account of the virtues is rather dedicated to showing

---

[40] With regard to virtue, Smith, Cousin claimed, "confuses it with respect for social propriety... In this theory virtue no longer seems to be virtue; it is no longer undertaken for its own sake; it becomes a matter of politeness and propriety; and if by chance propriety and politeness appear to demand the sacrifice of very serious duties in favour of ones which are not serious, who can say whether one would have the strength to refuse to offer this sacrifice to public opinion?" (Cousin, *Lectures on the History of Moral Philosophy in the Eighteenth Century* [1840], reprinted in Wood, ed. *Adam Smith: Critical Assessments*, vol. 4, pp. 114–15). The claim that Smith assumes "that virtue is identical with propriety" has been more recently restated and developed in Vincent Hope, "Smith's Demigod," in *Philosophers of the Scottish Enlightenment*, ed. Hope (Edinburgh: Edinburgh University Press, 1984), esp. 157, 160, 166.

[41] For the claim that Smith's interest in nobility is merely "a vestige of the classical ideals that according to Mandeville make no sense in commercial society," see Justman, *Autonomous Male*, 111. The language of the vestigial is also to be found in Minowitz, *Profits, Priests, and Princes*, 7, 13, 19, 22, 56, 79, 147, 226, 255; and Cropsey, *Polity and Economy*, xii and 92.

[42] On these claims, see especially the literature cited in Chapter 4, Notes 4 and 5.

how both forms of virtue might be harmonized, thereby maximizing the benefits of each separate category as well as ameliorating the deficiencies of each category left unto itself.

Smith's interest in the revivification of a certain vision of human greatness and nobility against a pervasive modern mediocrity anticipates certain of Nietzsche's efforts in a similar vein. At the same time, Smith's substantive understanding of nobility is far different from that of Nietzsche. In particular, for Smith the concept of moral nobility is itself seemingly paradoxically infused with a solicitude for the needs of the poor and the weak; Smith's achievement with regard to the redefinition of nobility is his harmonization of a commitment to excellence with the spirit of egalitarianism.[43] Just how Smith does this is addressed in later chapters. Here we need to attend to a final aspect of corruption which informs this conception of virtue: his concern that commercialization promotes not only atomization and social fragmentation but also an indifference to the poor. In particular, Smith's concern is that success in the marketplace has as its necessary concomitant the eradication of our natural solicitude for the well-being of our neighbors. In the strongest terms (terms invited by Smith's own treatment), commercialization paradoxically promotes both amelioration of the material conditions of the poor, as noted earlier, and an increasing indifference to the beneficiaries of this amelioration; commercial success, that is, can undermine sympathy.[44]

[43] Cf. Dwyer's claim that Smith's development of the impartial spectator marks his "rejection of the real community in favor of someone resembling a Nietzschean 'übermensch'" ("Theory and Discourse: The 6th Edition of *The Theory of Moral Sentiments*," in *Virtuous Discourse* (Edinburgh: John Donald, 1987), p. 183). Also, by "egalitarianism" I mean something less than what analytic philosophers mean by the term and something other than what is implied by recent scholars who have also applied the term to Smith. McLean has claimed that Smith understood economics to be "a radically egalitarian discipline" that aims to minimize or eliminate distinctions of ranks (*Adam Smith, Radical and Egalitarian*, 80). David Levy and Sandra Peart have identified Smith with egalitarianism on the rather different grounds that Smith is best classified as a thinker who "sufficiently trusts the subject to make unimpeded economic and political choices" rather than insisting on "somehow coercing specific choices and overriding preferences" in the manner of "analytical hierarchicalism" (*The "Vanity of the Philosopher": From Equality to Hierarchy in Post-Classical Economics* (Ann Arbor: University of Michigan Press, 2005), xvi; see also 4, 131–41). My own application of the label of "egalitarian" to Smith refers only to his concern for the well-being of the poor that is commonly associated with egalitarianism today. Insofar as Smith himself privileges concern for the poor over realization of perfect or absolute equality, in contemporary parlance his position is perhaps more accurately described as "prioritarian" rather than egalitarian; see, e.g., Derek Parfit, "Equality or Priority?" *Ratio* 10 (1997): 201–20.

[44] Some will hear in this formulation an echo of the notorious *Adam Smith Problem*. I side, however, with those treatments of *Das Problem* that regard it as a misunderstanding of

Smith's conception of commerce's effects on sympathy is the product of his analysis of the way in which commerce promotes ethical atomism culminating in social fragmentation. He lays the foundation of this conception in his analysis of changes in social relations as a result of economic progress. In his discussion of stadial theory in the *Lectures on Jurisprudence*, he observes that in "the more early and simple times" as opposed to "more luxurious times," families "continued in the same house and contributed their part to the maintaining a common stock." In wealthier societies, however, it becomes common for sons to "separate from the family of the father as soon as they are married" (LJA i.95). Smith then goes on to develop the implications of this small piece of armchair sociology in the sixth edition of *The Theory of Moral Sentiments*, where he observes that, in pastoral ages, extensive domestic cohabitation is necessary for reasons of "common defence" as well as economic necessity. Yet these arrangements had a clear reciprocal ethical effect: "They are all, from the highest to the lowest, of more or less importance to one another. Their concord strengthens their necessary association; their discord always weakens, and might destroy it." Smith's claim here is that the "intercourse" natural to precommercial societies promoted a specific type of social and moral identification, one founded not only on an "extensive regard to kindred" but also on a form of familial acceptance whose egalitarianism he underlines by insisting on the fact that under such conditions even a highland chief would recognize "the poorest man of his clan, as his cousin and relation" (TMS VI.ii.1.12). Smith uses this portrait of close, reciprocal, egalitarian ties of affection characteristic of rude ages as a standard by which to gauge the effects of commercial progress:

In commercial countries, where the authority of law is always perfectly sufficient to protect the meanest man in the state, the descendants of the same family, having no such motive for keeping together, naturally separate and disperse, as interest or inclination may direct. They soon cease to be of importance to one another; and, in a few generations, not only lose all care about one another, but all remembrance of their common origin, and of the connection which took place among their ancestors. (TMS VI.ii.1.13)

both the nature and relationship of self-love and sympathy, or the self-regarding and the other-regarding virtues; as I argue later, Smith's effort to reconcile these categories in fact animates his virtue theory. My claim here is somewhat different: not that sympathy and self-interest are in tension, but that inequality is inimical to sympathy, and that commercial societies, insofar as they require some degree of inequality, also necessarily inhibit a certain degree of sympathy. For particularly helpful reconsiderations of *Das Problem*, see Montes, *Smith in Context*, 15–56; and Otteson, *Marketplace of Life*, 2–4 and 93–100.

Smith's point here is hardly to lionize premodern aristocracies; he has lit-tle good to say about aristocratic familial identification, which he thinks founded on "the most frivolous and childish of all vanities" (TMS VI.ii.1.13). His claim is rather that commercialization and democratization – whose ben-efits he clearly valued – are yet in certain instances inimical to the values of "care" and "connection."

Smith's discussion of the effects of stadial progress on the family thus provides a window into one of the most penetrating aspects of his diagnosis of the ethical effects of commercialization, namely its effects on sympathy. Smith delivers the heart of this side of his doctrine in observing that "those persons most excite our compassion and are most apt to affect our sympathy who most resemble ourselves, and the greater the difference the less we are affected by them" (LJA iii.109). This claim is remarkable for at least two reasons. First, it reveals another point of contact with Rousseau and Tocqueville. In each of their theories, the concept of the *semblable* looms large. The concept is notoriously difficult to translate into English, but it roughly describes a social identity that is rooted in the mutual recognition of sameness. Such a conception is capable of being used either for good (as in the case of the reciprocal civic friendships of the Genevans, described by Rousseau in the dedication of the *Second Discourse* and the conclusion of the *Letter to d'Alembert*) or for bad (as in the oppressive homogeneity of the Americans described by Tocqueville in the conclusion of *Democracy in America*).[45] Smith suggests that the concept is crucial, for it seems to be the case that there is a direct correlation between the degrees of our con-sciousness of our "resemblance" to others and the degrees of our capacity for both compassion for and sympathy with them. This in turn reveals a second reason why the observation is crucial. It is well known that Smith considered persistence of wealth inequalities to be a fundamental, even if lamentable, prerequisite for economic growth. Yet now Smith claims that such inequalities, even if instrumentally necessary for opulence, inhibit our most distinctively human trait, namely our capacity for sympathy.

In developing this claim Smith applies a central point from his moral philosophy to his political philosophy. Several excellent studies have shown that, in Smith's system, the strength of all sympathetic attachments is directly

---

[45] See Rousseau, *Discourse on Inequality*, in *Discourses*, trans. Gourevitch, 114–23; Rousseau, *Letter to d'Alembert*, trans. Bloom (Ithaca: Cornell University Press, 1960), 135-6n; Toc-queville, *Democracy in America*, II.iv.6-8. On Tocqueville's use of the concept, see esp. Manent, *Tocqueville and the Nature of Democracy*, trans. John Waggoner (Lanham, MD: Rowman and Littlefield, 1996), 48–52, 61–65.

proportional to the proximity of the spectator to the person principally concerned.[46] But also deserving explicit recognition is that Smith's political theory rests on the same observation, with distance measured not in terms of spatial propinquity but in terms of social status and material rank. Smith details the effects of this operation in numerous places. One important discussion comes in the *Lectures on Jurisprudence*, in a discussion of the difference between a farmer and a nobleman in their relations to servants. Here Smith argues that the nobleman is "much farther removed" from the condition of his servant than the farmer, who "generally works along with his servant; they eat together, and are little different." This fact fundamentally determines their differing relations with the members of their households; as the noble's relationships with his servants are founded on a "disproportion," indeed one "so great that he will hardly look on him as being of the same kind," he consequently thinks his servant "has little title even to the ordinary enjoyments of life" and indeed "feels but little for his misfortunes" (LJA iii.108–109). The conditions of Roman slaves further prove the point. In the early days of the republic, in which inequalities of wealth were more moderate, slave treatment was more humane. But when "more advanced in riches and refinement," their treatment became. This leads Smith to pause on a paradox: namely that the treatment of the poor worsens even as the material condition of society – and hence their own material condition – improves. "The more society is improved the greater is the misery of a slavish condition; they are treated much better in the rude periods of mankind than in the more improved. Opulence and refinement tend greatly to increase their misery." All of this leads Smith, rightly considered one of our greatest champions of both commerce and liberty, to pause on a sobering thought:

Opulence and freedom, the two greatest blessings men can possess, tend greatly to the misery of this body of men, which in most countries where slavery is allowed makes by far the greatest part. A humane man would wish therefore if slavery has to be generally established that these greatest blessings, being incompatible with the happiness of the greatest part of mankind, were never to take place. (LJA iii.109–111; cf. LJB 136–37)

Coupled with his explicit reminder just before that slavery has so far been abolished in only a very small part of the globe (LJA iii.101), Smith's

---

[46] On this point, see especially Russell Nieli, "Spheres of Intimacy and the Adam Smith Problem," *Journal of the History of Ideas* 47 (1986): 611–24, esp. 619–24; Eugene Heath, "The Commerce of Sympathy: Adam Smith on the Emergence of Morals," *Journal of the History of Philosophy* 33 (1995): 447–66, esp. 455–57; and Forman-Barzilai, "Sympathy in Space(s)," 189–217.

implication seems to be that the social conditions of the vast majority of the world are not yet fit for the greatest blessings now enjoyed by only a fortunate few.

Against this claim it might be argued that the radical disproportion between the conditions of the few and those of the many characteristic of precommercial ages has at least been narrowed, if not wholly eradicated, by commercial modernity, and hence that Smith's concerns regarding inequality's evisceration of sympathy are today misplaced or obsolete. Yet Smith himself argues quite the opposite. Across his corpus, his comments on the capacity for reciprocal identification across modern society's classes are decidedly pessimistic. One unexpected place Smith develops these is in his analysis of comedy in LRBL. His principal claim here is that the "foundation of ridicule" lies in the unexpected inversion of the high and the low (LRBL i.108; LRBL i.110; LRBL i.117). The success of such an inversion, however, he explains, rests on a peculiar aspect of our natural psychology, namely our propensity to admire our superiors and to despise our inferiors: "Whatever we see that is great or noble excites our admiration and amazement, and whatever is little or mean on the other hand excites our contempt" (LRBL i.107). Herein of course lies the foundation of the psychology of emulation and identification on which much of Smith's economics is built. Yet unlike TMS and WN, which largely emphasize the practical and material collective benefits of the psychology of emulation, LRBL gives us the darker obverse side, the effects of our contempt of the "little and mean." The main effect of such contempt is to further inhibit our capacity for sympathy:

There is in human nature a servility which inclines us to adore our superiors and an inhumanity which disposes us to contempt and trample under foot our inferiors. We are too much accustomed to the misfortunes of people below or equal with ourselves to be greatly affected by them. But the misfortunes of the great both as they seem connected with the welfare of a multitude and as [they seem] we are apt to pay great respect and attention to our superiors however unworthy are what chiefly affect us. Nay such is the temper of men, that we are rather disposed to laugh at the misfortunes of our inferiors than take part in them. (LRBL ii.90)

The restatement of this point in the paragraph that follows makes even clearer the drastic implications of inequality for our capacity for sympathy: "we are rather apt to make sport of the misfortunes of our inferiors than sympathise with them" (LRBL ii.91).

Smith further elaborates on the effects of this disposition in *The Theory of Moral Sentiments*. In TMS II he observes that although men are "naturally sympathetic," they yet "feel so little for another, with whom they have no

49

particular connexion, in comparison of what they feel for themselves" (TMS II.ii.3.4; cf. TMS I.i.4.7). TMS I.iii.2 is famous for its forthright presentation of the positive effects of the fact, as noted elsewhere, that "our sympathy with our superiours [is] greater than that with our equals or inferiors" (LJB 12–13). Here we indeed not only learn that vanity is the impetus for commercial aspirations, but we also learn much about how the world beholds the rich man (and how he regards their regard), always conscious that he is "observed by all the world," that "every body is eager to look at him," that "in a great assembly he is the person upon whom all direct their eyes," and that he is "the object of the observation and fellow-feeling of every body about him." The optimist is meant to take this ubiquitous solicitude for recognition as the seed of a healthy emulation that encourages pursuit of similar paths and similar rewards. Yet Smith also spares no opportunity to emphasize the destructive effects of the obverse disposition, for the same disposition that promotes the lionization of the wealthy strips the poor of their dignity:

The poor man, on the contrary, is ashamed of his poverty. He feels that it either places him out of the sight of mankind, or, that if they take any notice of him, they have, however, scarce any fellow-feeling with the misery and distress which he suffers. He is mortified upon both accounts; for though to be overlooked, and to be disapproved of, are things entirely different, yet as obscurity covers us from the daylight of honour and approbation, to feel that we are taken no notice of, necessarily damps the most agreeable hope, and disappoints the most ardent desire, of human nature. The poor man goes out and comes in unheeded, and when in the midst of a crowd is in the same obscurity as if shut up in his own hovel. Those humble cares and painful attentions which occupy those in his situation, afford no amusement to the dissipated and the gay. They turn away their eyes from him, or if the extremity of his distress forces them to look at him, it is only to spurn so disagreeable an object from among them. The fortunate and the proud wonder at the insolence of human wretchedness, that it should dare to present itself before them, and with the loathsome aspect of its misery presume to disturb the serenity of their happiness. (TMS I.iii.2.1)

Here Smith perhaps even goes beyond Rousseau. Rousseau's solicitude for the poor is well known (though not unchallenged),[47] yet his consistent claim is that the solicitude for recognition is an adventitious desire not natural to man. But for Smith the denial of such recognition is not simply a frustration of an artificial need but rather an assault on human dignity itself. Thus, after describing the indignity of the defeated Perseus being led captive in the victory procession of Aemilius Paulus, Smith is moved to observe that

[47] An excellent reconsideration of Rousseau's reputation for distributivism in light of his actual textual claims is provided in Fleischacker, *Short History of Distributive Justice*, 56–61.

"compared with the contempt of mankind, all other external evils are easily supported" (TMS I.iii.2.12). But this is precisely the position of the poor in commercial society, Smith insists, whose position is so contemptible that the fortunate are compelled to avert their eyes. It is thus something more than a mere claim of injustice to which Smith is appealing when he calls our attention to the position of the modern laborer and the fact that "he who as it were supports the whole frame of society and furnishes the means of the convenience and ease of all the rest is himself possessed of a very small share and is buried in obscurity." His obscurity is at least as painful as any material injustice; he suffers not simply because "he bears on his shoulders the whole of mankind" while he enjoys the fewest advantages, but because "unable to sustain the load" he is "buried by the weight of it and thrust down into the lowest parts of the earth," and indeed "buried out of sight" (LJA vi.28; ED 5; cf. LJB 213).[48]

With this in place we can see the full effects of commerce on moral sentiments. The foundational principle of Smith's theory of moral sentiments is of course the desire for mutual sympathy founded on a fellow-feeling with the misery and the joy of others (TMS I.i.1.3). Throughout his book, Smith insists that this fellow-feeling is a natural and nearly universal response to our apprehension of adversity in particular: "we sympathize with the sorrow of our fellow-creature whenever we see his distress" (TMS II.i.2.5). Yet this otherwise universal sympathy simply does not hold before poverty: "The mere want of fortune, mere poverty, excites little compassion. Its complaints are too apt to be the objects rather of contempt than of fellow-feeling. We despise a beggar; and, though his importunities may extort an alms from us, he is scarce ever the object of any serious commiseration" (TMS III.3.18). Such a disposition is of course not without a certain utility of its own: appreciating the reticence of others to sympathize with our plights is of course an important incentive for cultivating self-command (see, e.g., TMS I.iii.1.9), and presumably the aversion to apprehending beggars encourages in us the industry that precludes resort to beggary. Yet Smith will not have us forget that increases in inequality also tend to encourage both "compassion" for the rich (TMS I.iii.2.2; TMS I.iii.2.6; TMS I.iii.2.9) and "indifference of men about the misery of their inferiors" (TMS I.iii.2.2).

---

[48] Amartya Sen presents an interesting contemporary application of Smith's concepts of "social exclusion" as developed here; see, e.g., his "Conceptualizing and Measuring Poverty," in *Poverty and Inequality*, ed. David B. Grusky and Ravi Kanbur (Stanford: Stanford University Press, 2006), 35–38, 44. See also Heilbroner, who calls helpful attention to Smith's account of indifference to poverty in TMS III.3 and I.iii.2 ("Socialization of the Individual in Smith," 130–31).

We are left then with a tension: on the one hand, Smith in several places insists that the growth of inequality in commercial society inhibits sympathy and the recognition of human dignity. On the other hand, Smith is not only a sincere believer in commercial society's material benefits but also consistently argues that the psychology that drives both commercial growth and moral corruption – our admiration for our superiors and our contempt for our inferiors – is too entrenched to be excised. This leaves him in a certain spot. On the one hand, he shares the concerns of the "whining and melancholy moralists" (TMS III.3.9) but thinks their schemes of reformation naïve and impractical. On the other hand, he shares the admiration of partisans of the system of natural liberty but finds their complacent acceptance of its deficiencies similarly untenable. To move beyond this impasse, Smith took it upon himself to chart a moderate and middle path, one that might ameliorate the most destructive features of commercial corruption and preserve the maximal gains of markets. Those ills, as defined in this chapter, might be briefly summarized here as a set of specific concerns: the explosion of *egocentrism*, manifesting itself in *vanity* and *love of superiority*; the encouragement of *restlessness* and *anxiety* induced by this new-found solicitude for superiority; the growth in *inauthenticity* and *duplicity* toward others induced by vanity; a growing *indifference to nobility* and *acceptance of moral mediocrity* as a consequence of solicitude for the pleasures of commercial society; an encouragement of *atomistic individualism* and concomitant weakening of reciprocal social ties as a result of attaining of commercial society's pleasures; and, finally, the *inhibition of our capacity for sympathy* and an *indifference to the condition of our inferiors* as a consequence of our solicitude for superiors. It is quite a list: selfishness, restlessness, anxiety, inauthenticity, duplicity, mediocrity, alienation, and indifference. Yet it is precisely these problems that constitute the question to which Smith's conception of virtue is intended as an answer.[49]

---

[49] My formulation of this point is indebted to Robert Pippin, "What Is the Question for which Hegel's Theory of Recognition is the Answer?" *European Journal of Philosophy* 8 (2000): 155–72.

2

THE SOLUTION: MORAL PHILOSOPHY

LIBERAL INDIVIDUALISM AND VIRTUE ETHICS

Having identified the central problem that Smith's conception of virtue was intended to address, it remains for us to examine the substance and the methods of his answer. This chapter focuses on his answer's methods. In so doing, it argues that the moral theory presented in the sixth edition of *The Theory of Moral Sentiments* is best understood as a contribution to the eighteenth-century virtue ethical tradition and is misunderstood when interpreted as an incipient contribution to either of the other two main schools of contemporary moral philosophy – utilitarianism and deontology – which also trace their modern origins to the latter half of the eighteenth century, and with which Smith has sometimes been associated.

In this century, virtue ethics has emerged principally as a late-stage rival to both utilitarian or consequentialist ethical approaches on the one hand and deontological or neo-Kantian approaches on the other. In contrast to these systems, which evaluate actions on the grounds of their capacity to maximize good effects (as consequentialism does) or on the grounds of their adherence to universally valid and rationally derived moral rules (as deontology does), virtue ethicists focus on evaluating characters and the specific virtues and vices that contribute to the composition of good and bad characters. In shifting attention from actions to characters, virtue ethicists are often said to replace the question of "what should I do?" with "what should I be?"[1] The inspiration for this turn is often credited to the

---

[1] The growing literature on virtue ethics is usefully surveyed and its central claims presented in Gregory Trianosky, "What Is Virtue Ethics All About? Recent Work on the Virtues," *American Philosophical Quarterly* 27 (1990): 335–44; Roger Crisp, "Modern Moral Philosophy and the Virtues," in *How Should One Live?*, ed. Crisp (Oxford: Oxford University Press, 1996), 1–18; Karen Stohr and Christopher Wellman, "Recent Work on Virtue Ethics," *American Philosophical Quarterly* 39 (2002): 49–72; David Copp and David Sobel, "Morality and Virtue: An Assessment of Some Recent Work in Virtue Ethics," *Ethics* 114

resurgence of neo-Aristotelianism.[2] To a lesser extent, and more recently, the antecedents of contemporary virtue ethics have been traced to eighteenth-century British moral philosophy, and particularly to Hutcheson and Hume.[3] But to these names a third needs to be added, for among the intentions of *The Theory of Moral Sentiments* (and the sixth edition in particular) is to describe an alternative approach to ethics, one that directs attention away from both moral rules and utility maximization and instead refocuses it on the cultivation of character. Furthermore, like contemporary virtue ethicists, Smith too is indebted to Aristotle.[4] These debts, however, are not our

(2004): 514–54; and Julia Annas, "Virtue Ethics," in *Oxford Handbook of Ethical Theory*, ed. Copp, 515–36. For important challenges to virtue ethics as a coherent alternative to consequentialism and deontology, see esp. Martha Nussbaum, "Virtue Ethics: A Misleading Category?" *Journal of Ethics* 3 (1999): 163–201; and Jane Singleton, "Virtue Ethics, Kantian Ethics, and Consequentialism," *Journal of Philosophical Research* 27 (2002): 537–51.

[2] The recovery of Aristotle's approach to ethics is the departure point for several of the seminal statements of virtue ethics; see, e.g., G. E. M. Anscombe's 1958 essay "Modern Moral Philosophy" (reprinted in *Virtue Ethics*, ed. Crisp and Slote, 26–44). Aristotle's place as the originator of the virtue ethics tradition is underlined by MacIntyre in several of his writings; see, e.g., his entry "Virtue Ethics," in *Encyclopedia of Ethics*, ed. L. C. Becker and C. B. Becker, 2nd ed. (London: Routledge, 2001), vol. 3, pp. 1757–63. For critiques of the misappropriation of Aristotle by modern virtue ethicists on the grounds that their theories overemphasize Aristotle's egoism and neglect his understanding of the place of politics in human flourishing, see Peter Simpson, "Contemporary Virtue Ethics and Aristotle," *Review of Metaphysics* 45 (1992): 503–24; and Stephen Buckle, "Aristotle's *Republic* or, Why Aristotle's Ethics Is Not Virtue Ethics," *Philosophy* 77 (2002): 565–95.

[3] Stephen Darwall's reader, for example, includes selections from three philosophers prior to the twentieth century: Aristotle, Hutcheson, and Hume; see Darwall, ed., *Virtue Ethics* (Oxford: Blackwell, 2003); and MacIntyre, "Virtue Ethics," 1760. On Hume's virtue ethics, see esp. Marcia Homiak, "Does Hume Have an Ethics of Virtue? Some Observations on Character and Reasoning in Hume and Aristotle," *Proceedings of the Twentieth World Congress of Philosophy* 7 (2000): 191–201; Christine Swanton, "Can Hume Be Read as a Virtue Ethicist?" *Hume Studies* 33 (2007): 91–113; and Jacqueline Taylor, "Hume on Beauty and Virtue," in *A Companion to Hume*, ed. Elizabeth Radcliffe (London: Blackwell, 2008), 273–92. For a more critical evaluation, see Rosalind Hursthouse, "Virtue Ethics and Human Nature," *Hume Studies* 25 (1999): esp. 80–81. Douglas Den Uyl also makes a strong case for Shaftesbury as a "classical virtue ethicist" in his "Shaftesbury and the Modern Problem of Virtue," *Social Philosophy and Policy* 15 (1998): 276ff.

[4] Recent commentators have helpfully developed Smith's debts to Aristotle on a striking range of other points beyond those examined here. On justice, see Laurence Berns, "Aristotle and Adam Smith on Justice: Cooperation Between Ancients and Moderns?" *Review of Metaphysics* 48 (1994): 71–90; on friendship, see Den Uyl and Griswold, "Adam Smith on Friendship and Love," *Review of Metaphysics* 49 (1996): 609–38; on the commercial virtues, see Martin J. Calkins and Patricia H. Werhane, "Adam Smith, Aristotle, and the Virtues of Commerce," *Journal of Value Inquiry* 32 (1998): 43–60; on practical wisdom, see Fleischacker, *Third Concept of Liberty*, 125–39, and Maria Alejandra Carrasco, "Adam Smith's Reconstruction of Practical Reason," *Review of Metaphysics* 58 (2004): 81–116; on

focus here.[5] Rather, our goal is to show that Smith not only anticipates several aspects of modern virtue ethics but also that the development and articulation of his practical intervention in the debate over the proper remedy for commercial society's ills employs a virtue ethical approach.[6]

Doing so requires recovery of one of the most neglected aspects of Smith's ethics. Smith is well known for having divided ethics into two questions: "wherein does virtue consist?" and "by what power or faculty in the mind is it, that this character, whatever it be, is recommended to us?" (TMS VII.i.2). Studies of his ethics tend to emphasize the sophistication of his treatment of the latter question and minimize the perspicuity of his response to the former.[7] Yet Smith takes pains to stress the priority of the first question, calling the second the "next question of importance," "a mere

self-command and the mean, see Gloria Vivenza, *Adam Smith and the Classics: The Classical Heritage in Adam Smith's Thought* (Oxford: Oxford University Press, 2001 [1984]), 46–50, and Montes, *Smith in Context*, 81–86; on the best regime, see Alvey, *Adam Smith: Optimist or Pessimist*, esp. 163–64; and on rhetoric, see the studies cited in Chapter 3, Note 20.

[5] I treat these debts at greater length in my essay "Adam Smith, Aristotle, and Virtue Ethics," in *New Voices on Adam Smith*, ed. Montes and Schliesser (London: Routledge, 2006), 17–39; see also Chapter 3, this volume.

[6] Herein lies one of the contributions of the present study. Several other commentators have also identified Smith with a virtue ethical approach; see esp. Vincent Hope, *Virtue by Consensus: The Moral Philosophy of Hutcheson, Hume, and Adam Smith* (Oxford: Clarendon Press, 1989), 83–88; Griswold, *Smith and the Virtues of Enlightenment*, esp. 50, 185, 229ff., 265, 288, and 358; Deirdre McCloskey, *The Bourgeois Virtues: Ethics for an Age of Commerce* (Chicago: University of Chicago Press, 2006); 306–7, and in "Adam Smith, the Last of the Former Virtue Ethicists," *History of Political Economy* 40 (2008): 43–71; Robert C. Solomon, "Free Enterprise, Sympathy, and Virtue," in *Moral Markets: The Critical Role of Values in the Economy*, ed. Paul J. Zak (Princeton: Princeton University Press, 2008), 20; Montes, *Smith in Context*, 11, 96; and Robert Shaver, "Virtues, Utility, and Rules," in *Cambridge Companion*, 208; but cf. Haakonssen, "Introduction: The Coherence of Smith's Thought," in *Cambridge Companion*, 15. My own approach does not pretend that Smith gives an adequate or full-fledged virtue theory (whatever that may be), but rather that he adopts elements of this approach in responding to a specific political problem. The value of his contribution thus lies not simply in the way in which he answers contemporary problems in virtue theory, but rather in the substantive answer he gives to a substantive moral and political problem and the methodological example he offers of how moral philosophy might meet practical problems.

[7] Representative is Raphael's judgment that Smith's answer to the virtue question is "disappointingly thin" as compared to his "ingenious and well-constructed solution" to the judgment question; see his *Impartial Spectator*, 71, cf. 10–11, 68–69, and his "Adam Smith 1790: The Man Recalled; the Philosopher Revived," in *Adam Smith Reviewed*, ed. Peter Jones and Andrew S. Skinner (Edinburgh: Edinburgh University Press, 1992), 108–112. In this vein see also the suggestion that "if we want guidance on how to live the good life, we should look elsewhere" than Smith (Haakonssen and Winch, "The Legacy of Adam Smith," in *Cambridge Companion*, 385); as well as the suggestion that Smith's ethics is silent on the "'art of living'" and "rules out the exclusive identification of happiness with a

matter of philosophical curiosity" – one that, while "of the greatest importance in speculation, is of none in practice" (TMS VII.iii.intro.1; TMS
VII.iii.intro.3). Smith's emphasis on the priority of the virtue question, coupled with its relative underemphasis in the literature, prompts the present
effort to elucidate his conception of "the excellent and praise-worthy character" (TMS VII.i.2; TMS VII.ii.1) and the methods necessary to apprehend and cultivate such a character. In an effort to explain how a virtue
ethical approach shapes his inquiry on this front, this chapter then has three
goals: first, to demonstrate the importance of Smith's normative, humanistic
conception of philosophy; second, to examine his distinction between the
two branches of moral philosophy, ethics and natural jurisprudence; and
third, to demonstrate that he consciously argued against incipient versions
of deontology and utilitarianism and crafted his approach to normative ethics
from a virtue ethical standpoint.

In uncovering these debts to virtue ethics I do not wish to argue that
Smith offers us pat solutions to the most vexing problems in contemporary
virtue theory debates, but rather that the value of his approach lies in his
demonstration of the possibility – and even the necessity – of synthesizing
virtue ethics and liberal individualism. This aspiration marks Smith as unique
in both his day and ours. His belief that it is both possible and necessary
to ennoble modern commercial liberalism through a recovery of virtue
distinguishes him both from eighteenth-century proponents of commercial
society, such as Mandeville, who claim that virtue is unnecessary for a
flourishing polity, and the eighteenth-century critics of commercial society,
such as Rousseau, who suggest that the recovery of virtue necessary for

unique kind of life" (Pratap Mehta, "Self-Interest and Other Interests," in *Cambridge Companion*, 265–66). My own position, developed in what follows, is much closer to that of
Vivienne Brown, who emphasizes that Smith's answer to the "what is virtue" question, his
distinction between praise and praiseworthiness, and his account of the wise and virtuous
man would all "need to be drained of normative import before Haakonssen and Winch's
interpretation could be made plausible"; see Brown's review of the *Cambridge Companion*
in *Economics and Philosophy* 24 (2008): 262. In a similar vein, see Schliesser's critique of
this antinormative reading as reliant on "a very anachronistic version of the fact-value
distinction" (http://ndpr.nd.edu/review.cfm?id=10823). Haakonssen and Winch's view is
also implicitly contested in Ann Firth's claim that Smith, like Kant, "wants his readers and
students to dedicate themselves to the attainment of inner moral purity" ("Adam Smith's
Moral Philosophy as Ethical Self-Formation," in *New Perspectives on Adam Smith's "The
Theory of Moral Sentiments,"* ed. Geoff Cockfield, Ann Firth, and John Laurent (Chel-
tenham: Edward Elgar, 2007), 120). I might contest the suggestion that Smith's normative
ideal is best described as "purity," but Firth seems right to emphasize that Smith's ethical
ideals, and particularly his portrait of the wise and virtuous man, were intended to provide
incentives for self-betterment.

human flourishing requires the rejection of commercial liberalism. Similar suspicions of incommensurability persist today, evident in claims that the concept of the self upon which liberal individualism is based is inimical to the creation of communities that form the necessary context for the exercise of genuine virtue, that it is inimical to the other-directed virtues that distinguish modern virtue ethics from mere egocentrism, and that it promotes a concern for utility maximization and self-aggrandizement incompatible with virtue. Smith grants that any form of liberal individualism that in fact led to such consequences would be inimical to virtue; his entire critique of commercial corruption, as examined earlier, is founded on this concept. Yet unlike many critics today, Smith distinguishes corruptions of liberal individualism from a conception of liberalism both more stable and more likely to promote virtue. Smith grants that this conception is "egocentric" insofar as it takes the goods of the self as its point of departure, but in so doing it only replicates the foundation shared by other ethics of virtue. His commercial liberalism is predicated not on an attenuated vision of the self driven by self-interest, but rather on the conviction that the conditions of material security and freedom that commercial liberalism provides offer the optimal context for the cultivation of character to which an ethics of virtue aims.

SOCIAL SCIENCE VERSUS MORAL PHILOSOPHY

Before we turn to the nature of Smith's virtue ethics, a pressing question must be addressed. The obstacles to an appreciation of his virtue ethics stem only in part from competing readings of his moral theory as utilitarian or deontological. A much broader obstacle is to be found in the well-received and prevalent view that Smith's enterprise is not normative, but "scientific." This position has taken a variety of forms, ranging from broad claims that Smith is a father of modern social science and the Scottish "science of man," to specific claims that his approach to ethical and economic inquiry is descriptive or phenomenological and best understood as an objective, qualitatively neutral effort to understand human phenomena from the standpoint of the detached scientific observer.[8] What unites these claims is the conviction that

---

[8] A forgotten pioneer of this approach was Albion W. Small, *Adam Smith and Modern Sociology: A Study in the Methodology of the Social Sciences* (Chicago: University of Chicago Press, 1907), esp. 20–21, 81–83, 146–47. Developed and influential expositions of and commentaries on this view are to be found in T. D. Campbell, *Adam Smith's Science of Morals* (London: George Allen and Unwin, 1971), esp. 19–21, 46, 51–52, 234–36; Raphael, "Adam Smith: Philosophy, Science, and Social Science," in *Philosophers of the Enlightenment*, ed. S. C. Brown (Sussex: Harvester Press, 1977), 83–89; Andrew S. Skinner, *A System of Social Science*

Smith is more concerned to observe and explain than judge or intervene, and it is principally on these grounds that his contributions to modern social science have been taken to be so pioneering. It should be noted, however, that this characterization has not been accepted tout court; recent years have seen several challenges to the reductionism to which such a conception of Smith's philosophical method potentially points. Several of these question the possibility of an absolute separation of the normative and descriptive elements in Smith's social science, suggesting that his methods are an amalgamation of these elements.[9] Our appreciation of such has in fact advanced so far as to make it plausible to suggest that the old *Adam Smith Problem* has been replaced by a much more interesting reconciliatory question: namely the question of how Smith was able to synthesize the normative and descriptive aspects of his social science.[10] This question in any case seems more promising

(Oxford: Clarendon Press, 1979); Winch, *Adam Smith's Politics*, 6; Haakonssen, *Science of a Legislator*, 6, and "Introduction," in *Cambridge Companion*, 4; Minowitz, *Profits, Priests and Princes*, 2–3, 129; Craig Smith, *Adam Smith's Political Philosophy: The Invisible Hand and Spontaneous Order* (London: Routledge, 2006), 164–66; Forman-Barzilai, "Sympathy in Space(s)," 191. The most thoroughgoing study of Smith's commitment to the "empirical" and ostensible antipathy to the "abstract" with which I am familiar is Milton L. Myers, *The Soul of Modern Economic Man* (Chicago: University of Chicago Press, 1983), esp. 95–97, 107–8, 118–19.

[9] J. Ralph Lindgren importantly sought to expose the "myth" of Smith as social scientist by painting him as a "profoundly humane philosopher" (*The Social Philosophy of Adam Smith* (The Hague: Martinus Nijhoff, 1973), 15–19). This position has been further developed in several important subsequent studies, including Muller, *Smith in His Time and Ours*, 48–49, 93; Griswold, *Smith and the Virtues of Enlightenment*, 72–73; Fleischacker, *Smith's Wealth of Nations*, 34–36, and Fleischacker, "Smith's Ambiguities: A Response to Emma Rothschild's *Economic Sentiments*," *Adam Smith Review* 1 (2004): 141–49; and Berry, "Smith and Science," in *Cambridge Companion*, 130–34. Evensky's development of Smith's hopeful and humanistic commitment to social improvement is of particular note (see, e.g., *Smith's Moral Philosophy*, 15–16, 31–32, 77, 108, 148, 312); I discuss these aspects of Evensky's work at greater length in a book review published in *Revue de philosophie économique* 8 (2007): 123–28. Also important in this context is Evensky's claim that Smith may be a Newtonian, but he is one who yet appreciates the "fundamental difference between the human condition and the natural world that surrounds it" (*Smith's Moral Philosophy*, 7); and Alvey's claim that Smith resisted positivism, and instead understood himself to be "a moral philosopher who aimed to improve society morally, in part to achieve human perfection as an end in itself, and in part to achieve social order" ("Moral Education as a Means to Human Perfection and Social Order: Adam Smith's View of Education in Commercial Society," *History of the Human Sciences* 14 (2001): 2). Illuminating studies of the ways in which Smith was appropriated by later rational choice theorists and economists are to be found in Sonja Amadae, *Rationalizing Capitalist Democracy: The Cold War Origins of Rational Choice Liberalism* (Chicago: University of Chicago Press, 2003), 193–219; and Evensky's chapter on "Chicago Smith Versus Kirkcaldy Smith," in *Smith's Moral Philosophy*, 245–64.

[10] This tension is suggested in Winch's account of the debate over whether "the explanatory style of the proto-social scientist, operating in a proto-positivist manner, is incompatible

than the simple question of whether TMS is ultimately *either* normative *or* descriptive; recognizing that between its covers one finds efforts in each direction, our task is to explain how Smith understood these approaches to cohere. The key to such may well lie in the recognition of two additional facts: first, Smith's prescriptive modes tend to be associated with his discussions of the virtue question and his analytic modes with the judgment question; second, the normative elements are decidedly more pronounced in the sixth than in previous editions. Together these facts suggest that Smith's embrace of both descriptive and prescriptive methodologies is driven less by any explicit theoretical reconciliation (a reconciliation that he conspicuously fails to provide) than by the simple fact that such an embrace is compelled by the nature of the comprehensive problem that he set for himself – the identification and resolution of the problem of commercial corruption. In this sense, his embrace of both normative and scientific analysis is less evidence of any tension or inconsistency in his approach but rather evidence of his recognition that they are separate and equally necessary sides of a single comprehensive project; his normative response to the problem of commercial corruption, that is, suggests his awareness of the insufficiency of the scientific mode of analysis alone to respond fully to corruption. This insufficiency in turn compelled his (and, in turn, compels our) consideration of normative remedies grounded in a prescriptive account of virtue rather than descriptive or scientific accounts of institutional design.

To restate Smith's remedies in a more detailed way: it has long been recognized that the institutional proposals set forth in Book V of the *Wealth of Nations* were largely conceived as responses to the corruption problem with which we are engaged. In these institutional proposals Smith makes clear precisely what he has in mind when he proclaims that corruption "deserve[s]

with the normative moral and political concerns of republicanism" ("Commercial Realities, Republican Principles," 298) and in his "Adam Smith: Scottish Moral Philosopher as Political Economist," *Historical Journal* 35 (1992): 95; see also Shaver, "Virtues, Utility, and Rules," in *Cambridge Companion*, 195–96. Helpful on the ways in which Smith's social science embraces both positivistic and normative commitments is Frederick Neuhouser, "*Wealth of Nations* and Social Science," *Adam Smith Review* 2 (2006): 236–38. A particularly excellent discussion of the seeming tension between the descriptive and the normative elements in Smith's project can be found in Otteson, *Marketplace of Life*, esp. 10–11 and 202–3, and see also his persuasive account of Smith's synthesis at pp. 220–39, which offers a useful correction to a too-common propensity to read his comment on his "present inquiry" at TMS II.i.5.10 as a self-conscious methodological pronouncement on the whole of TMS, and thus an endorsement of positivism (esp. pp. 224, 236–39). I treat this passage at greater length in my forthcoming essay "Skepticism and Naturalism in Adam Smith," in *Essays on Adam Smith's Philosophy*, ed. Vivienne Brown and Samuel Fleischacker (London: Routledge, 2009).

the most serious attention of government" and that "some attention of government is necessary in order to prevent the almost entire corruption and degeneracy of the great body of the people" (WN V.i.f.60; WN V.i.f.49). In explaining how government might attend to this problem, Smith sets forth a science of institutional design that anticipates certain elements of the science developed by Madison and other architects of the American constitution, with the most prominent of these being his proposals for expanded military training, for the public encouragement of theaters, for controlling the effects of religious faction through freedom of expression, and an expansive and unprecedented proposal for public education at state expense.[11] This final proposal has garnered the most attention from Smith's readers – much of it critical. Indeed ever since Marx, Smith's educational proposals, radical as they may have been for his age, have been largely considered insufficient to meet the enormous challenges of corruption; education, it is often argued, is too slight a bandage for the gaping wound Smith himself describes. Several arguments to the contrary have been set forth, but on the whole, this critique of his educational proposal remains common and persuasive to many.[12]

[11] For an overview of Smith's institutional approach, see especially Nathan Rosenberg, "Some Institutional Aspects of the *Wealth of Nations*," *Journal of Political Economy* 68 (1960): 559, 569–70. Smith's views on the need for political institutions to remedy the lacunae in natural order in particular has been especially helpfully developed in Lauren Brubaker, "Adam Smith on Natural Liberty and Moral Corruption: The Wisdom of Nature and Folly of Legislators?" in *Enlightening Revolutions: Essays in Honor of Ralph Lerner*, ed. Svetozar Minkov (Lanham, MD: Lexington Books, 2006), 191–217; and Brubaker, "Does the 'Wisdom of Nature' Need Help?" in *New Voices*, ed. Montes and Schliesser, 168–92. For treatments of specific aspects of the institutional proposal, see, on Smith and the militia and military service, Richard B. Sher, "Adam Ferguson, Adam Smith, and the Problem of National Defense," *Journal of Modern History* 61 (1989): 240–68 (esp. the helpful analysis of WN V.i.f.60 at 255, which dovetails with my own earlier analysis), and Montes, *Smith in Context*, 61–69; on Smith's arguments for religious pluralism as a means of countervailing sectarian factionalism (and Madison's debts to these arguments), see Fleischacker, "Adam Smith's Reception among the American Founders, 1776–1790," *William and Mary Quarterly*, 3rd ser., 59 (2002): 897–924, esp. 907–15, and Brubaker, "Smith on Natural Liberty," 210–12; on freedom of religion and its relationship to political liberty, see esp. Griswold, *Smith and the Virtues of Enlightenment*, 266–92; on Smith and the theater, see my essay "From Geneva to Glasgow."

[12] See, e.g., Cropsey, *Polity and Economy*, 106; and Heilbroner's dismissal of the educational solution as "utter folly" in "Paradox of Progress," 538. More positive assessments of the sufficiency of the educational proposals to mitigate the effects of commercial corruption can be found, e.g., in Alvey, "Moral Education as a Means to Human Perfection," 9–12; Force, *Self-Interest Before Smith*, 251–52; Brian Smith, "Smith, Leisure, and the Division of Labor," 24, 35–38, 43; Rasmussen, *Problems and Promise*, 12, 108–11, 129, 163; and esp. West, "Adam Smith on the Cultural Effects of Specialization: Splenetics versus Economics," *History of Political Economy* 28 (1996): 100; West, "Adam Smith and Alienation:

But what have not been emphasized are the implications of this critique. If indeed the institutions of WN V are insufficient to meet the challenges of commercial society, three options readily present themselves: first, to accept complacently the failure of the political science of institutional design and to resign ourselves to the prospect that the corruption problem is irresolvable and inescapable; second, to revisit our political science and propose a more comprehensive and hopefully more successful institutional remedy; or third, to restrain the urge for immediate action from the conviction that nature, in its wisdom, will in time remedy the ill consequences of previous human action. Smith nods, at various times, in each direction, as several excellent studies have shown.[13] Yet these three options hardly exhaust the entire range of available possibilities. Smith's corpus, as it has come to us, suggests another: namely the possibility that he considered this specific problem from a quite different angle, employing a quite different methodology. Indeed the

Wealth Increases, Men Decay?" in *Essays on Adam Smith*, ed. Wilson and Skinner, 540, and West, "Smith and Rousseau's *Discourse*," 56. According to West, part of the reason such educational institutions are sufficient to meet the problem is simply that the problem is less pressing than often thought. This view has been extended in two recent detailed studies. Hill, in the course of her helpful account of Smith's argument for the ways in which specialization promotes interdependence, liberty, and security, argues that although Smith recognized specialization's deleterious effects, he regarded these with "complacency" and as "of relatively low importance in the grand scheme of things," considering them inconveniences "far outweighed by the benefits" of specialization, "soluble within prevailing social relations," and sufficiently insubstantial that Smith's educational proposals were "perfectly adequate" to meet their challenges ("Smith, Ferguson and Marx," 345–48, 356–58); see also her claim in response to Pack and Heilbroner that the proper cure for the ills of progress is "more progress" ("Smith and Corruption," 647). Similarly, Maria Pia Paganelli's excellent exposition of the ways in which self-interest promotes excessive self-preference and anxiety and undermines social order suggests these negative effects are in appearance only, and that TMS in fact "does not seem to present any serious criticism of self-interest," for in it, self-interest is "always successfully constrained" ("The Adam Smith Problem in Reverse: Self-Interest in *The Wealth of Nations* and *The Theory of Moral Sentiments*," *History of Political Economy* 40 (2008): esp. 370–76). Such a view may obviate criticisms of Smith's educational proposals by rendering such institutions unnecessary, yet seems difficult to square with Smith's concerns in the sixth edition.

[13] For the first view – and particularly for the claim that "rather than furnishing philosophical weapons against moral decay and political incapacity," Smith's works "offer full and complete surrender" – see Gallagher, *Rule of the Rich*, 71; cf. 78, 90, 94. For the second view, in addition to the studies of the "science of the legislator" cited in Chapter 4, Note 14, see the accounts of Smith's vision of "philosophical and political statesmanship" as nature's helper in Brubaker, "Does the 'Wisdom of Nature' Need Help?" in *New Voices*, ed. Montes and Schliesser, 169–73, 185–87; and "Smith on Natural Liberty," in *Enlightening Revolutions*, ed. Minkov, 206–10. For the third view, see the studies of unintended order in Otteson, *Marketplace of Life*, esp. 101–33; and Craig Smith, *Smith's Political Philosophy*, esp. 1–14, 164–68.

very fact of his execution of TMS VI in the sixth edition is evidence of his recognition of the inadequacy of quietism in the face of commercial society's most pressing ills, as well as the limits of social science in establishing a remedy for the unanticipated consequences of its own inventions. TMS VI, that is, is an attempt to solve, via moral philosophy, precisely the problem that was bequeathed by economics and which political science proved unable to solve in WN V.

TWO TYPES OF MORAL PHILOSOPHY: NATURAL JURISPRUDENCE VERSUS ETHICS

The claim that Smith turned to moral philosophy to solve a political problem invites several questions: among them, what sort of moral philosophy did Smith employ to solve this problem? Putting matters this way returns us to another crucial albeit underemphasized distinction. At the end of TMS, Smith claims that "the two useful parts of moral philosophy" are "Ethics and Jurisprudence" (TMS VII.iv.34). The distinction is made in the course of an argument to exclude casuistry from legitimate moral philosophy. Yet this distinction does significant work in his theory, because it concludes his argument that moral philosophy's two "useful parts" are distinguished by differing ends and methods. Recent scholarship, in the wake of Haakonssen's pioneering work, has focused largely on Smith's natural jurisprudence, in part to provide an alternative to civic humanist accounts of his political thought.[14] Yet appreciation of the role of virtue in his moral and political philosophy – while indeed a virtue different from that of the republican paradigm – requires an examination of his conception of the methods of "the science which is properly called Ethics" as compared to those of "what might properly be called natural jurisprudence" (TMS VII.iv.6; TMS VII.iv.37).

Smith presents his fullest account of the differing methods of these sciences in the final section of the final part of TMS. His account distinguishes "two

[14] In addition to Haakonssen's path-breaking *Science of a Legislator*, see also his essays "What Might Properly Be Called Natural Jurisprudence?" in *The Origins and Nature of the Scottish Enlightenment*, ed. R. H. Campbell and Andrew S. Skinner (Edinburgh: John Donald, 1982), 205–25 (and especially 222n9, where a system built on the negative virtue of justice is said to have by necessity a stronger normative character than a system of positive virtues); and "Natural Law and Moral Realism: The Scottish Synthesis," in *Studies in the Philosophy of the Scottish Enlightenment*, ed. M. A. Stewart (Oxford: Oxford University Press, 1990). On the relationship between the two schools, see esp. Pocock, "Cambridge Paradigms and Scotch Philosophers," in *Wealth and Virtue*, ed. Hont and Ignatieff; cf. Berry, "Smith and the Virtues of Commerce," in *NOMOS XXXIV: Virtue*, 76; and Berry, "Smith Under Strain," 459. For a recent argument for the recovery of civic humanism against the jurisprudential approach, see Montes, *Smith in Context*, esp. 11, 57–58, 92.

different manners" of treating ethical rules (TMS VII.iv.2). The first he associates with those philosophers who focus on justice and aim to articulate rules for just action that are "accurate in the highest degree, and admit of no exceptions or modifications" (TMS III.6.10). Theorists of justice can (indeed must) establish such rules for reasons that concern both the nature and significance of the phenomena they study. Their significance is familiar; Smith's analogy of the virtues to parts of a building – with beneficence as a mere ornament and justice the pillar that supports the whole – is the foundation of his argument for why the observance of justice can be mandated by legal force, whereas the practice of the other virtues cannot (TMS II.ii.3.4; TMS II.ii.1.5 and 7). Yet this quintessentially liberal argument for the priority of justice constitutes only half of his argument for separating justice from the social virtues. Justice also requires separate treatment for reasons that concern the nature of its subject. It is this less obvious reason that underlies Smith's repeated insistence that justice "is the only virtue with regard to which such exact rules can properly be given," that its rules "are the only rules of morality which are precise and accurate" and "those of all the other virtues are loose, vague, and indeterminate," and his claim that to expect the same rigorous adherence to the rules for other virtues as we do for justice would be "the most absurd and ridiculous pedantry" (TMS VII.iv.7; TMS VII.iv.1; TMS III.6.9). Jurisprudence can be reduced to a science because its phenomena can be treated scientifically; they in fact meet Smith's own criterion on this front, a criterion set forth in his review of Platonic science, in which he claims that "the objects of science, and of all the steady judgments of the understanding, must be permanent, unchangeable, always existent, and liable neither to generation nor corruption, nor alteration of any kind" (HALM 2). Smith's own partially executed quest to establish "a theory of the general principles which ought to run through and be the foundation of the laws of all nations" is itself an attempt at a "scientific" discourse that would meet this definition's criteria (TMS VII.iv.37; cf. LJB 1). But it is equally clear that ethical phenomena that concern extrajudicial matters do not meet this standard, as evident in Smith's treatment of custom in TMS V, among other discussions.[15]

---

[15] HALM 2 poses a challenge. Although Smith clearly gives his description of science in the first person here, one wonders whether he is speaking in his own name or in Plato's (or the Platonists') name. But even if the latter, the essential point still stands: Smith's aim is to separate ethics – an "Aristotelian" science of particulars – from the "Platonic" or universal orientations characteristic of either the physical sciences or a universal science of natural jurisprudence.

As a consequence, Smith suggests that the methods required of ethicists differ from those required of natural lawyers, and the conflation of these methods has led to unnecessary confusion within moral philosophy as a whole. Hence he divides the methods of treating moral rules into those of "critics," on the one hand, who applied to their study of all virtues "that loose method to which they were naturally directed by the consideration of one species of virtues," and on the other, those of "grammarians" who, in treating the virtues, "universally endeavoured to introduce into their precepts that sort of accuracy of which only some of them are susceptible" (TMS VII.iv.2). Each method is in some measure in the wrong insofar as it applies to the whole of its inquiry methods appropriate only to a part of it. Smith's own method of inquiry in TMS suggests that he thinks the method of the critics better suited to the subject matter of ethical inquiry (and indeed particularly to the subject matter of Part VI) and that of the grammarians suited to justice, the proper object of jurisprudence.[16] He develops this point in his critique of the casuists. Both "the casuists of the middle and latter ages of the Christian church, as well as all those who in this and in the preceding century have treated of what is called natural jurisprudence" are grammarians who "do not content themselves with characterizing in this general manner that tenor of conduct which they would recommend to us, but endeavour to lay down exact and precise rules for the direction of every circumstance of our behaviour" (TMS VII.iv.7). Yet natural lawyers seeking to establish rules of justice used this method more successfully than did those casuists who sought "to prescribe rules for the conduct of a good man" (TMS VII.iv.8).[17] Smith cannot condone such methods for such ends – hence his critique of the casuists for attempting "to no purpose, to direct by precise rules what it belongs to feeling and sentiment only to judge of." As contributions to ethics their works are essentially worthless: "dry and disagreeable," prone to impose "frivolous accuracy" on "subjects which do not admit of it," abounding "in abstruse and metaphysical distinctions," but ultimately "incapable of exciting in the heart any of those emotions which it is the principal use of books of morality to excite." Their worst fault is that they fail to achieve the normative aim that Smith insists is the proper goal

---

[16] Smith's recognition that the nature of justice requires that it be treated in a manner different from the other ethical virtues anticipates and thereby avoids one of the most common objections to contemporary virtue ethics, namely that it fails to provide a sufficient defense for justice itself; see, e.g., Stohr and Wellman, "Recent Work," 68.

[17] For excellent discussions of the origins and operation of these general rules, see Haakonssen, *Science of a Legislator*, 61–62; Brown, *Smith's Discourse*, 82–86; and Fleischacker, *Third Concept of Liberty*, esp. 41–55.

of ethics and hence they are "as useless as they are commonly tiresome," as "none of them tend to animate us to what is generous and noble" and none "tend to soften us to what is gentle and humane" (TMS VII.iv.33).[18]

Herein lies the distinctive aspect of Smith's "ethical" rather than "jurisprudential" approach to moral philosophy in TMS. Smith insists not only that moral discourses should properly have normative effects but also that a rule-bound morality is ineffective at achieving such effects, owing to a characteristic tendency toward ethical reductionism in actual circumstances. He calls attention to this reductionism in his discussion of the impossibility of discovering an ethical general rule "that will apply to all cases without exception." He takes as an example the difficulties associated with the question of the ethical obligation to keep one's word in varying situations – an example that Kant would soon make famous (and indeed argue to a quite opposite conclusion) in his discussion of lying.[19] From the perspective of "the common sentiments of mankind," Smith claims, it is "evidently impossible" to determine how and when and to what degree an extorted promise should be kept: "This would vary according to the characters of the persons, according to their circumstances, according to the solemnity of the promise, and even according to the incidents of the rencounter" (TMS VII.iv.12). He reiterates this in Part VI. Here the example concerns the proper method of recompensing benefactors, and the lesson is the same: it is "altogether impossible" to "determine by any precise rules" proper conduct amidst conflicting obligations. Rules are of no help: "These it is often impossible to accommodate to all the different shades and gradations of circumstance, character, and situation, to differences and distinctions which, though not imperceptible, are, by their nicety and delicacy, often altogether undefinable" (TMS VI.ii.1.22).

Smith's argument against casuistry thus culminates in the argument that the sort of reductionism characteristic of rulebound approaches fails to respond adequately to the individual circumstances that are necessarily

---

[18] In this respect, Smith sides with Hutcheson rather than Hume, implicitly agreeing with his teacher that "warmth in the cause of virtue" is no vice in a philosopher, and denying Hume's claim that it is "impossible to conjoin" the perspectives of the scientific "anatomist" and the normative "painter"; see the well-known letter of Hume to Hutcheson, 17 September 1739, in *The Letters of David Hume*, ed. J. Y. T. Greig (Oxford: Clarendon Press, 1932), vol. 1, p. 32. In this vein see also Phillipson's helpful suggestion that Smith sided with Hutcheson in regarding "the Stoic and Augustinian longing for virtue as a fundamental moral need which would have to be satisfied if men and women were to be truly sociable" ("Language, Sociability, and History: Some Reflections on the Foundations of Adam Smith's Science of Man," in *Economy, Polity, and Society: British Intellectual History 1750–1950*, ed. Stefan Collini, Richard Whatmore, and Brian Young (Cambridge: Cambridge University Press, 2000), 72–74).

[19] Kant, *Groundwork of the Metaphysics of Morals*, Ak 4:402–3.

unique to each ethical situation. Yet his orientation in light of this under-standing is perhaps unexpected. One route he might have taken would have been to shift focus from rules to judgment and to develop an account of practical wisdom capable of responding to the nuances of discrete situations; some recent studies have done much in fact to illuminate Smith's account of the practical wisdom that might help an agent navigate such terrain.[20] Yet Smith also offers an additional category: not only is he interested in cultivating our capacity for practical deliberation and reasoned choice, but he also seeks to cultivate our appreciation of how ideal characters, possessed of both ethical and deliberative excellence, will act in such situations. In some sense this approach is suggested in his interest in not simply virtue, but in "the character of virtue" – a concept that embraces not only the charac-ter virtues but also the study of virtuous characters. As we shall see, TMS VI offers – alongside studies of prudence, magnanimity, and beneficence – portraits of "the prudent man," "the wise and virtuous man," and "the mag-nanimous man" (TMS VI.i.7ff; TMS VI.iii.25; TMS VI.iii.44).[21] Smith's ethical inquiry in this respect takes its bearings from the same methods and objectives that he associates with classical ethical inquiry and especially with Aristotle and Cicero. Like the ancients – and unlike the medieval casuists and modern natural lawyers – Smith aims to "present us rather with a general idea of the perfection we ought to aim at, than afford us any certain and infallible directions for acquiring it" (TMS VII.iv.1; TMS III.6.11).

Our full argument on this front has to wait; for now we only mark the dis-tinction between ethics and natural jurisprudence, as well as Smith's repeated

---

[20] For helpful treatments of Smith's conception of practical wisdom, and particularly his conception of the reciprocal relationship between reason and sentiment, see especially Carrasco, "Smith's Reconstruction of Practical Reason," esp. 83–90, 112–14; and Fleis-chacker, *Third Concept of Liberty*, esp. 125–39. A more critical perspective is offered in Den Uyl, *The Virtue of Prudence* (New York: Peter Lang, 1991), 123–41.

[21] This point is beginning to attract more attention. Vivenza explicitly describes Part VI as a "gallery of 'characters'" (*Smith and the Classics*, 60). Other important studies of the import of character in Smith include Paddy Bullard's ms. "'Physiognomy of the Mind': Conceptions of Character from the Augustans to Adam Smith"; and Colin Heydt, "'A Delicate and an Accurate Pencil': Adam Smith, Description, and Philosophy as Moral Education," *History of Philosophy Quarterly* 25 (2008): 57–73, in which Smith's aim is said to be "to depict a *typified individual*" rather than to depict "the *quality itself*" (61; italics original), and Smith himself is said to "follow the lead of the ancient moralists" (58). Heydt's analysis is particularly helpful in calling attention to Smith's efforts as a moral "diagnostician" who seeks to improve our capacity to recognize the virtues, in keeping with classical approaches (see esp. 63, 67), though he sharply distinguishes Smith's ethics from classical commitments to the promotion of human flourishing and self-perfection (59) in a way that I do not (see Chapter 6, this volume).

insistence that TMS is conceived in the frame of the former rather than the latter, as suggested in his repeated claim that whereas natural jurisprudence is "by far the most important" of the sciences and the "least cultivated," it yet "belongs not to our present subject to enter into any detail" on it (TMS VI.ii.intro.2; cf. TMS VII.iv.37). The very fact that Smith chose not to treat justice in his study of "the character of virtue" in Part VI is further indicative of the separation he sought to effect. This in itself provides a window into not only his political thought but also his moral philosophy, and particularly into his vision of the best society. Smith is famous for having argued that justice is not only necessary for the stability of society, but that it is also "but a negative virtue," one which "does no real positive good," and which can often be fulfilled "by sitting still and doing nothing" (TMS II.ii.1.9). The priority of this negative virtue is often taken as a main indication of his preference for a liberal social order. Yet the negative virtue of justice is nearly wholly absent from his study of the character of virtue; here Smith's focus is on "the foundation of that order which nature seems to have traced out for the distribution of our good offices, or for the direction and employment of our very limited powers of beneficence" (TMS VI.ii.intro.2). To put the point more strongly: at the expected place in TMS VI, Smith appears less interested in minimizing the harms that are the product of failing to adhere to the negative virtue of justice than in maximizing the benefits that are the product of proper adherence to the active virtues. This marks a sharp difference from the dominant modes of inquiry of WN and LJ. These inquiries are dedicated to accounting for forms of social organization that promote justice and avoid injustice by building on the 'low but solid' foundation of "mercenary exchange of good offices according to an agreed valuation" (TMS II.ii.3.2), an image memorialized in TMS in its sketch of a dutiful but dysfunctional family bound by "the mutual exchange of all essential good offices" (TMS VI.ii.1.8). Smith is aware, however, of another approach that sets its sights much higher. A stable society can be built on the pursuit of mutual self-interest, but for those interested in the society that "flourishes and is happy" – the type of society that is naturally attractive to the virtue ethicist – the needs of individuals are satisfied not by the mechanical operations of reciprocal self-interest, but "from love, from gratitude, from friendship, and esteem" (TMS II.ii.3.1). The central category of Smith's virtue ethics is thus not the self-interest characteristic of the political and economic systems he defends but a more nuanced understanding of self-love and the dispositions to which it gives rise, and the goal of this virtue ethics is not to minimize harms or injustices but to maximize the benefits of mutual affection.

THREE TYPES OF ETHICS: UTILITARIANISM, DEONTOLOGY, AND VIRTUE ETHICS

Having drawn two distinctions in this chapter already, we are now poised to draw a third. Our inquiry to this point has argued that, in TMS, Smith's discourse is that of the moral philosopher rather than the social scientist and, furthermore, that as a moral philosopher his discourse is that of the ethicist rather than the natural lawyer. But putting the question this way necessitates another distinction: what sort of ethicist was Smith? In our day, the study of normative ethics is dominated by three rival schools: utilitarianism, deontology, and virtue ethics. To claim that eighteenth-century ethics was similarly dominated by the same three schools would be both anachronistic and reductionist. At the same time, these categories can be useful in helping to navigate the eighteenth century, particularly in light of the fact that two of the principal ethical systems of its second half, those of Hume and Kant, have often been regarded as expressions of incipient versions of utilitarianism and deontology, respectively. And while it would be too much to claim that Smith provides a "system" that rivals theirs, evaluating his ethics against their categories can help us see what is distinctive in his own. In so doing it becomes clear that Smith sought to distinguish his approach from the incipient versions of utilitarianism and deontology with which he was familiar.

Smith's argument against utilitarianism is largely contained in TMS IV.1, as is well known.[22] Yet the aim of this chapter is not simply to argue against utilitarianism as one might today; that is to say, its principal goal is not simply to counter the claim that the proper standard for evaluating actions is their capacity for utility-maximizing effects. Both here and elsewhere Smith avoids developing his position in terms of a debate over absolute moral standards.[23]

---

[22] TMS IV.1 has given rise to a number of competing readings. Some have argued that Smith is best seen through a utilitarian lens; see Campbell, *Smith's Science of Morals*, esp. 205 and 219; and Fred Rosen, "The Idea of Utility in Adam Smith's *Theory of Moral Sentiments*," *History of European Ideas* 26 (2000): 79–103. For challenges to this view, see esp. Marie Martin, "Utility and Morality: Adam Smith's Critique of Hume," *Hume Studies* 16 (1990): 107–20; and Pack and Schliesser, "Smith's Humean Criticism," 52–54. See also the helpful review of this debate in Montes, *Smith in Context*, 114–15.

[23] Thus Haakonssen's claim that Smith "did not raise the question of a validating foundation for morality"; see his introductions to his edition of TMS (Cambridge: Cambridge University Press, 2002), vii–viii; and to the *Cambridge Companion*, 4–5. For the full extension of this claim, see Haakonssen and Winch, "Legacy of Adam Smith," in *Cambridge Companion*, esp. 381 and 384–86; cf. Carola von Villiez, "Double Standard – Naturally! Smith and Rawls: A Comparison of Methods," in *New Voices*, ed. Montes and Schliesser, 124, 134.

In TMS IV.1 in particular his aims are simultaneously more modest and more ambitious. Their modesty lies in the fact that Smith does not deny the goodness of utility maximization, but rather suggests that to posit utility maximization as either the sole or the ultimate standard of ethical value overlooks the moral significance of beauty; such reductionism precludes a comprehensive understanding of the multiple phenomena involved in moral judgment. Yet this claim, however modestly phrased, is ambitious. Smith's project to recover beauty as a legitimate category of moral judgment is substantively parallel to a central aim of his moral and political inquiry into the nature of virtue. As we have seen, among Smith's goals on this front is to recover the concept of nobility from threats posed to it by materialism. His attempt to recover beauty from the reductionism of utilitarianism is therefore both substantively similar to and indeed a prerequisite for his normative efforts to recover moral beauty.

The evidence for this claim lies in Smith's simultaneous efforts to recover both "beauty" and "nobility" in TMS IV.1. The chapter introduces itself as a response to an unnamed Hume, particularly to Hume's claim that utility is always pleasing because it suggests to our imagination, on apprehending an object, "the pleasure or conveniency which it is fitted to promote" (TMS IV.1.2). Against this position, Smith argues that what "has not, so far as I know, been yet taken notice of by any body" is that the beauty of utility, and the capacity for utility in particular – what Smith tends to call its "fitness" – is often more valued than the actual achievement or production of useful ends (TMS IV.1.3; TMS IV.2.3). This argument is significant for several reasons. Most famously it serves as the foundation of Smith's argument concerning the relationship of economic growth to human psychology; indeed the chapter that begins as a counter to utilitarianism famously ends with Smith's most notorious (and compressed) account of the unintended beneficial consequences of the invisible hand, here guiding the ruling passions of the poor man's son and the proud and unfeeling landlord. Yet other important work is also being done here. Smith's concern is to resist the reductionism characteristic of utilitarianism; thus, he claims that "it seems impossible that the approbation of virtue should be a sentiment of the same kind with that by which we approve of a convenient and well-contrived building; or that we should have no other reason for praising a man than that for which we commend a chest of drawers" (TMS IV.2.4). Smith is blunt: men, quite simply, are not armoires, and thus any theory of our admiration of their virtue must not only account for their utility, but also for "the unexpected, and on that account the great, the noble, and exalted propriety of such actions" (TMS IV.2.11).

Smith's strategy here is to confront the deflationary and reductionist ten-dencies of utilitarianism with the fact that they fail to account for our love of nobility and beauty. It is indeed on this theme that his argument in TMS IV turns. Yet this claim seems odd on its face. The examples Smith initially proposes to recover beauty seem hardly noble by any definition, but down-right petty: the man pained lest a door not be placed in the middle of a house (TMS IV.1.1); the man troubled by the disorder of the chairs in his hall (TMS IV.1.4); the man disconcerted by the relative unreliability of his cheap watch (TMS IV.1.5). But as in his analogy of the pin factory, here too "trifling" illustrations are being used to convey a larger point. His claim in each case is that a basic disposition, the love of beauty, has been misdirected. This claim is particularly evident in his account of the watch-owner. Smith makes clear that solicitude for the watch's excellence is of no comparative advantage to its owner: "the person so nice with regard to this machine, will not always be found either more scrupulously punctual than other men." It is thus not the love of utility that explains such a man's love of fine watches, but another love altogether: "what interests him is not so much the attain-ment of this piece of knowledge, as the perfection of the machine which serves to attain it" (TMS IV.1.5). Put differently, at the heart of even so petty a materialist as the watch-lover lies a disdain of the ordinary and a love of the beauty characteristic of perfection. The point is reiterated powerfully in the next paragraph. Smith famously despises and devalues "trinkets of frivolous utility" – "baubles," he calls them – whose "whole utility is cer-tainly not worth the fatigue of bearing the burden" (TMS IV.1.6). The love of such trinkets, of course, is central to the argument concerning luxury consumption and economic growth here presented. But this argument also has another side. In framing his discussion not simply in terms of luxury but in terms of love of beauty, Smith suggests that there might be something more than vulgar selfishness at work in the heart of the lover of luxuries. The desire to possess and consume such trinkets yet reflects a native love of the beautiful – a disposition that is both natural and admirable, however corrupted its manifestation may be here.

The next question for Smith is how this disposition might be rescued from the base forms it commonly takes. This question governs much of the remainder of the argument of TMS IV. Elsewhere we will need to address the best-known aspects of this argument – the poor man's son and the invisible hand – but here we concentrate on the way in which Smith appeals to and cultivates this otherwise misdirected love of the beautiful and noble. His principal aim in this respect is to show the political utility of a redirected form of this disposition. Thus he follows his study of the poor man's son and the selfish landlord by observing that "the same principle, the same love of system, the same regard to the beauty of order, of art and contrivance, frequently serves to recommend those institutions which tend to promote the public welfare." Put more strongly: the same disposition that finds its expression in watch collecting in some can be redirected to assist in the promotion of public prosperity in others. Furthermore, Smith thinks this disposition more effective at generating public spirit and promoting public welfare than either sympathy or humanity. Hence he observes that "from a certain spirit of system, however, from a certain love of art and contrivance, we sometimes seem to value the means more than the end, and to be eager to promote the happiness of our fellow-creatures, rather from a view to perfect and improve a certain beautiful and orderly system, than from any immediate sense or feeling of what they either suffer or enjoy." Thus his striking claim:

When a patriot exerts himself for the improvement of any part of the public police, his conduct does not always arise from pure sympathy with the happiness of those who are to reap the benefit of it. It is not commonly from a fellow-feeling with carriers and waggoners that a public-spirited man encourages the mending of high roads. When the legislature establishes premiums and other encouragements to advance the linen or woollen manufactures, its conduct seldom proceeds from pure sympathy with the wearer of cheap or fine cloth, and much less from that with the manufacturer or merchant. The perfection of police, the extension of trade and manufactures, are noble and magnificent objects. The contemplation of them pleases us, and we are interested in whatever can tend to advance them. (TMS IV.1.11)

This claim is remarkable for at least two reasons. Smith has often been celebrated and criticized for having contributed to the modern substitution of sentiment for reason. But here his explicit claim is that humanity or sympathy or fellow-feeling with the suffering are too weak to effect substantive political action; a well-crafted appeal to a love of the beautiful, however, offers a remedy for the deficiency of the softer, social sentiments. Second, the themes of the preceding passage are so banal as to be boring, focusing as it does on such topics in public administration as textile production, highway maintenance, and trade regulation. Yet it is precisely the "perfection" of these seemingly mundane objects that Smith calls "noble and magnificent" and "beautiful and grand." In making such claims, Smith reiterates a point first made in his discussion of the poor man's son. The poor man's son is likewise fixated on mundane external goods, but their appearance is dramatically translated by his imagination into "something grand and beautiful and noble, of which the attainment is well worth all the toil and anxiety which we are so apt to bestow upon it" (TMS IV.1.9, 11). In each case, Smith's aim is to show that our native longing for beauty or nobility, particularly when magnified by the imagination, remains a powerful source of human motivation – far more powerful than utilitarianism recognizes.

Smith's argument against utilitarianism is thus complex; rather than rejecting it as a whole, his claim is that while it holds in certain cases it lacks the comprehensiveness that its adherents occasionally claim for it – as evidenced by its failure to account for the love of beauty. His argument against deontology takes a similar form. Smith praises a moral code based on general rules at several places, perhaps most pointedly in his assertion that, in the absence of general rules, "there is no man whose conduct can be much depended upon" (TMS III.5.2). On the grounds of such claims, a reading of his ethics through the deontological lens has emerged.[24] Yet Smith's no-less-frequent qualifications of the effectiveness of a rule-grounded ethics reveal an ambivalence that ultimately prevents us from classifying his ethics as fully deontological.

Smith's principal discussion of the central concepts of deontology is to be found at TMS III.4–6. In introducing his discussion of general rules, Smith begins from a quite Kantian point of departure. The principal justification for an ethics of general rules is its effectiveness at overcoming what Smith calls "self-deceit, this fatal weakness of mankind," which is "the source of half the disorders of human life" (TMS III.4.6). As for Kant, for Smith the chief problem in practical ethics is the egotistic distortion of judgment that occurs when individuals are judges in their own cases and "every thing appears magnified and misrepresented by self-love" (TMS III.4.3). In one sense, Smith classifies this as a problem of judgment, the second question of TMS VII.i.2, rather than as a problem of virtue: "So partial are the views of mankind with regard to the propriety of their own conduct, both at the time of action and after it; and so difficult is it for them to view it in the light in which any indifferent spectator would consider it" (TMS III.4.5). The distortion of judgment by egoism will thus to some degree require recourse to the impartial spectator, the central category of the judgment question, as well as

[24] See most recently Ernst Tugendhat, "Universalistically Approved Intersubjective Attitudes: Adam Smith" (trans. Bernard Schriebl) *Adam Smith Review* 1 (2004): 88–104. MacIntyre explicitly identifies Smith as an advocate of virtue as "rule-following"; see *After Virtue*, 234–35. Montes identifies specific elements of Smith's theory as deontological (see *Smith in Context*, 54n, 98, 108–13, 128) and also provides a helpful comparison of Smith to Kant (see *Smith in Context*, 114–22). The historical links between Smith and Kant have been most thoroughly traced in Fleischacker, "Philosophy in Moral Practice: Kant and Adam Smith," *Kant-Studien* 82 (1991): 249–69; and his "Values Behind the Market: Kant's Response to the *Wealth of Nations*," *History of Political Thought* 17 (1996): 379–407; as well as his *Third Concept of Liberty*; cf. Valihora, "Judgement of Judgement," 155–61.

to the rehabilitation of self-love through a reconsideration of the character of virtue. But in the present inquiry, a more immediate question requires attention: namely, how does Smith's conception of the utility of general rules in judgment compare to that of Kant and to deontological ethics more generally?

Kant and Smith alike seek to curb the effects of egotistic self-preference in self-judgment and thereby lift what Smith famously calls "the mysterious veil of self-delusion" (TMS III.4.4). Both indeed would agree that "general rules of conduct, when they have been fixed in our mind by habitual reflection, are of great use in correcting the misrepresentations of self-love concerning what is fit and proper to be done in our particular situation" (TMS III.4.12). Yet Smith and Kant describe quite different paths to this end. Their main differences are two. First, Smith's account of the origins of general rules is empirical, and hence a posteriori.[25] Although he agrees with Kant that nature has not left men "altogether without a remedy" and "abandoned us entirely to the delusions of self-love," his remedy is hardly Kant's: "Our continual observations upon the conduct of others, insensibly lead us to form to ourselves certain general rules concerning what is fit and proper either to be done or to be avoided" (TMS III.4.7). Smith continually returns to this theme in what follows, emphasizing that the origin of general rules is to be traced to experience rather than reason – hence his insistence that the general rules that determine standards for both praise and blame "can be formed no other way than by observing what actions actually and in fact excite them" (TMS III.4.10). This line of argument reaches its peak in his observation that

It is thus that the general rules of morality are formed. They are ultimately founded upon experience of what, in particular instances, our moral faculties, our natural sense of merit and propriety, approve, or disapprove of. We do not originally approve or condemn particular actions; because, upon examination, they appear to be agreeable or inconsistent with a certain general rule. The general rule, on the contrary, is formed, by finding from experience, that all actions of a certain kind, or circumstanced in a certain manner, are approved or disapproved of. (TMS III.4.8; cf. TMS III.4.9)

This observation does a great deal of work in Smith's theory. First, in emphasizing the fact that general rules are the product of experience and not reason, Smith reiterates his distance from Kant's a priori mandates. Second, Smith reveals his distance from even non-Kantian forms of deontology in insisting that general rules, however derived, are not unto themselves the principal

---

[25] A helpful discussion of this point is offered in Raphael, *Impartial Spectator*, 55–56.

standards for morality; as was true in his argument against utilitarianism, Smith's strategy here is to suggest that such a focus on discovering a unitary absolute standard for morality reduces the complex and multiple phenomena of moral judgment to crude simplifications. And finally, by suggesting that the construction of general rules necessarily requires both acuity of observation and precision of judgment, Smith implies that morality has for its prerequisite the cultivation of perceptual skills and a capacity for the synthesis of the multiple and disparate data derived from such discrete and repeated perceptions. All of this suggests a very different way of doing ethics, one that is self-consciously set forth as an alternative to rival approaches. Thus he insists that circumstances have "misled several very eminent authors, to draw up their systems in such a manner, as if they had supposed that the original judgments of mankind with regard to right and wrong, were formed like the decisions of a court of judicatory, by considering first the general rule, and then, secondly, whether the particular action under consideration fell properly within its comprehension" (TMS III.4.11). His system, on the contrary, seeks to be less reductionist. Thus, although it remains true that Smith perhaps has no "metaphysics of morals" and indeed fails to speak to the concerns of contemporary metaethics, his "failure" on this front hardly relegates him to the ranks of mere describers of empirical moral phenomena.[26] As his critique of deontology makes clear, to be even a "scientific" or sociological student of morality one must abandon the "neutral" view and instead apply the natural human capacity for the appreciation of the discrete particularity of individual situations.[27] Smith, it might be said, seeks to occupy a middle ground between the reductionism of deontology or casuistry on the one hand, and the relativism of pluralism on the other.[28]

If Smith's departure from Kant's conception of the origins of general rules can be said to form the first leg of his disagreement with deontology, his departure from Kant's conception of the universal applicability of such rules constitutes the other. Again, on its face this claim seems odd. As we read on into TMS III.5, Smith's defense of general rules appears to grow more strident. But this appearance is deceiving; what Smith in fact comes to defend is not general rules as universally applicable (as, say, with Kant's

---

[26] See Haakonssen's claim that Smith "does not have access to a universal morality nor is an underlying logos any part of his concern" ("Introduction," in *Cambridge Companion*, 9).

[27] My views here are influenced by my study of Isaiah Berlin's conception of political judgment; see my "Political Science and Political Understanding: Isaiah Berlin on the Nature of Political Inquiry," *American Political Science Review* 98 (2004): 327–39.

[28] The question of the possibility of Smith's own relativism is important, and one I take up at greater length in Chapter 5, Section 2.

notion of the categorical imperative), but rather a morality of general rules as a particular sort of morality appropriate for a particular segment of humanity. In launching this defense we thus find Smith in the interesting position of becoming an enthusiastic champion of what he admits is a decidedly second-best moral system. The evidence for the claim lies in his description of the audience of systems of general rules. His explicit claim is that a regard for general rules, or "what is properly called a sense of duty," is not merely "a principle of the greatest consequence in human life" but, more pointedly, "the only principle by which the bulk of mankind are capable of directing their actions"; the morality of general rules, that is, is indispensable in shaping the "coarse clay of which the bulk of mankind are formed," if not for those "of the happiest mould" (TMS III.5.1). Such a claim, in conjunction with his differentiation of the loose system of aristocratic morality from the strict system of morals for "common people" (WN V.i.g.12), provides evidence for a view of Smith as advocating hierarchies, or a two-tiered system of morality with different standards for different classes.[29] This of course poses a challenge to a strict egalitarian reading of Smith. Yet it fails to touch the most radical aspect of his position in this respect: namely his claim that the results of a morality of general rules are second best.

Smith most clearly presents the deficiency of actions governed by general rules in his accounts of affection. He seems to begin optimistically, presenting rule following as a substitute for affection and claiming that, when affections are suppressed by accident or circumstance, "respect for the general rule will frequently, in some measure, supply their place, and produce something which, though not altogether the same, may bear, however, a very considerable resemblance to those affections." Yet even in emphasizing the utility of this substitute, Smith emphasizes that it falls considerably short of the original. This is perhaps most clearly presented in his account of a society built on "the mutual exchange of all essential good offices," in which social orders may reflect an "external appearance of decent regard" yet lack "that cordial satisfaction, that delicious sympathy, that confidential openness and ease, which naturally take place in the conversation of those who have lived long and familiarly with one another." Furthermore, the bonds that hold together the citizens of such a society are fragile, for "with such persons, respect for the general rule can at best produce only a cold and affected civility (a very slender semblance of real regard); and even this, the slightest

[29] This view has come to be associated with Norbert Waszek, "Two Concepts of Morality: A Distinction of Adam Smith's Ethics and Its Stoic Origin," *Journal of the History of Ideas* 45 (1984): 591–606; but see also Vivenza's reminder that the Stoics were hardly the only classical source to embrace a two-tiered conception (*Smith and the Classics*, 194n10).

offence, the smallest opposition of interest, commonly puts an end to alto-gether" (TMS VI.ii.1.8–9). In TMS III.5, Smith makes the same point in his portraits of the dutiful friend and dutiful wife who maintain relationships from propriety rather than affection. If not "the very first of their kinds" these are "perhaps the second," he suggests, calling particular attention to their conspicuous lack of affection in noting that even if they "may have the most serious and earnest desire to fulfill every part of their duty, yet they will fail in many nice and delicate regards, they will miss many opportunities of obliging, which they could never have overlooked if they had possessed the sentiment that is proper to their situation" (TMS III.5.1). Smith clearly has limited esteem for the friend who loves "merely from a cold sense of duty, and without any affection to his person," or the indifferent wife who fails to love her husband but strives "to act as if she felt it" (TMS III.5.1; TMS III.6.4). Such willed or earnest dedication to duty is on some level preferable to indifference or hatred, and perhaps even admirable insofar as it requires constancy. At the same time, it falls considerably short of virtue. In this Smith anticipates a well-known contemporary argument against deon-tology; indeed his examples of the dutiful but unloving wife and friend will remind some of the example of the man who visits his friend in the hospital only out of a cold sense of duty rather than concern. Smith agrees that "surely there is something lacking here – and lacking in moral merit or value," insofar as such ostensibly virtuous behavior specifically precludes "love, friendship, affection, fellow feeling, and community."[30]

Smith's argument against deontology concludes – and his argument for virtue ethics begins – with the reintroduction of his distinction between the grammarians and the critics in TMS III.6. The chapter begins with a discussion of the difference between situations that call for actions driven by a sense of duty and respect for general rules and those that call for action driven by sentiment or affection (TMS III.6.1). Smith's general claim is that although we should be quick to indulge the sentiments in situations that elicit softer or social sentiments, we should be equally quick to act from duty in situations that elicit harsher passions. To this he also adds the important observation that the pursuit of the petty goods of self-interest is best regulated by rules, whereas the pursuit of the greater goods of grandeur and ambition are best prompted by sentiment – an observation that will

---

[30] Stocker, "Schizophrenia of Modern Ethical Theories," 73–74; and see p. 77 for the claim that this is a consequence of economic individualism. Smith employs his own example of a sickbed visit for another purpose at TMS III.3.23.

need to be reconsidered in his later accounts of prudence and magnanimity (TMS III.6.6–7). But here his aim is to show that a deontological respect for rules cannot account for our admiration of specific individual virtues. Smith begins this argument by reiterating the same point made in his argument against casuistry, namely that rules for virtues seem in general "loose and inaccurate, and to admit of ten thousand exceptions," and hence "it is evident, that no general rule can be laid down, by which a precise answer can, in all cases, be given to any of these questions." In particular, "the general rules of almost all the virtues, the general rules which determine what are the offices of prudence, of charity, of generosity, of gratitude, of friendship, are in many respects loose and inaccurate, admit of many exceptions, and require so many modifications, that it is scarce possible to regulate our conduct entirely by a regard to them" (TMS III.6.9). Now, as at TMS VII.iv, Smith qualifies this remark with the observation that justice, alone among the virtues, can admit of being so treated, and indeed he forthrightly calls for a "sacred" and "reverential and religious regard" to justice's general rules (TMS III.6.10). Yet this does not hold for all the virtues:

The rules of justice may be compared to the rules of grammar; the rules of the other virtues, to the rules which critics lay down for the attainment of what is sublime and elegant in composition. The one, are precise, accurate, and indispensable. The other, are loose, vague, and indeterminate, and present us rather with a general idea of the perfection we ought to aim at, than afford us any certain and infallible directions for acquiring it. A man may learn to write grammatically by rule, with the most absolute infallibility; and so, perhaps, he may be taught to act justly. But there are no rules whose observance will infallibly lead us to the attainment of elegance or sublimity in writing; though there are some which may help us, in some measure, to correct and ascertain the vague ideas which we might otherwise have entertained of those perfections. And there are no rules by the knowledge of which we can infallibly be taught to act upon all occasions with prudence, with just magnanimity, or proper beneficence: though there are some which may enable us to correct and ascertain, in several respects, the imperfect ideas which we might otherwise have entertained of those virtues. (TMS III.6.11)

In restating his fundamental distinction between the grammarians and the critics, Smith develops two additional angles. In the statement examined previously, Smith's aim was to separate his approach from that of the natural lawyers; there the debate was among two schools of moral philosophy. Having resolved that debate, he now seeks to give priority to a particular approach within ethics, an approach that privileges a capacity to discern – and thereby to make manifest in our actions and characters – the "sublime and elegant."

The remainder of our inquiry is dedicated to this approach and its methods of creating and instilling "a general idea of the perfection we ought to aim at," particularly as revealed in Smith's treatments of the three perfections specified here: "prudence," "just magnanimity," and "proper beneficence."

VIRTUE ETHICS: MODERN, ANCIENT, AND SMITHEAN

With Smith's critiques of utilitarianism and deontology in place we can now turn to the ethical system he offers in their stead. His predilection is for a virtue ethics that focuses on the education and cultivation of character. His preference for such a system, in turn, leads him to reject contemporary approaches to ethics in favor of a consciously "classical" approach. Smith's skepticism toward modern ethics in fact runs deep. In a well-known if enigmatic passage in LRBL he argues that, when combined, the systems of Lucian and Jonathan Swift "form a system of morality from whence more sound and just rules of life for all the various characters of men may be drawn than from most set systems of morality" (LRBL i.125). Striking and strange as this synthesis is, even more so is Smith's description of the conditions of modern moral philosophy that necessitate it. His principal concern is that "the thoughts of most men of genius in this country have of late inclined to abstract and speculative reasonings which perhaps tend very little to the bettering of our practise" – a lament that the second scribe records by noting that "even the practical sciences of politics and morality or ethics have of late been treated too much in a speculative manner" (LRBL i.101–102). This propensity to privilege the speculative to the practical is what necessitates the recovery of the methods of Lucian and Swift, the latter of whom was "more inclined to prosecute what was immediately beneficial," and thus "all his writings are adapted to the present time, either in ridiculing some prevailing vice or folly or exposing some particular character" (LRBL i.102). Swift is admirable for three reasons: for his concerted engagement with the immediate problems of his day; for his dedication to normative interventions in ethical matters, as reflected in his concern to "better the practice" of his audience; and for his focus on the specifics of characters and situations as opposed to general admonitions to virtue.[31] Smith is particularly insistent on this final point and returns to it at the conclusion of this same lecture, insisting that it is precisely a preference for specifics and particulars over "vague and general declamations suited to any virtue whatever" that renders

---

[31] I develop these debts at greater length in my essay "Style and Sentiment: Smith and Swift," *Adam Smith Review* 4 (2008): 88–105.

Addison "an excellent model to those whose particular business it is to teach morality, in opposition to a very different manner which prevails at present" (LRBL v.124–25; cf. LRBL i.125). He further insists on this point in another sweeping critique of philosophical ethics in TMS:

> When a philosopher goes to examine why humanity is approved of, or cruelty condemned, he does not always form to himself, in a very clear and distinct manner, the conception of any one particular action either of cruelty or of humanity, but is commonly contented with the vague and indeterminate idea which the general names of those qualities suggest to him. But it is in particular instances only that the propriety or impropriety, the merit or demerit of actions is very obvious and discernible. It is only when particular examples are given that we perceive distinctly either the concord or disagreement between our own affections and those of the agent, or feel a social gratitude arise towards him in the one case, or a sympathetic resentment in the other. When we consider virtue and vice in an abstract and general manner, the qualities by which they excite these several sentiments seem in a great measure to disappear, and the sentiments themselves become less obvious and discernible. (TMS IV.2.2)

Smith's aim here is something more than a mere vindication of ordinary life before the refinements of philosophy. Fairly or unfairly, his critique of modern moral philosophy in LRBL and his critique of philosophers in TMS each center on the claim that philosophers favor the abstract over the particular, and that such abstraction renders the ethical systems built upon it incapable of effecting the normative intervention that Smith considers the proper goal of ethics.

In taking such a stand, Smith thus seeks to do more than merely give voice to a lament. Even as he shows where and how modern moral philosophy fails, he also argues that ancient moral philosophy often succeeds on this same front. Indeed his well-known ancient "turn" – an orientation that has received a great deal of attention in recent years – can largely be traced to his conviction of the superiority of ancient ethics with regard to its focus on normativity and particularity.[32] Much of this interest in classical ethics stems directly from Smith's preference for the ethical methods of the critics, which he explicitly associates with "all the ancient moralists." Unlike the deontologists, the ancients "have not affected to lay down many precise rules

---

[32] These debts – which extend well beyond Smith's interest in Stoicism – were of course well known even to an earlier age of scholarship (see, e.g., W. R. Scott, *Greek Influence on Adam Smith* (Athens: Pyrsos, 1939)) but have received frequent and careful treatment in recent years. In addition to the studies cited earlier in this chapter in Note 4, see the helpful overview provided in Vivenza, "Reading Adam Smith in the Light of the Classics," *Adam Smith Review* I (2004): 107–24.

that are to hold good unexceptionably in all particular cases." Their goals were rather to determine

first, wherein consists the sentiment of the heart, upon which each particular virtue is founded, what sort of internal feeling or emotion it is which constitutes the essence of friendship, of humanity, of generosity, of justice, of magnanimity, and of all the other virtues, as well as of the vices which are opposed to them: and, secondly, what is the general way of acting, the ordinary tone and tenor of conduct to which each of those sentiments would direct us, or how it is that a friendly, a generous, a brave, a just, and a humane man, would, upon ordinary occasions, choose to act. (TMS VII.iv.3)

Such a formulation is important for at least two reasons. First, in emphasizing the ancient focus on the "particular" foundations of the individual virtues and on the question of how a possessor of the virtues would "choose to act," Smith calls attention to the sensitivity of the ancients to the particularity and the normativity that the moderns overlooked. Indeed the review of the "ancient moralists" that follows emphasizes both aspects; hence Smith's claim is not only that the ancients forego the "nice exactness" characteristic of casuistry in favor of a focus on character description (TMS VII.iv.34; TMS VII.iv.3) but also that the ancients sought to "present us with agreeable and lively pictures of manners" to "inflame our natural love of virtue, and increase our abhorrence of vice" and thereby "help both to correct and to ascertain our natural sentiments with regard to the propriety of conduct, and suggesting many nice and delicate attentions, form us to a more exact justness of behaviour, than what, without such instruction, we should have been apt to think of." Thus the goal of "Cicero, in the first book of his Offices" and "Aristotle in the practical parts of his Ethics" is said to be to set forth prescriptions, which when dressed with "the embellishments of eloquence," prove "capable of producing upon the flexibility of youth, the noblest and most lasting impressions" that confirm in such an audience the noblest and most useful habits (TMS VII.iv.5–6). Smith thus chiefly admires the ancient moralists for bridging the divide between particularity and practice. But his expression of his admiration is also important for a second reason. His main earlier description of the question of ancient ethics is the same formulation that he uses to describe his own ethics; that is to say, the ancient focus on "the ordinary tone and tenor of conduct" is replicated in his conviction that the question of the nature of virtue is properly an investigation into "the tone of temper, and tenour of conduct, which constitutes the excellent and praise-worthy character" (TMS VII.iv.3; TMS VII.i.2). And with this in place we can see clearly his debts to the ancient moralists, for it is from them that he inherits both the conviction that the end of ethics is normative intervention and the conviction that the proper means of ethics is the illustration of particulars embellished by rhetoric – two convictions central to both the organization and intentions of TMS VI.

A final aspect of ancient ethics that elicited Smith's admiration also needs to be mentioned. In his discussion of public education in WN, Smith provides his most direct contrast of "the ancient moral philosophy" and "the modern philosophy." In the former, the focus lies on "the happiness and perfection of a man, considered not only as an individual, but as the member of a family, of a state, and of the great society of mankind." In the latter, in contrast, the duties of ordinary life were considered "as chiefly subservient to the happiness of a life to come" – the necessary consequence of the eclipse of moral philosophy by theology. As a result, the ancient emphasis on the relationship of "the perfection of virtue" to "the most perfect happiness in this life" was replaced by an ascetic morality focused on the afterlife, with the consequence that ethics degenerated into a "debased system of moral philosophy," and moral philosophy became "by far the most corrupted" of philosophy's branches (WN V.i.f.30–31). Smith's own opinions on the utility of faith in the afterlife are complex, and not always in sharp contrast with the position being disparaged here (see, e.g., TMS II.ii.3.12). But what is clear is that Smith was decidedly sympathetic to the ancients' understanding that virtue is a prerequisite for happiness, which he glosses as the claim that the ancients "very justly represented virtue; that is, wise, just, firm, and temperate conduct; not only as the most probable, but as the certain and infallible road to happiness even in this life" (TMS VII.ii.1.28). Among our most important goals in what follows is to demonstrate that Smith himself held this conviction. One of the central aims of TMS VI was to recover precisely this "classical" understanding that virtue might provide a surer route to happiness than the system of materialist acquisition that so often threatens it. Put differently, Smith's conception of virtue is at once a methodological intervention in a philosophical debate over the proper methods and ends of ethics as well as a substantive intervention in a political debate over the proper means of remedying the ills of commercial civilization.

3

INTERLUDE: THE WHAT AND THE HOW OF TMS VI

THE WHAT: SMITH'S "PRACTICAL SYSTEM OF MORALITY"

To this point our focus has been diagnostic; our aim, that is, has been to identify the two principal ills, one political and the other philosophical, that concerned Smith with regard to the question of virtue. Now we must turn from the diagnostic to the therapeutic. Smith's study of the character of virtue in TMS VI seeks to propose remedies for both the political problem of commercial corruption and the corruption of modern ethics. To appreciate these proposed remedies, it is necessary to examine briefly the context and intentions of the sixth edition revisions.

TMS VI is the longest of the five major revisions and additions to which Smith calls his readers' attention in the Advertisement prefaced to the 1790 publication of the sixth edition (see TMS Advertisement.1).[1] Yet scholars

---

[1] The Advertisement claims that the "principal alterations" made in the sixth edition are to I.iii.3 and III.1–4; that it has "brought together" (in VII.ii.1) several passages on Stoicism that had previously been "scattered about"; that in it are "thrown together" some additional observations on "the duty and principle of veracity" (in VII.iv); and that the present Part VI is "altogether new." The Advertisement is interestingly silent on (or seeks to downplay as "of no great moment") two other major substantive revisions in the sixth edition, on the substance of which see Chapter 6, Note 22. Collating Smith's account of his revisions with that given by the editors in the textual apparatus to the Glasgow edition and my own examination of the fifth and sixth editions, we can conclude that, aside from the minor revisions noted by the editors in Appendix 1 and throughout the Glasgow edition, substantive revisions to the sixth edition fall into one of three categories. Significant additions can be found at I.iii.2.9; I.iii.3.1–8; II.ii.3.12; II.iii.3.4–5; III.1.2; III.2.1–4, 6–9, 10–35; III.3.1, 5–6, 8, 10, 12–45; III.4.1, 4; all of VI; VII.ii.1.18, 21–22, 23–47, 49; and VII.iv.23–28, 29–31 (breaks in sequential ordering indicate the interpolation of older material). Significant revisions to or reordering of preexisting material can be found at III.2.31–32; III.4.1; V.1.6; VII.ii.1.20–21, 23; and VII.ii.4.6. Material dropped in the sixth edition includes passages in or after I.iii.1.9n; I.iii.2.9; II.ii.3.12; III.1.7; III.3.11; VII.ii.1.17; VII.ii.1.19; and VII.iv.28. I hope the inclusion of this list will aid readers by sparing them my constant repetition of the locution "added/revised/dropped in the sixth

have reached differing assessments of the significance and sophistication of these revisions. The least charitable view holds that the sixth edition revisions are the pointless pottering of an "elderly and unwell" Smith who wrote in an elliptical style even in his prime (a view that seems to vindicate Smith's own claim that "very little can be either expected or hoped from the old man" (TMS VI.ii.1.3)).[2] Others have argued that the sixth edition merely brings into even greater relief claims already present, if less developed, in earlier editions.[3] But between these two poles – the sixth edition as new but insignificant, or as significant but not new – lies a third alternative, one that calls attention to both its novelty and significance.

That Smith himself thought his revisions significant is beyond doubt. His extant correspondence from the period in question makes this clear. Apologizing for the delay in delivering his final manuscript, Smith begs his publisher's forgiveness on the grounds that "the subject has grown upon me" (CAS 287). This growth is evident from the trajectory of his references to the revisions in his correspondence. In his first comment on them, Smith merely mentions "a few alterations to make of no great consequence" (CAS 244). But three years later, in 1788, this casual attitude would give way to urgency, with Smith now writing to his publisher that he is engaged in "the most intense application," making "many additions and corrections" to all parts of the work (CAS 276). The toll such application took on him is evident in his admission that as a consequence of his hard labor he was "obliged to

edition." This list also adds to the otherwise excellent account given in the introduction to the Glasgow edition (at pp. 43–44) Smith's previously undocumented changes at TMS VII.ii.1.21, which are in fact not merely additions of new material but an expansion of part of the passage that in editions 1–5 followed the present TMS VII.ii.1.17 and is listed as withdrawn in the Glasgow edition (see pp. 273–74). In the sixth edition (and hence the Glasgow text), VII.ii.1.21 preserves intact, with minor variations, a key phrase from the "withdrawn" material ("If he preferred . . ."). On the substantive significance of this passage, see Chapter 5, Note 51.

[2] See, e.g., Viner, "Adam Smith and Laissez-Faire," in Jacob Hollander et al., *Adam Smith, 1776–1926* (Chicago: University of Chicago Press, 1928), 138; and Dwyer's reference to Smith's "complex, tortuous and occasionally convoluted revision" ("Ethics and Economics," 679). At the same time, Smith's age is something of a red herring; if the principal revisions for the sixth edition were made between late 1787 and late 1789, as his correspondence indicates, Smith would have been only 64 when he began and only 66 when he finished.

[3] See, for example, Griswold, *Smith and the Virtues of Enlightenment*, 28; Otteson, *Marketplace of Life*, 14; cf. Montes, *Smith in Context*, 19n7 and 128. A brief but helpful overview of the various scholarly views on the degree to which the sixth edition revisions attest to the evolution of Smith's theological commitments is provided in Alvey, "The 'New View' of Adam Smith and the Development of His Views over Time," in *New Perspectives*, ed. Cockfield et al., 77–79.

return" to his post at the Custom House to find some relaxation – an irony compounded by the fact that he had left this same position only months earlier to devote himself to writing full-time (CAS 287). Smith's admission testifies to the degree of seriousness and strain the revisions elicited; indeed it is with regard to them that he confessed, "I am a slow a very slow workman, who do and undo everything I write at least half a dozen of times before I can be tolerably pleased with it" (CAS 276). This perfectionism would prove to impact his productivity as well as his health. Smith is well known to have had, prior to his decision to revise TMS, "two other great works upon the anvil," described in 1785 as a "theory and history of law and government" and a "philosophical history" of the arts and sciences (CAS 248). Some attention has been given to his failure to complete these projects.[4] But on some level, Smith's decision to devote his remaining time and energies to revisiting TMS must have played a significant, if not principal, role in his abandoning of the "several other works which I have projected and in which I have made some progress" in favor of attempting to "leave those I have already published in the best and most perfect state behind me" (CAS 276).

Smith's solicitude for this project is thus sufficient to demand an equal solicitude on the part of his readers; Part VI deserves our attention if only because it demanded so much of his. But Part VI is mostly worthy of engagement for its substance. Studies of the sixth edition often note that, taken collectively, its revisions suggest a more realistic, if not more pessimistic, assessment of commercial society than is to be found in Smith's earlier writings. One of the most influential formulations of this position argues that in 1790 Smith's main aim was to engage "the dilemma of either a 'commercial culture' or a 'liberal civilization'" by reconsidering his earlier assessments of prudential bourgeois accumulation.[5] This position has been further developed in the claim that prior to 1790 he had grown "progressively disillusioned

---

[4] See Griswold, "On the Incompleteness of Adam Smith's System," *Adam Smith Review* 2 (2006): 181–86, and *Smith and the Virtues of Enlightenment*, 33–39 and 257–58; and the response offered in Ian S. Ross, "Reply to Charles Griswold: 'On the Incompleteness of Adam Smith's System'," *Adam Smith Review* 2 (2006): 187–91; as well as Maureen Harkin, "Adam Smith's Missing History: Primitives, Progress, and Problems of Genre," *English Literary History* 72 (2005): 429–51.

[5] Laurence Dickey, "Historicizing the 'Adam Smith Problem': Conceptual, Historiographical, and Textual Issues," *Journal of Modern History* 58 (1986): 591n82 (which also distances Smith from liberal, republican, and natural jurisprudential traditions) and 608; on the ways in which the sixth edition's critical analysis of the prudent man reflects Smith's increasing pessimism toward commercialization and the bourgeois virtues, see esp. 589–92, 598–99, and 609; as well as Dwyer, "Theory and Discourse," 173–75, which identifies as the "main worry" of the sixth edition "the excessive ambition of the middling ranks in social life" (173) (though cf. the response given by Raphael to Dickey on this point in his "Adam

with capitalism," prompting his "increasing concern about the destructive characteristics of commercial capitalism," and a pessimism which "intensified in the intervening period between the completion of *Wealth of Nations* and the final edition of *Theory of Moral Sentiments* in 1790."[6] These studies also call attention to some of the specific causes of concern for Smith in 1790, noting in particular his concern that the principles of "socialization" via sympathy defined in earlier editions were in fact "working all too well," rendering citizens of commercial societies incapable of resisting conformity to cultural norms, in addition to the fact that the elevation of common life and commercial greed may threaten or diminish the possibility of genuine virtue.[7] As statements of the problems Smith sought to confront in 1790, these studies are extremely helpful in capturing some (if not all) of his concerns. But they leave another question unanswered: in what sense can Smith's revisions be said to constitute a coherent response to these problems? On this front the literature is less persuasive. Rightly noting that the sixth edition revisions emphasize the problem of corruption and the necessity of recovering virtue, these studies tend to suggest that the 1790 revisions are the clearest manifestation of Smith's civic humanism or republicanism.[8] As

Smith 1790," 106–8, which argues that the sixth edition sets forth "sociological reports" rather than Smith's "personal views" (108)).

[6] See Dwyer, "Ethics and Economics," 662–64, 666, 679; and Phillipson's claim that in the sixth edition Smith's "faith in the civilising powers of commerce seems muted," leading him to call for "a more austere, more Epictetan Stoicism" ("Language, Sociability, and History," 83–84). It should also be noted that Smith's theoretical shift would likely have had an empirical foundation. In several places his writings testify to his awareness of the dramatic boom in Glaswegian commerce during the third quarter of the eighteenth century (see, e.g., WN I.ix.9; WN II.ii.41; WN II.iii.12) and, given this awareness, it is difficult to believe he would not have been acutely aware of and influenced by the fact that Glasgow's commercial explosion coincided with a deterioration of social conditions that in time gave rise to Europe's most profound case of urban destitution. In his review of Glasgow in the 1750s and 1760s, W. R. Scott observes that "the picture of the times is one of strong lights and some deep shadows," noting that rises in graft, theft, arson, and violent crime all accompanied the rapid progress of opulence; see Scott, *Adam Smith as Student and Professor* (Glasgow: Jackson, Son and Co., 1937), 79; cf. T. M. Devine, "The Urban Crisis," in *Glasgow*, ed. T. M. Devine and Gordon Jackson (Manchester: Manchester University Press, 1995), vol. 1, pp. 402–16; and Dwyer, "Ethics and Economics," 682–83.

[7] On the former problem, see esp. Dickey, "Historicizing the 'Adam Smith Problem',", 604; Dwyer, "Theory and Discourse," 170–72; and Peter France, "Rousseau, Adam Smith and the Education of the Self," in *Moy Qui Me Voy*, ed. George Craig and Margaret McGowan (Oxford: Oxford University Press, 1989), 40–41, 49. On the latter problem, see esp. Dwyer, "Ethics and Economics," 681, 684.

[8] See, e.g., Dwyer, "Ethics and Economics," 674 and 678; Evensky, *Smith's Moral Philosophy*, esp. 21–22, 204–6, 212; Force, *Self-Interest Before Smith*, 162–63; and Montes, *Smith in Context*, 96. Even Dickey, who explicitly distances Smith from the republican paradigm,

argued before, there are good reasons to believe Smith's theory of virtue cannot be assimilated to this paradigm. But more importantly, what is lacking in this account is an explanation of how exactly the specific conception of virtue proposed in TMS VI might remedy the specific corruptions diagnosed and emphasized in previous editions and elsewhere in the sixth edition. Put differently, what is needed is first an elucidation of the relationship of the critical projects of TMS I.iii.3 (examined earlier) and TMS III.1–4 (to be examined later) to the constructive project of TMS VI. Second, in addition to an account of the connections between TMS VI and the work as a whole, the internal logic and coherence of TMS VI also demands explanation. In an effort to illuminate this coherence, this chapter examines the methods that Smith's analysis of the "character of virtue" employs, focusing particularly on the conceptions of rhetoric, dialectical organization, and self-love on which it depends. By so doing, I aim not only to reveal the coherence and sophistication of this "complete new sixth part containing a practical system of morality, under the title of the Character of Virtue," but also to demonstrate the depth of Smith's mature conviction that a "system of natural liberty" requires this "practical system of morality" as a necessary concomitant (CAS 287).

THE HOW: RHETORIC, AUDIENCE, AND THE METHODS OF PRACTICAL ETHICS

The sophistication of Smith's practical system of ethics is most evident in its use of rhetoric. The subtlety of Smith's rhetoric is now well appreciated, thanks to several recent studies.[9] My goal is to build on such studies by examining the way in which Smith employed in his practical ethics several of the specific rhetorical concepts and techniques that he describes at greater length in LRBL. To better achieve this end and also to draw out some of the ways in which his system of practical ethics fits into a broader virtue ethical tradition, this section focuses on a comparison of Smith's ethical rhetoric to that of Aristotle. By so doing, I hope to offer a reconsideration

yet frames Smith's concern in 1790 as the loss of "public spiritedness" ("Historicizing the 'Adam Smith Problem'," 591).

[9] See especially Brown, *Smith's Discourse*; Griswold, *Smith and the Virtues of Enlightenment*, esp. 40–75; Stephen J. McKenna, *Adam Smith: The Rhetoric of Propriety* (Albany: State University of New York Press, 2006); and Mark Salber Phillips, "Adam Smith, Belletrist," in *Cambridge Companion*, 57–78. For a more focused treatment of the relationship of Smith's conception of rhetoric to his understanding of economic activity, see Andreas Kalyvas and Ira Katznelson, "The Rhetoric of the Market: Adam Smith on Recognition, Speech, and Exchange," *Review of Politics* 63 (2001): 549–78.

of Smith's debts to antiquity beyond his oft-noted debts to Stoicism and Epicureanism by suggesting some further points of contact between Smith and Aristotelianism.[10]

To start at the beginning: Smith's conception of his moral system as "practical" is itself evidence of a departure point similar to that of Aristotle. The normative goals of Smith's own theory in this respect are decidedly similar to Aristotle's familiar and repeated claim that the principal goal of ethical inquiry is our improvement in fact.[11] But, perhaps more importantly, Smith and Aristotle share an understanding of the nature of the phenomena of ethical inquiry. In this respect, Smith's claim that the science of ethics "does not admit of the most accurate precision" (TMS VII.iv.6; cf. TMS III.2.18; TMS VII.iv.33) recalls Aristotle's claim that the level of precision that can be expected in other types of inquiry can hardly be expected in ethics owing to the nature of its subject matter.[12] Ethics may be a science, but it is hardly a science on par with the natural sciences. Furthermore, Smith's reservations toward the efficacy of an ethics of general rules is in keeping with Aristotle's claim that the aim of ethics is less to establish general rules for action than to cultivate the judgment or the practical wisdom necessary for right actions in particular situations.[13] Both Smith and Aristotle thus agree that "precision" is not a proper goal for ethics; indeed Smith's distinction of grammarians from critics is anticipated in Aristotle's distinction of the rough-and-ready science of carpenters from the more precise science of geometricians and his parallel claim that the same degree of exactness cannot be expected of both orators and mathematicians.[14]

---

[10] Smith has been previously identified as "an Aristotelian philosopher"; see, e.g., Solomon, "Free Enterprise, Sympathy, and Virtue," 17–18. Others remain more skeptical; see, e.g., Carrasco, "Smith's Reconstruction of Practical Reason," 98. Most seem to agree that Smith shares Aristotle's interest in the virtues; the issue is whether and to what degree Smith subscribes to a teleology comparable to that of Aristotle; hence David Raynor's claim that Smith and Hume are *"updated* Aristotelians without the teleology" ("Adam Smith and the Virtues," *Adam Smith Review* 2 (2006): 245; italics original); cf. Griswold, *Smith and the Virtues of Enlightenment*, 58, 111, 130; Den Uyl and Griswold, "Smith on Friendship and Love," 616; and MacIntyre, *Whose Justice? Which Rationality?* (Notre Dame: University of Notre Dame Press, 1988), esp. 328–29.

[11] *Nicomachean Ethics*, 1103b26–31; 1179a33–1179b4. My paraphrases here and later are drawn from Rackham's Loeb translation of the *Ethics* and Kennedy's Oxford translation of the *Rhetoric.*

[12] See *Nicomachean Ethics*, 1094b11–14; 1098a26–29; 1103b34–1104a11.

[13] See *Nicomachean Ethics*, 1104a5; 1109b18–23; 1126a31–1126b4; see also Nancy Sherman, *The Fabric of Character: Aristotle's Theory of Virtue* (Oxford: Clarendon Press, 1989), 13ff., for a helpful development of this claim.

[14] *Nicomachean Ethics*, 1098a29–32; 1094b25–27.

What most binds Smith to Aristotle is their shared understanding of how authors might most effectively present ethical premises to their audiences. Given the imprecision of the subject matter of ethics, Aristotle teaches that moralists do better to present broad outlines of the truth rather than exacting definitions, particularly at the outset.[15] His own *Ethics* of course does just this. Starting with the given, his inquiry begins with a "rough sketch," drawn from what is already familiar to his audience, and fills this in over time as it moves gradually from common opinion to truth, thereby distinguishing itself from those approaches that take first principles as a starting point.[16] This approach, while necessary because of the subject matter of ethics, is also necessary because of the nature of the audience to which ethical treatises are directed. None but the best-disposed students can be led to virtue through theoretical accounts alone, Aristotle insists, as most men are driven by love of gain and pleasure rather than love of the noble.[17] If one hopes to steer such an audience to the love of nobility, it is thus necessary to appeal, at least at the outset, to their instinctive inclinations and opinions.[18] Indeed it is on these grounds that Aristotle concludes that the rhetorical style of ethical treatises should differ from that of metaphysical treatises. Most men, unable to reason from distant starting points or to see many things at once, are moved only by more immediate appeals, he explains, and long, intricate arguments built on universals will always have much less sway with them than arguments grounded in particulars already familiar from experience.[19]

Smith's approach to ethics embraces a number of features central to Aristotle's approach.[20] His emphasis on particulars is especially pronounced; as we saw earlier in the discussion of modern philosophy, Smith is skeptical of "abstraction" in ethics and consistently endorses the use of moral particulars. His review of Aristotle in TMS calls attention to this point, endorsing Aristotle alongside other ancient moralists who teach that the most effective way of depicting the "invisible features" of internal passions is "by describing the effects which they produce without, the alterations which they occasion

---

[15] *Nicomachean Ethics*, 1094a24–26; 1098a20–26.

[16] *Nicomachean Ethics*, 1145b2–7; 1095a30-b4.

[17] *Nicomachean Ethics*, 1179b4–16.

[18] *Nicomachean Ethics*, 1098b9–12; and *Rhetoric*, 1356b33–1357a4.

[19] *Rhetoric*, 1357a1; 1395b25–1396a1.

[20] For additional treatments of Smith's debts to Aristotle's rhetoric, see Griswold, *Smith and the Virtues of Enlightenment*, 56–58 (especially useful on Smith's "quasi-Aristotelian insistence on pre-theoretical moral knowledge" or *endoxa*, as is Calkins and Werhane, "Smith, Aristotle and the Virtues of Commerce," 51); and McKenna, *Rhetoric of Propriety*, 3–44, 78n2, 92–93, 96, 120, 127, 131, 137–38.

in the countenance, in the air and external behaviour, the resolutions they suggest, the actions they prompt to" (TMS VII.iv.5). The same claim is also emphasized in LRBL, in which it is suggested that the most effective method of capturing a popular audience's attention is to focus on "some minute circumstances" (LRBL v.172) – hence Smith's praise of Demosthenes, who never spoke in the abstract but always of specific individuals (LRBL ii.227). This thought also governs Smith's accounts of the optimal method of painting characters, in which he claims that the "great error" often made is that of "making them too general," for the real challenge is not simply to describe the relative degrees of virtue or vice in a character, but to describe their "peculiar tinges" in a specific instance (LRBL i.200; LRBL i.190–91; cf. LRBL i.24; LRBL ii.37). Smith's aim here is to distinguish an ethics content to describe "general tenor of conduct" from one that makes a more concerted effort to go about "descending into particulars" (LRBL i.193).[21]

Smith's emphasis on particulars – especially particulars that can be "shown" – has important implications for his construction of TMS VI. TMS VI explicitly presents itself as a consideration of what happens when we "consider the character of any individual" – that is to say, it presents itself not as an analysis of virtue, but as a study of the methods by which "we naturally view it" (TMS VI.intro.1). But Smith's interest in particular appearances over abstractions is also important for another reason. To speak to particulars is to speak in a manner befitting a certain type of audience. Fittingness is indeed an important and oft-emphasized component of Smith's conception of rhetoric, and he makes clear that good rhetoric must be well suited to the natures of the author, the audience, and the circumstances (LRBL i.76–79; cf. LRBL i.99 and LRBL i.137). But what makes this teaching distinctive and distinctively Aristotelian is Smith's understanding of the relationship of particularity to fittingness in popular ethical discourses. At the conclusion of one of his lectures, he explains that the method of inquiry and composition that is "undoubtedly the best in all matters of science" is yet inappropriate to rhetorical discourse, owing to their different audiences. Like Aristotle, Smith insists that "the arguments that are to be used before a people cannot be very intricate"; such arguments ought to be "so evident as not to require any elaborate explanation" and must contain "no nicety nor refinement, no metaphysical arguments" (LRBL ii.135, 138). Also like Aristotle he insists

---

[21] Though even in focusing on particulars we should take care to note that Smith warns against losing the forest for the trees; thus his caution that while it is easy to get occasionally caught up in "nice and minute particularities," the real challenge is to sail between the Scylla of pedantry and the Charybdis of abstraction (see LRBL i.191).

that the people to which these arguments are commonly directed "have no pleasure in these abstruse deductions; their interest, and the practicability and honourableness of the thing recommended is what alone will sway with them and is seldom to be shown in a long deduction of arguments" (LRBL ii.135).

Put differently, for both Smith and Aristotle, ethics is a rhetorical and dialectical process rather than a deductive process – one which calls for persuasion rather than either conviction or mere demonstration.[22] At the same time, even if ethics is not deductive, that is not to say that Smith understood it as scattershot or haphazard. On the contrary, Smith continually suggests that, even if logical deduction is not a proper goal in ethics, the order and arrangement of subject matter is yet fundamental to ethical treatises. It is here that Smith's commitment to dialectic emerges, and indeed it is in their joint commitment to dialectic that the fundamental similarity of his ethics to that of Aristotle lies. Aristotle's use of dialectic is well known and particularly evident in his presentation and arrangement of the virtues in Books III and IV of the *Nicomachean Ethics*, the trajectory of which can be said to trace an ascent from the lower and more common virtues to virtues both rarer and nobler.[23] Smith's arrangement of his account of the virtues in Part VI of TMS follows a similar ascending trajectory. Part of this is because of Smith's interest in order. Order is a great and repeated theme of his rhetoric lectures, which teach that a good writer requires three capacities: complete knowledge of his subject matter; facility at painting his ideas in the most expressive, fitting manner; and ability to "arrange all the parts of his subject in their proper order" (LRBL i.104–5). Order particularly enables an author to carry his readers from point to point, guiding them from first glimpses to final revelation; like the good poet, the good writer strives to "accommodate all his circumstances so as that they tend to

---

[22] For this locution, see Rousseau, *Social Contract*, II.7, para. 9; and Christopher Kelly, "'To Persuade Without Convincing': The Language of Rousseau's Legislator," *American Journal of Political Science* 31 (1987): 321–35.

[23] My understanding of Aristotle's dialectical account of the virtues and his appeal to *endoxa* is particularly indebted to the studies of Aristide Tessitore and Harry Jaffa. Particularly helpful is Jaffa's observation that "Aristotle is thoroughly consistent throughout; but his consistency is intelligible only when it is seen that the conception of courage is subjected to a *development*, starting from a relatively crude beginning. The ultimate conception is only intelligible if it is reached through the intermediate stages. But just because the succeeding stages go beyond the preceding stages, certain inconsistencies seem to appear if everything that is true of the one is premised as being equally true of the other" (*Thomism and Aristotelianism* (Chicago: University of Chicago Press, 1952), pp. 79–80 (italics original); see also 114–15); and Tessitore, *Reading Aristotle's Ethics: Virtue, Rhetoric, and Political Philosophy* (Albany: State University of New York Press, 1996), esp. 19.

bring about the main event either directly or indirectly" (LRBL ii.82). Smith indeed repeatedly claims in the lectures that such concatenate compositions are vastly superior to disconnected works in which ideas are haphazardly treated "in the order they happen to cast up to us" – hence his preference for the "Newtonian" method, in which we "lay down certain principles known or proved in the beginning, from whence we account for the several phenomena, connecting all together by the same chain." This method is not only "undoubtedly the most philosophical," but it is also more engaging and "gives us a pleasure to see the phenomena which we reckoned the most unaccountable all deduced from some principle (commonly a well known one) and all united in one chain, far superior to what we feel from the unconnected method" (LRBL ii.133–35).[24]

Smith's teachings on order in LRBL are crucial to his composition of TMS VI. Hence, my main claim on this front is that Smith's organization of his account of the virtues in his system of practical morality is not only shaped by the principles of order described in LRBL but also reflects an Aristotelian commitment to the use of dialectic to persuade an audience to follow in their own self-cultivating practices an ascent from the lesser to the nobler virtues. Furthermore, Smith's ascending account of the virtues in Part VI is united by a chain: specifically self-love. Such a claim builds on a now-familiar and well-established view of Smith as a dialectical thinker – a view that, while rarely given centrality, is held by a broad scholarly consensus.[25] This view now needs to be brought to TMS VI itself, the specific virtues of which are organized around an ascent from a low or vulgar form of self-love to one higher and nobler.

---

[24] To be clear: Smith presents this formulation not as an endorsement of Aristotle but as an argument against him; his praises of Newton are framed as endorsements of the superiority of such a method to (what he took to be) Aristotle's "unconnected" method.

[25] On the place of dialectic in Smith's work, see esp. Skinner, *System of Social Science*, 45; Den Uyl and Griswold, "Smith on Friendship and Love," 611 and 635; Lerner, "Love of Fame and the Constitution of Liberty," in *Geschichte und Recht: Festschrift für Gerald Stourzh zum 70 Geburtstag*, ed. T. Angerer et al. (Vienna: Böhlau Verlag, 1999), 65; and Haakonssen, "Introduction," in *Cambridge Companion*, 17. Griswold, however, presents the most thorough account of the role of dialectic in Smith's philosophy (see *Smith and the Virtues of Enlightenment*, 20, 74, 111, 193–94, 225, 229n3, 256, 301, 317, 331, 347, and 359); his observation that TMS is a "story that unfolds in steps" (61) is particularly helpful; cf. Raphael, "Adam Smith 1790," 108–9. My aim is to extend this conception to a reading of Smith's scheme of the virtues in TMS VI, thereby further developing and extending A. L. Macfie's largely unheralded claim that TMS sets forth a "theory of graduated individual values" and a "psychological account of the progress from vanity to magnanimity" (*The Individual in Society* (London: George Allen and Unwin, 1967), 54, 72); cf. Glenn R. Morrow, *The Ethical and Economic Theories of Adam Smith* (New York: Longmans, Green, 1923), 51.

THE HOW: THE ASCENT OF SELF-LOVE IN THREE STAGES

How then does this dialectic operate in practice in TMS VI? On its face, it seems plain. The section headings of Part VI suggest it is divided into treatments of three discrete virtues in three separate sections, with one section each devoted to prudence, to benevolence, and to self-command. This division has led to the frequent suggestion that TMS VI constitutes Smith's treatment of three of the four "cardinal virtues," justice being treated separately for reasons examined earlier.[26] Yet the convenient division afforded by the chapter headings only imperfectly describes the actual organization of the substance of Part VI. In point of fact – and for reasons described more fully in subsequent chapters – the organization of TMS VI is better captured not by the chapter headings but rather by the organization of the virtues set forth in Smith's most direct statement of the reasons for the insufficiency of the understanding of virtue as rule following. His claim there, as we saw, is that "there are no rules by the knowledge of which we can infallibly be taught to act upon all occasions with prudence, with just magnanimity, or proper beneficence" (TMS III.6.11). This list of virtues differs in a subtle but decisive way from the list implied by the section headings often said to constitute Smith's canon of the "cardinal virtues." Four differences are particularly noteworthy: first, Smith's substitution of magnanimity for self-command; second, his substitution of beneficence for benevolence; third, his qualifiers of "just" magnanimity and "proper" beneficence (qualifications that suggest his awareness of pernicious as well as virtuous forms of these dispositions); and fourth, his reordering of magnanimity between prudence and beneficence.

Such fine distinctions cannot but seem pedantic on their face. They are, however, crucially important for two specific reasons beyond the simple

---

[26] See, e.g., McCloskey, "Adam Smith, the Last of the Former Virtue Ethicists," 51. On Smith's "cardinal virtues," see, e.g., Cropsey, *Polity and Economy*, 43; Hope, *Virtue by Consensus*, 106; Athol Fitzgibbons, *Adam Smith's System of Liberty, Wealth, and Virtue: The Moral and Political Foundations of The Wealth of Nations* (Oxford: Clarendon Press, 1995), 104–6; Heydt, "'Delicate and Accurate Pencil'," 60; Haakonssen, "Introduction" to *Cambridge Companion*, 17; Raphael, *Impartial Spectator*, 73–80; as well as the several pieces cited at Montes, *Smith in Context*, 70–71. Montes also offers a helpful comparison of Smith's canonical virtues to the cardinal virtues tradition (see *Smith in Context*, 69–75). Smith groups the four virtues together in several places (see, e.g., TMS VI.i.15; TMS VI.iii.1; TMS VI.iii.11), though he himself uses the phrase "cardinal virtues" only to refer to Plato's and Cicero's systems and never to his own (see TMS VII.ii.1.9 and TMS VII.iv.5). In this vein see also the helpful warning against identifying Smith with the cardinal virtues tradition in Vivenza, *Smith and the Classics*, 195 and n.

reason that this revised list better captures the movement and organization of Part VI. First, the revised list better enables us to see exactly how Smith's account of the character of virtue in TMS VI forms a response to the problems of commercial corruption. Thus where the list of the cardinal virtues helpfully describes in general terms Smith's conception of the various excellences of character, the revised list of virtues clarifies the specific ways in which he conceived of the discrete virtues as targeted responses to the various discrete challenges posed by commercial corruption. Briefly, Smith's account of the virtue of prudence is conceived as a remedy for the vices of restlessness and anxiety induced by commercial vanity; his account of the virtue of magnanimity is conceived as a remedy for the vices of mediocrity and conformism induced by commercial materialism; and his account of beneficence is conceived as a remedy for the vices of alienation, indifference, and inhibition of sympathy that are the consequences of commercial individualism. The intimate relationship between these diagnosed ills and these proposed remedies attests at once to Smith's commitment to normativity and his concern, befitting an admirer of Swift, to develop remedies for the most pressing problems of his day.[27]

The revised list of the virtues is also important for a second reason. Not only does this list help us better see the way in which the specific virtues of TMS VI were intended as responses to specific problems, but it also helps us better see the internal unity of its theory of the virtues. Smith's three principal character virtues of prudence, magnanimity, and beneficence are each discrete manifestations of a specific disposition on a continuum of self-love that extends from the low to the high.[28] To put it slightly differently: in the same way that Smith's theory of the historical stages of economic development relies on his well-known "four stages" theory, his theory of individual moral development rests on what might be thought of as a "three stages" theory – one that traces the moral ascent of the individual in a manner

[27] It should also be noted that the categories of Smith's treatment of other virtue systems in TMS VII more closely follow the list of virtues noted in TMS III.6.11 rather than the conventional list of the cardinal virtues. Thus, TMS VII lacks sections on justice and self-command in focusing rather on prudence (TMS VII.ii.2), benevolence (TMS VII.ii.3), and propriety (TMS VII.ii.1) – the last of which is in fact not a treatment of the sort of propriety that Smith elsewhere describes, but of magnanimity, which is here largely equated with propriety (see, e.g., TMS VII.ii.4.2 and 5).

[28] In this respect I agree with Skinner's claim that TMS VI ought to be read as "a full treatment of the complex psychology of self-love" ("Adam Smith: Ethics and Self-Love," in *Adam Smith Reviewed*, ed. Jones and Skinner, 144). Skinner notes that this treatment is especially to be found in Part VI, yet his own detailed treatment is developed largely independently of reference to TMS VI.

analogous to his account of the material ascent of civilization. Furthermore, self-love plays the same role in this stadial moral account as the means of production plays in the stadial material account; that is to say, in each theory, the stage of development is determined by and ultimately defined by the discrete expression given to the main category of the chain that unifies the theory. Specifically, TMS VI traces an ascent from a comparatively low self-love characteristic of prudent men focused on acquiring the external goods of wealth and reputation, to the comparatively high self-love of magnanimous men focused on acquiring the external goods of honor, glory, and fame, to the genuinely noble self-love of the wise and virtuous man of proper beneficence who transcends the limiting dispositions characteristic of his predecessors. Such a conception of the relationship of self-love to virtue also marks Smith as unique in both his day and ours. Today, magnanimity carries resonances of self-abnegation and self-sacrifice. This conception, however, clashes sharply with Smith's decidedly classical understanding; his magnanimity focuses not on the denial of the self but on the cultivation of the best parts of the self. So too his conception of beneficence. Beneficence, in Smith, is not simply the privileging of other-regard at the expense of self-regard (though it will of course require some degree of such). For insofar as the beneficent life is the best life and the proper aim of those seeking genuine excellence and happiness, it is less the opposite of self-love than the proper end of those who most care about their own good and seek to transcend self-love's more limiting forms. Smith's conception of the elevation and ennoblement of self-love thus marks his affinities with the classical tradition of moral education and reveals the degree to which he sought to go beyond both familiar debates on liberal self-interest and republican civic virtue characteristic of eighteenth-century British political thought, as well as familiar debates on egoism and altruism characteristic of eighteenth-century British moral philosophy and contemporary ethics alike.[29]

The argument just sketched must stand or fall on its capacity to illuminate the organization and substance of TMS VI. Yet Part VI is not the only place in TMS that this three-stage ascent is described. In his argument against "licentious systems" in TMS VII, Smith not only distinguishes his conception

---

[29] Some recent work has, however, done much to question the irreconcilability of self-love and virtue. Two excellent discussions by contemporary philosophers that disambiguate self-love from both self-preference and egoism, and reconcile it (to varying degrees) with altruism, can be found in Robert Merrihew Adams, *A Theory of Virtue: Excellence in Being for the Good* (Oxford: Oxford University Press, 2006), 95–111; and Richard Kraut, *What Is Good and Why: The Ethics of Well-Being* (Cambridge, MA: Harvard University Press, 2007), 48–57.

of self-love from Mandeville's conception of self-interest but also presents, briefly and clearly, the three stages of moral development upon which the ascending practical morality of Part VI is built. In this sense, his debate with Mandeville in TMS VII provides an anticipation in microcosm of his own more extended argument in TMS VI and thus deserves our attention both as a useful preparative for the study of his developed account of the character of virtue, and for the insight it provides into his most forthright confrontation with the problem of commercial corruption that he inherited in part from Rousseau.[30]

Smith's central argument against Mandeville is that he reduces all psychological motives to the love of praise and "considers whatever is done from a sense of propriety, from a regard to what is commendable and praise-worthy, as being done from a love of praise and commendation, or as he calls it from vanity" (TMS VII.ii.4.7).[31] Beneficence, on this view, is merely an appearance, a mask designed to conceal an actor's self-interested motives and help him better elicit the praises he seeks. This assumption, Smith explains, led Mandeville to regard "every thing as vanity which has any reference, either to what are, or to what ought to be the sentiments of others" (TMS VII.ii.4.12). Yet it is precisely this reduction of all actions to praise-seeking that Smith rejects. Against the cry that all is vanity, Smith argues "that the desire of doing what is honourable and noble, of rendering ourselves the proper objects of esteem and approbation, cannot with any propriety be called vanity." In this distinction lies one of his most fundamental moves: the separation of the type of individual actuated by a sincere desire to deserve praise by acting honorably and nobly from the one "who is not contented with the silent sentiments of esteem and approbation," who requires instead "noisy expressions and acclamations," and "who is never satisfied but when his own praises are ringing in his ears." Whatever its potential material benefits, the desire for undeserved praise, or vanity, Smith dismisses here as a "frivolous passion" of "the lowest and the least of mankind" (TMS VII.ii.4.8).[32] The effect of this distinction is to identify two different classes of

[30] Winch seems right to say that "when Smith was dealing openly and covertly with Mandeville in the TMS, he was also answering some of Rousseau's arguments"; *Riches and Poverty*, 60. Smith himself of course explicitly assimilated Rousseau and Mandeville in the introductory portion of his *Edinburgh Review* essay; for detailed treatments of this connection, see Schliesser, "Smith's Conception of Philosophy," in *New Voices*, ed. Montes and Schliesser, 343–47; and Rasmussen, *Problems and Promise*, 59–66.

[31] See especially Winch, *Riches and Poverty*, 69–70; Hont and Ignatieff, "Needs and Justice," in *Wealth and Virtue*, ed. Hont and Ignatieff, 12.

[32] In light of this claim it seems too strong to say, as many have, that Smith considers "the selfish activity of the individual" to be "a positive factor, almost a 'virtue'"; see, e.g.,

individuals, themselves distinguished by their degree of susceptibility or dedication to two different dispositions. The vain are known by their "frivolous desire of praise at any rate," where lovers of true glory are distinguished by "the desire of acquiring honour and esteem by really deserving those sentiments"; where the former would have esteem at any cost, the latter desire only "esteem for what is really estimable" (TMS VII.ii.4.9). Lovers of true glory thus care to deserve as well as to claim, and are thus more admirable, Smith insists. But Smith also argues that they are happier than the vain. Thus we are told that the vain praise-seekers are tormented by precisely the anxiety-inducing and tranquility-inhibiting solicitude for esteem that Smith thinks vitiates commercial society more generally; hence the vain man is "restless and impatient," he is "always anxious to obtain new expressions of esteem," he "solicits with the most anxious importunity all external marks of respect," and he "is never to be satisfied, is full of jealousy and suspicion that we do not esteem him so much as he desires, because he has some secret consciousness that he desires more than he deserves" (TMS VII.ii.4.8–9).

The love of true glory is thus superior to vanity. Yet the love of true glory is not the highest or most admirable disposition; the love of true glory, albeit superior to the mere love of praise, is itself yet inferior to a third and highest disposition, that of the "love of virtue." The significance of this position can be seen by comparing it to those taken by certain of Smith's contemporaries. Hume – whose ethics are often assumed to be commensurate with Smith's – claimed that "to love the glory of virtuous deeds is a sure proof of the love of virtue."[33] Yet it is precisely this conflation of solicitude for glory with the love of virtue that Smith is concerned to resist in distinguishing this third-level orientation. His own conception of the love of virtue is in fact less similar to that of Hume than to that of Rousseau. Rousseau, it has been argued, similarly describes a love of "merited" glory that is superior to unmitigated

Colletti, *From Rousseau to Lenin*, 213; see also Colletti's claim that although Smith sees the dangers of inequality, he is yet "absorbed above all by the idea of economic development" (156). While Smith of course recognized the economic utility of self-interest, here and elsewhere he unambiguously distinguishes self-interest's utility from virtue's nobility. So too his claim against Mandeville calls into question the suggestion that he was content to "explore the paths of economic growth (commerce) without being troubled by the salvation of the human soul," or that he sought to "follow the path of economic analysis beyond moral considerations"; see Jimena Hurtado Prieto, "The Risks of an Economic Agent: A Rousseauian Reading of Adam Smith," *Columbian Economic Journal* 1 (2003): 217; and "Bernard Mandeville's Heir: Adam Smith or Jean-Jacques Rousseau on the Possibility of Economic Analysis," *European Journal of the History of Economic Thought* 11 (2004): 1.

[33] Hume, "Of the Dignity or Meanness of Human Nature," in *Essays, Moral, Political, and Literary*, ed. Eugene F. Miller (Indianapolis: Liberty Fund, 1985), 86.

amour-propre, but it is yet limited insofar as it "makes one draw the sentiment of one's existence from the opinions of others rather than from oneself."[34] The love of true or merited glory is thus a refinement of self-love; yet if one seeks genuine self-sufficiency, a form of life must be discovered that "can only be realized by passing through and then transcending *amour-propre*," as did the Jean-Jacques portrayed in Rousseau's autobiographical writings.[35] This same ideal – which at once unexpectedly aligns Smith with Rousseau and separates him from Hume – lies at the heart of Smith's understanding of virtue and is most clearly presented in his account of the love of virtue in his response to Mandeville.[36]

Smith here presents the love of virtue as a remedy for a problem that plagues the love of true glory. The love of true glory was presented as a remedy for a problem that plagues the mere love of praise or vanity; this remedy was founded on the distinction between claiming and deserving and, from the perspective of the lover of true glory, that distinction appeared to be sufficient. Yet having achieved his initial goal of revealing the vulgarity of praise-seeking that is indifferent to desert, Smith now turns to concentrate on what is both genuinely noble and genuinely problematic in the love of glory itself. In its defense Smith argues that the love of true glory shares with the love of virtue the fact that "both aim at really being what is honourable and noble" – hence the "affinities" between the three discrete stages that he describes in this argument, with the first two bound by a desire for claiming recognition not shared by the third, and the second two bound by a desire for deserving recognition not shared by the first. Yet this shared commitment to desert common to the second and third stages is vitiated by the potentially stronger commitment to claiming that binds the second stage to the first. Smith makes this clear in explicitly assimilating the love of true glory and the love of praise on the grounds that each takes "some reference to the sentiments of others." The lover of true glory is thus a divided man, torn between a concern to deserve esteem and a concern to attain the esteem he deserves. To be a lover of virtue, on the other hand, is to be wholly dedicated to the first objective and wholly indifferent to the second – to be a man who acts "solely from a regard to what is right and fit to be done," even if honor, praise, esteem, glory or fame "should never be bestowed upon him." Such a person, Smith pointedly insists, is thus driven principally by

---

[34] Melzer, *Natural Goodness of Man*, 257–58.

[35] Cooper, *Rousseau, Nature, and the Good Life*, 130, 173–74.

[36] A helpful parallel account of how Smith's "intensely felt sense of decline and nostalgia" serves to "not infrequently align Smith more closely with Rousseau than with Hume" is offered in Harkin, "Smith's Missing History," 443.

"the desire of rendering ourselves the proper objects of honour and esteem; or of becoming what is honourable and estimable." Put differently: in his case a desire to appear is wholly subordinated to a desire to be; indifferent to the recognition of others, he cares only to act as he ought, even in the full consciousness that his actions will likely never be appreciated with the esteem they deserve. Herein lies the reason why the lover of true glory comes in at second rank: "while he desires to merit approbation," he is "at the same time anxious to obtain it" – a disposition which, although more admirable than vanity, yet attests to some degree of "human infirmity." The "very great difference" that separates the lover of virtue from the lover of true glory lies then in his indifference to recognition – a disposition, Smith claims, that is not only the happiest, as it is "altogether secure and independent of fortune, and of the caprice of those he lives with," but also "the most sublime and godlike motive which human nature is even capable of conceiving" (TMS VII.ii.4.9–10).[37]

The three stages of self-love that Smith describes in his response to Mandeville at TMS VII.ii.4 – the love of praise, the love of true glory, and the love of virtue – represent an incipient version of the account of the substance of and relationships between the three ethical virtues of prudence, just magnanimity, and proper beneficence that are the focus of TMS VI. This comparison helps us see that Smith's theory of the virtues is unified by its grounding in a common center – namely the continuum of self-love – which provides it with an internal theoretical consistency even as it presents itself as a practical attempt to mitigate or ameliorate the specific ethical ills of commercial society, positing prudence to regulate the excesses of the love of praise and esteem, just magnanimity to regulate the excesses of the love of true glory, and proper beneficence to overcome individualism and enable us to achieve the best and happiest life of perfect moral nobility. And it is in this final point that Smith's most radical claim lies. Smith's ethics is today almost universally regarded as an endorsement of a system of social

---

[37] My argument thus extends a position that has been helpfully developed by both Waszek and Dickey. Waszek emphasizes Smith's "two-level approach" as a moral philosopher, distinguishing popular propriety from the "praiseworthy path of 'perfect virtue' that is open to a small élite"; "Two Concepts of Morality," 591ff.). Dickey emphasizes that, over the course of his revisions to TMS between 1759 and 1790, Smith joined to his emphasis on the inferior commercial virtues an interest in the elite virtues ("Historicizing the 'Adam Smith Problem'," esp. 597–99). My own understanding of the relationship between these levels most closely agrees with Muller's helpful claim that "implicit in Smith's works is the assumption that superior virtue, insofar as it is susceptible to cultivation, can be developed through exposing those who have developed the inferior virtues through institutional means to the stimulus of moral philosophy" (Muller, *Smith in His Time and Ours*, 165).

constructions and reciprocal adjustments of ethical behaviors via a train of self-conscious exchanges of observations and judgments between actors and spectators. Yet this aspect of his project, although crucial to his system – and evident particularly in his accounts of sympathy and moral judgment (e.g., TMS I.i) and of the ethical socialization of the self (e.g., TMS III.1) – is only half of his project. What I want to argue in what follows is that Smith's system of practical ethics indeed takes such processes as a departure point, but that its goal is not merely the establishment of an intersubjective ethics of mutual recognition but the transcendence of a dependence on recognition via the cultivation of the love of virtue. Smith makes this aim clear in a separate sixth edition revision to which we will have reason to return later. In TMS III.2, Smith restates precisely the same three-level distinction that he initially set forth in his argument against Mandeville, distinguishing again the practice of undeserved praise-claiming ("the most contemptible vanity") from a desire for merited and deserved praise ("the love of just fame, of true glory") from the wholehearted concern for self-approbation irrespective of actual praise ("the love of virtue"). The happiest and best life, he unambiguously reiterates, is the third, which looks on recognition and praise and even true glory as unnecessary; its self-approbation "stands in need of no confirmation from the approbation of other men. It is alone sufficient, and he is contented with it. This self-approbation, if not the only, is at least the principal object, about which he can or ought to be anxious. The love of it, is the love of virtue" (TMS III.2.8). Smith's argument against Mandeville in TMS VII is thus explicitly reiterated in the sixth edition revisions to Part III. But in the sixth edition, the role of this three-tiered conception of moral education is hardly limited to Part III, because the practical morality of Part VI is also built on this model. It too culminates in the love of virtue, and Smith's consistent interest in it across parts and editions suggests he regarded it less as an abstract ideal than as the proper object of moral education, and indeed the sole object worthy of the ambitions of those who seek to live the best possible life.

4

PRUDENCE, OR COMMERCIAL VIRTUE

THE CHALLENGE: FROM PRAISE TO PRUDENCE

In Part VI of TMS, Smith introduces the virtue of prudence as a remedy for the vices induced by the love of praise, the basic form of untutored self-love. His concern to remedy these vices is itself the product of his nuanced assessment of the love of praise – an assessment that balances an appreciation of the material and social benefits of the love of praise with an appreciation of the psychological and political disturbances that such a love frequently encourages. Smith's account of prudence has as its principal goal the maximization of these benefits and the minimization of their costs.[1] In this respect his account goes beyond familiar conceptions. It has long been recognized that his account of prudence provides a window on commercial man.[2] Yet the aim of his account is hardly to champion "the accumulating capitalist who is the driving force of the *Wealth of Nations*,"[3] nor is it simply to offer a defense of "bourgeois virtues" – a project with which Smith's name has increasingly come to be associated.[4] And neither is it only a plea for

[1] In discussing prudence here I refer only to the ethical virtue described in TMS VI.i. Although Smith's conception of moral judgment elsewhere offers a developed account of the role of prudential judgment or practical reason in helping us perceive the good in discrete ethical situations (on which see the studies cited at Chapter 2, Note 20), his treatment of prudence as an ethical virtue in TMS VI.i is less concerned with judgment or deliberation than with the dispositions useful in practical private life. On this difference, see especially the treatment of Smith's revaluation of classical prudence from an intellectual to a moral virtue in Den Uyl, *Virtue of Prudence*, esp. 124, 129, 141; and Raphael, *Impartial Spectator*, 61.

[2] Thus Cropsey calls prudence "the commercial virtue par excellence" (*Polity and Economy*, 47); cf. Griswold, *Smith and the Virtues of Enlightenment*, 203–7.

[3] Heilbroner, "Socialization of the Individual in Smith," 124; see also Hirschman, *Passions and Interests*, 100.

[4] Smith's championing of the bourgeois virtues is a theme of McCloskey's *Bourgeois Virtues* (see 8, 407) and extends back to McCloskey, "Bourgeois Virtue," *American Scholar* 63

moderation or middling virtue, though it surely is that in part.[5] Rather, Smith's account of prudence sets forth a model moral character for the admiration and emulation of citizens of commercial society – one specifically designed to preempt the particular ills and preserve the particular beneficial inclinations characteristic of such citizens.

The main benefit Smith sees in the love of praise, or vanity, is the stimulus such a love provides to economic growth and distributive justice. This benefit is emphasized in Smith's two most conspicuous personifications of social benefactors animated by vanity. The first is his well-known account of the "proud and unfeeling landlord" driven by "vain and insatiable desires," whose retainers "derive from his luxury and caprice, that share of the necessaries of life, which they would in vain have expected from his humanity or his justice" (TMS IV.1.10). The most conspicuous treatment of vanity in WN teaches the same lesson via its notorious account of how the attempt to gratify "the most childish, the meanest and the most sordid of all vanities" led feudal lords lusting for diamond buckles to trade away their superiority (WN III.iv.10; WN III.iv.17). And although there has been considerable debate over the degree to which Smith remained attached to a model of

(1994): 177–91; McCloskey, however, is careful to distance Smith from the "Prudence Only" view that she attributes to Smith's latter-day admirers (see, e.g., 117–19). For other explicit identifications of Smith with bourgeois virtue, see esp. Minowitz, *Profits, Priests and Princes*, esp. 2, 13, 79–86, 138, 172, 186; Muller, *Smith in His Time and Ours*, 165–66; Calkins and Werhane, "Smith, Aristotle and the Virtues of Commerce," 43; and Justman's claim that TMS is "the closest thing to an authorized version of the morality of bourgeois society" (*Autonomous Male*, 3; cf. 47); cf. David Brooks, "A Moral Philosophy for Middle-Class America," *New York Times*, 15 October 2006. A counterargument is offered in Dwyer, "Ethics and Economics," 663 and 671. For response, see Winch, *Adam Smith's Politics*, 180–81. Of available interpretations, my own position on this front is closest to Alvey's in his *Adam Smith: Optimist or Pessimist?*, which nicely demonstrates that although Smith is obviously receptive to the "commercial or bourgeois virtues" (61), his conception of virtue on the whole is "not reducible to simply bourgeois terms" (120) and that Smith himself cannot be reduced to a "bourgeois apologist" (203) as he also embraces "non-bourgeois virtues" (184). Rare among Smith commentators, Alvey also calls explicit attention to Smith's attachments to nobility and transcendent standards (see, e.g., 53, 196–97, 202; cf. Scott, *Greek Influence on Smith*, 8; Friedman, *Moral Consequences of Growth*, 55). In a similar vein, Schliesser notes Smith's emphasis at TMS IV.1.10 on the "*ennobling by-products*" of commercial society ("Smith's Conception of Philosophy," in *New Voices*, ed. Montes and Schliesser, 351).

[5] The best studies of Smith's conception of the moderate virtues include Berry, "Smith and the Virtues of Commerce," in *NOMOS XXXIV: Virtue*, 69–88; Phillipson, "Smith as Civic Moralist," in *Wealth and Virtue*, ed. Hont and Ignatieff, 179–202; Henry C. Clark, "Conversation and Moderate Virtue in Adam Smith's *Theory of Moral Sentiments*," *Review of Politics* 54 (1992): esp. 193–97; Calkins and Werhane, "Smith, Aristotle and the Virtues of Commerce"; and Muller, *Smith in His Time and Ours*, 93–99 and 167–69.

economic growth as driven by luxury consumption and the "deceptions" of vanity by the time he came to write WN, both works clearly call conspicuous attention to instances in which the selfish consumption of the vain and superior had the beneficial if unintended consequence of a redistribution of wealth and power.[6]

Such statements would seem to align Smith more with Mandeville than Rousseau. Yet Smith's recognition of vanity's material benefits was tempered by his no-less-explicit recognition of its psychological and political consequences. These consequences, as we have seen, are twofold. First, the love of praise, when unregulated, induces an anxious restlessness that necessarily torments both its possessor and all those in his ambit. This, it would seem, is the necessary consequence of vanity's combination of the love of gain with solicitude for status and superiority. Seen thusly, the vanity that drives commercial society via the encouragement of status achievement through the pursuit of wealth can be regarded as a corrupted conjunction of the traditional virtue of pride and the traditional vice of *pleonexia*. In this respect Smith joins a train of thinkers from Pascal to Rousseau to Tocqueville who argue that the dangers of the pursuit of "the frivolous pleasures of vanity and superiority" lie in the psychological disturbances suffered by all who have the misfortune of "not knowing when they were well, when it was proper for them to sit still and to be contented" (TMS III.3.31).

Yet busyness, restlessness, and anxiety only constitute one side of the dangers of the pursuit of praise; in addition to these psychological effects Smith also notes a political effect: the development of incentives to inauthenticity and duplicity in personal relations. Here Smith again shares a fear common to Pascal and Rousseau: namely the fear that the solicitude for praise on which commerce depends is itself prone to induce inauthenticity once praise-pursuers come to realize that their goals are better achieved by duplicity than by honesty.[7] Smith's treatment of vanity in TMS VI calls attention to this fact. Not only does he bluntly claim that "the vain man is not sincere" (TMS VI.iii.36), he also repeatedly illustrates the vain man's "false

---

[6] For this debate, see especially Griswold, *Smith and the Virtues of Enlightenment*, 222–25 and 262–66, and the response offered in Fleischacker, *Smith's Wealth of Nations*, 104–18; cf. Rasmussen, *Problems and Promise*, 132–37. Vanity is of course present in WN even if less often and less explicitly emphasized: "With the greater part of rich people, the chief enjoyment of riches consists in the parade of riches, which in their eyes is never so complete as when they appear to possess those decisive marks of opulence which nobody can possess but themselves" (WN I.xi.c.31).

[7] See Pascal, *Pensées* (esp. 82 in the Brunschvicg edition); Rousseau, *Discourse on Inequality*, in *Discourses*, trans. Gourevitch, 170–1, 183–4; but cf. Tocqueville, *Democracy in America*, II.iii.18.

pretensions" (TMS VI.iii.36) and his conscientious cultivation of deception, "the illusions of vanity": "his vanity is delighted with viewing himself, not in the light in which you would view him if you knew all that he knows; but in that in which, he imagines, he has, by his own address, induced you actually to view him" (TMS VI.iii.37). Put bluntly, if vanity and the love of praise are in fact necessary for economic growth, Smith's analysis suggests that Rousseau was right to fear that in such a society a concern for appearances would supplant the love of virtue.

Smith's conception of prudence is designed to meet these two challenges – anxiety on the one hand and duplicity on the other. In so doing it provides us with good reasons to think that we might transcend the familiar paradox that the wealth of nations must be bought at a high cost to individuals. Smith's study of prudence, that is, suggests that the tragic view of commercial society in which material gain demands moral evisceration is incomplete.[8] Moreover, his study of prudence responds to the paradox inherited from his historical context. Mandeville is sometimes admired for having had the consistency to embrace commerce and dismiss virtue, just as Rousseau is sometimes admired for having had the integrity to embrace virtue and dismiss commerce – and admirers of each are likely to regard Smith as caught between attachments to two incompatible categories. Yet Smith's conception of prudence suggests a different view altogether and offers an alternative to Mandeville's complacent acceptance of commercial society in its viciousness as well as to Rousseau's enthusiastic rejection of commercial society for its viciousness. Indeed Smith's study of prudence in TMS VI might be taken as an implicit rejection of both the quietism of the former and the absolutism of the latter and an embrace in their stead of a commitment to a moderate normative intervention which may enable citizens of commercial society to circumvent a possible but not inevitable tragedy. The principal substantive aims of this account are then first to encourage habits of industry, steadiness, and moderation to ameliorate the anxiety, busyness, and restlessness encouraged by the love of praise; and second to educate and thereby redirect our love of praise away from the selfishness that leads to duplicity

---

[8] See, e.g., Griswold's claims that one of Smith's "key teachings" is that deception drives wealth pursuit, that "pathos is intrinsic to the human condition" as "human life is fundamentally theatrical," that deception necessarily leads to "unhappiness," that WN describes a world "governed by a systematic self-deception about its own ends," and that Smith thinks "we seem fated to unending striving, whether or not we are philosophers," even if modest partial remedies exist (*Smith and the Virtues of Enlightenment*, 16, 109, 222, 263, 347); see also Berry, "Smith Under Strain," 458–59; and Brubaker's discussion of Smith's hesitation to claim that progress is necessary by nature ("Does the 'Wisdom of Nature' Need Help?" in *New Voices*, ed. Montes and Schliesser, 182–84).

and inauthenticity via the encouragement of a more admirable desire to be esteemed for possessing genuine virtues. Smith's account is thus both optimistic and realistic; so far from seeking to extirpate the love of esteem, his more moderate and hopeful goal is to educate it in such a way that preserves the material benefits of the aggregate pursuit of individual self-interests while minimizing vanity's most pernicious effects on the happiness and tranquility of societies and individuals.

EDUCATING THE VAIN: FATHERS AND SONS

Smith's remedy for the problems posed by vanity, or the love of praise, rests on the fact that this disposition is, by nature, educable. Herein lies one aspect of the import of distinguishing self-love from self-interest. Commentators have frequently noted that Smith's interest is in the former rather than the latter, but the philosophical significance of this lies in the fact that self-interest – defined here as the desire to maximize material acquisitions – is fundamentally static, whereas self-love – here, in its most basic form, the desire to maximize a sense of self-worth via recognition – is susceptible to elevation via moral education.[9] And this susceptibility has an important political consequence. Rather than argue that vanity must be complacently accepted as a necessary vice of commerce (as Mandeville seems to suggest) or that vanity ought to be extirpated from our nature so that commercial society might be transcended (as a facile reading of the early Rousseau might seem to suggest), Smith's suggestion is both more hopeful and more moderate, and seeks rather an improvement that is also realizable.

This strategy governs Smith's education of vanity in his account of prudence in TMS VI. It is itself presaged in several other places in his corpus that, taken collectively, offer a parable of fathers and sons. The key text is his account of the most notorious son in his work, "the poor man's son, whom heaven in its anger has visited with ambition." This brilliant rhetorical set piece has deservedly commanded a great deal of attention.[10] Not only is its

[9] For the conflation of self-love and self-interest, see, e.g., Ronald H. Coase, "Adam Smith's View of Man," *Journal of Law and Economics* 19 (1976): 543–4; see also Samuel Hollander's claim that on Smith's view the "motive of 'self-love' is synonymous with that of 'prudence'" ("Adam Smith and the Self-Interest Axiom," *Journal of Law and Economics* 20 (1977): 138). More careful discriminations of self-love from self-interest are provided in Brown, *Smith's Discourse*, 94, 97; Werhane, *Smith and Modern Capitalism*, 29–32; and the especially helpful account in Fleischacker, *Smith's Wealth of Nations*, 90–100.

[10] For particularly helpful treatments, see Brubaker, "Smith on Natural Liberty," in *Enlightening Revolutions*, ed. Minkov, 196–201; and Fleischacker, *Smith's Wealth of Nations*, 105–11.

rhetoric striking – indeed perhaps here more than anywhere in TMS Smith practices the painterly techniques described in LRBL – but it also presents the heart of the ostensible tragedy of commercial society: the desire of the poor man's son to better his condition appears to be at once the condition necessary for collective social prosperity and the condition that guarantees his individual misery. Yet here we need to be careful. When read in light of Smith's further development of the themes of this story elsewhere – and particularly when read in light of his account of prudence in TMS VI – we discover good reasons to regard the story of the poor man's son less as a window into Smith's vision of the truth of the conditions of life in commercial society, and more as a cautionary tale that illustrates the possible or potential degradation of life in such a society, one that provides incentives for citizens of such a society to embrace the remedies proposed in his account of prudence.

What then are the problems at the heart of the story of the poor man's son, and how does Smith think they might best be managed? The chief problem, quite clearly, is his solicitude for praise and esteem. This solicitude is so pronounced in the account of the poor man's son that he can be regarded as a quintessential expression – and perhaps even as an exaggerated expression – of the drive for attention and recognition that TMS I.iii.2 established as the fundamental motive of commercial action. Smith invites such a consideration specifically by describing the poor man's son with phrases taken directly from his translation of the comparison of civilized man with the savage that concludes Rousseau's *Second Discourse*.[11] We are thus not surprised to find that the source of the misery of the poor man's son is precisely his susceptibility to the same *amour-propre* that Rousseau insists renders civilized man so miserable. Hence, Smith gives his account of the career of the poor man's son: "naturally indolent" and desiring only to be at ease, he "admires the condition of the rich" and pursues his commercial ambitions from the hopes that his success would enable him to enjoy the conveniences wealth affords, and consequently to "sit still contentedly, and be quiet, enjoying himself in the thought of the happiness and tranquility of his station." But herein lies his ironic tragedy: his love of tranquility leads him to pursue his goal in a manner specifically inimical to the achievement of that goal; like Rousseau's civilized man, his pursuit of "the idea of a certain artificial and elegant repose" comes at the cost of the sacrifice of a "real tranquility that is at all times in his power." Smith's account of the poor man's son's desperate and futile attempts to secure recognition – all of which

---

[11] See Justman, *Autonomous Male*, 60; Force, *Self-Interest Before Smith*, 158–59, 180.

result only in ever more anxiety, restlessness, and exhaustion – makes this clear. In devoting himself "for ever to the pursuit of wealth and greatness," he

submits in the first year, nay in the first month of his application, to more fatigue of body and more uneasiness of mind than he could have suffered through the whole of his life from the want of them. He studies to distinguish himself in some laborious profession. With the most unrelenting industry he labours night and day to acquire talents superior to all his competitors. He endeavours next to bring those talents into public view, and with equal assiduity solicits every opportunity of employment. For this purpose he makes his court to all mankind; he serves those whom he hates, and is obsequious to those whom he despises.

The poor man's son is Smith's quintessential expression of the "vanity" that drives the pursuit of "wealth and greatness" in order to "gratify that love of distinction so natural to man" (TMS IV.1.8). And Smith's lesson seems clear: the solicitude for the recognition elicited by the attainment of wealth or greatness necessarily leads to individual misery – clearly defined here as both anxiety and restlessness as well as inauthenticity and slavish abasement – whatever may be its socially beneficial consequences.

Yet this is hardly Smith's last word on the matter. For all the misery that vanity brings to the poor man's son, in other places he suggests that this same vanity, directed in a more prudent manner, can encourage the pursuit of other goods more conducive to both virtue and happiness. Interestingly Smith makes this claim twice in the course of giving advice to fathers of sons who seem to suffer from precisely the same malady that afflicts the poor man's son. The first instance is to be found in his correspondence. Throughout his life Smith took an interest in fatherhood that is notable in a childless bachelor; indeed across his works he dispenses parental advice, including the suggestions that the accompanying of his son to college is "the most sacred as well as the most important duty of a father," that the greatest responsibility of a father to his daughter is "to educate her in all sort of virtues and instill into her the purest morals and the chastest affections," and that parents should send their children neither to boarding schools nor on Grand Tours, each of which corrupt by removing children from the salutary surveillance of their parents and only deliver a parent "from so disagreeable an object as that of a son unemployed, neglected, and going to ruin before his eyes" (CAS 243; LJA iii.59; WN V.i.f.36; cf. CAS 37, 42; TMS VI.ii.1.10). Smith's most striking advice on this front was communicated to Lord Shelburne, whose younger son he taught and boarded at Glasgow. Lord Shelburne was hardly a poor man, yet Smith saw that his son clearly shared with the poor man's son a love of praise and recognition: "His regularity is tempered by a great desire of distinguishing himself by doing actions of éclat that will draw upon him the attention of the world. He is even animated by this passion to a degree that is a little hazardous and is capable of venturing to expose his talents, which are naturally excellent, before they are perfectly matured" (CAS 42). Yet Smith also predicted that, in spite of his vanity, in his maturity Shelburne's son was likely to become "firm, steady and resolute in an uncommon degree" and that "by the time he is five and twenty, whatever faults he has will be the faults of the grave and serious character, with all its faults the best of characters" (CAS 42; CAS 51).

What authorized Smith to see such mature promise in such youthful vanity? His seemingly paradoxical view is that the son's ethical development will occur not in spite of his vanity, but because of it. Such is the explicit suggestion made in his most direct advice to fathers of vain sons, which itself reads both as an injunction to Shelburne and as an explanatory key to the dialectical organization of TMS VI:

> The great secret of education is to direct vanity to proper objects. Never suffer him to value himself upon trivial accomplishments. But do not always discourage his pretensions to those that are of real importance. He would not pretend to them if he did not earnestly desire to possess them. Encourage this desire; afford him every means to facilitate the acquisition; and do not take too much offence, although he should sometimes assume the air of having attained it a little before the time. (TMS VI.iii.46)

Smith is fighting battles on several fronts here. Given the similarity of such an account to the account given to Lord Shelburne, it is plausible to speculate that the image of his son might have been before Smith as he wrote. But more importantly, this account provides a response to Rousseau. In *Emile*, Rousseau claims that *le grand secret de l'éducation* is to occupy pupils in both contemplative and active exercises that never leave vanity a chance to grow.[12] Smith's position is precisely the opposite: if vanity can be neither avoided nor extirpated, the most prudent and effective strategy for its management is to direct it in such a way that its ambitions are harnessed to provide incentive for virtue. Herein lies Smith's educative strategy. His response to Mandeville, we remember, distinguishes two discrete stages: the love of praise and the love of true glory. In TMS VI.iii.46, Smith returns to

---

[12] Rousseau, *Emile; or, On Education*, trans. Allan Bloom (New York: Basic Books, 1979), 202. *Emile* was first published in 1762, and Smith's library is known to have contained a first edition (see Hiroshi Mizuta, ed., *Adam Smith's Library* (Oxford: Oxford University Press, 2000), 217), and hence Smith may well have had Rousseau in mind; but cf. Locke, *Some Thoughts Concerning Education* (Oxford: Clarendon Press, 1989), 116, which uses the phrase in a context that closely anticipates Smith's use. Lindgren provides a brief account of the mechanisms of this process in his account of mentorship (*Social Philosophy of Smith*, 43).

this distinction, and suggests that in fact the proper goal of the moral educator and good father is precisely to effect an elevation from the first to the second category by addressing the most common passion of commercial society, "the desire of the esteem and admiration of other people," and refining it so that it might become "the real love of true glory; a passion which, if not the very best passion of human nature, is certainly one of the best." Thus Smith's own strategy as a moral educator: recognizing that vanity is often "no more than an attempt prematurely to usurp that glory before it is due," he seeks to cultivate it rather than suppress it, in the hope that in time the vain person will come to desire to be esteemed "for qualities and talents which are the natural and proper objects of esteem and admiration," and thus become "a real proficient in all those talents and virtues to which, at present, he may only be an ostentatious and empty pretender" (TMS VI.iii.46).

Smith's aim then is to cultivate vanity as an ally in the transcendence of vanity. Such a position suggests the complexity of his relationship to Rousseau. Earlier we noted the differences in Rousseau's and Smith's understandings of the great secret of education. But Rousseau well understood the methods Smith describes here; as commentators have explained, the method of "palliation," or the "homeopathic" emergence of a remedy from the disease itself, is fundamental to Rousseau's own practical politics and ethics and is particularly evident in his schemes for managing *amour-propre* in Geneva, Poland, and Corsica.[13] This same ideal, as is well known, forms a guiding principle of Smith's advice on practical political intervention, evident particularly in his preference for the moderate and accommodating "science of the legislator" to the extreme and intolerant methods of the "man of system."[14] But Smith's methods of moral education are founded on precisely the

[13] For excellent treatments of Rousseau's use of this method, see Jean Starobinski, *Blessings in Disguise; Or, The Morality of Evil* (Cambridge: Polity Press, 1993), 118–31; and Forman-Barzilai, "The Emergence of Contextualism in Rousseau's Political Thought: The Case of the Parisian Theatre in the *Lettre à d'Alembert,*" *History of Political Thought* 24 (2003): esp. 462–63.

[14] On the place of moderation and antiperfectionism in Smith's science of the legislator, see especially Haakonssen, *Science of a Legislator,* esp. 79–98; Griswold, *Smith and the Virtues of Enlightenment,* 301–10; Peter McNamara, *Political Economy and Statesmanship: Smith, Hamilton and the Foundation of the Commercial Republic* (DeKalb: Northern Illinois University Press, 1998), 87–92; Winch, *Riches and Poverty,* 90–123; Winch, "Science and the Legislator: Adam Smith and After," *Economic Journal* 93 (1983): 501–20; Muller, *Smith in His Time and Ours,* 84–92; and the recent discussion in Amit Ron, "Modern Natural Law Meets the Market: The Case of Adam Smith," *European Journal of Political Theory* 7 (2008): 117–36, esp. 121–25. I develop the parallels between Smith's and Rousseau's moderate legislative sciences on these fronts in my "From Geneva to Glasgow," esp. 178–79, 184–88; and "Enlightened Nation Building," esp. 220–23, 226–30.

same methods that he endorses in his comments on the proper methods of legislation. Both his advice to the father of a vain son as well as his approach to the education of the vain praise-lovers in TMS VI take as their point of departure the conviction that self-love is both inevitable and educable, and it is precisely on this foundation that his strategy for ameliorating corruption depends. With regard to the inevitability of self-love, Smith is careful never to claim that the love of esteem either could or should be extirpated; doing so, he well knows, would inhibit the individual's desire to better his condition. And with regard to vanity's educability, Smith's consistent claim is that the regulation of the love of praise by the virtue of prudence is the optimal means both of avoiding the tragedy of the poor man's son and of attaining the sort of happiness available to commercial men. By substituting a patient firmness and steady resolve for an otherwise destructive anxiety and restlessness, and by substituting a love of deserved esteem for otherwise obsequious and duplicitous fawning, Smith explains how the common citizens of commercial society might flourish, and not merely those few capable of seeing that "wealth and greatness are mere trinkets of frivolous utility" (TMS IV.1.8).

SELF-INTEREST RIGHTLY UNDERSTOOD

Smith's practical education of the love of praise via the cultivation of prudence in fact begins in TMS I and is extended in TMS VI. The two treatments are united by the claim that prudence, in enabling its possessor to overcome restlessness and inauthenticity, is a prerequisite for both individual and social flourishing. This dual scope of prudence is clearly revealed in Smith's claim that "the prudent, the equitable, the active, resolute, and sober character promises prosperity and satisfaction, both to the person himself and to every one connected with him," whereas "the rash, the insolent, the slothful, effeminate, and voluptuous, on the contrary, forebodes ruin to the individual, and misfortune to all who have any thing to do with him" (TMS IV.2.1). Smith's aim here is twofold: first, to draw a distinction between the patient and resolute character of the prudent man and the impatient and impulsive character of his opposite; and second, to demonstrate that the virtues of the one and the vices of the other have effects that are both individual and social. Smith's emphasis on the second aspect particularly reveals the insufficiencies of regarding the story of the poor man's son as his definitive teaching on the relationship of vanity to commercial growth and civic flourishing. Taken alone, the example of the poor man's son seems to suggest that headlong pursuit of self-interest is collectively beneficial though personally detrimental. This account needs to be supplemented or contextualized, however, by attention to several other accounts that present a more subtle and complex view. Far from suggesting that individual happiness and social flourishing are mutually exclusive, these instead distinguish two different methods of pursuing self-interest – one both self-destructive and socially- destructive, and the other beneficial to both society and the individual.

The ills of the destructive approach are presented in Smith's study of the foppish dilettante in TMS I. The "young nobleman" achieves his superiority, we are there told, not "by knowledge, by industry, by patience, by self-denial, or by virtue of any kind." In sharp contrast, "conscious how much he is observed" and how much "all his motions are attended to," he cultivates the appearance of propriety rather than the practice of virtue to attain the recognition that he seeks (TMS I.iii.2.4). So too "the man of rank and distinction" indifferent to glory and "contented with the humble renown" his appearance brings. He sets his sights low: "to figure at a ball is his great triumph, and to succeed in an intrigue of gallantry, his highest exploit." As a consequence, he too cultivates only a fine appearance and "possesses none of the virtues" characteristic of men of affairs, and "shudders with horror at the thought of any situation which demands the continual and long exertion of patience, industry, fortitude, and application of thought" (TMS I.iii.2.5). Smith's studies of the moral psychology of the tyrant further illustrate how the improper pursuit of esteem portends both individual and social misery. In the terms of the passage from TMS IV.2.1, where the dilettante exhibits the vices characteristic of the slothful and voluptuous, the would-be tyrant exhibits those of the rash and insolent:

With what impatience does the man of spirit and ambition, who is depressed by his situation, look round for some great opportunity to distinguish himself? No circumstances, which can afford this, appear to him undesirable. He even looks forward with satisfaction to the prospect of foreign war, or civil dissension; and, with secret transport and delight, sees through all the confusion and bloodshed which attend them, the probability of those wished-for occasions presenting themselves, in which he may draw upon himself the attention and admiration of mankind. (TMS I.iii.2.5)

Like the fop, the would-be tyrant is principally animated by the love of distinction and admiration, but in his capacity to promote individual and social misery he shows himself to be the fop's superior. His effects on society are obvious, and Smith vividly describes both his "fraud and falsehood" and his "perpetration of the most enormous crimes" from assassination to civil war. And Smith is no less quick to insist that the tyrant's personal misery equals the social miseries he perpetrates – hence his cautionary reminder that "though they should be so lucky as to attain that wished-for greatness, they are always most miserably disappointed in the happiness which they expect to enjoy in it," as their tranquility is perpetually disturbed by "the avenging furies of shame and remorse" (TMS I.iii.3.8). This fate, in conjunction with that of the fop, thus stands as a warning to any who would take from the story of the poor man's son the lesson that individual happiness and social flourishing can or should be disjoined. Furthermore, TMS I.iii.3.8 is an effort at damage control; even if one should prove indifferent to the subtle charms of the higher of the "two different roads" described at TMS I.iii.3.2, this warning may at least serve to render one hesitant to take the lowest of roads.

The stories of the fop and the tyrant also have a second advantage. Not only do they serve as evidence of Smith's conviction that pursuits of self-interest tend to affect individuals and societies in similar ways, but they also emphasize the utility of a specific set of character qualities in the pursuit of self-interest. Each story, that is, illustrates the consequences of a lack of industry, patience, and resolve: the fop lacks the resolve and industry to submit to extended and fatiguing labor, and the tyrant lacks the patience to pursue glory steadily and justly. But against these excesses, Smith defines a middle way that cultivates the patient resolve that the tyrant and fop lack. Thus, he explains that if a private man "hopes to distinguish himself," he must do so by "more important virtues":

He must cultivate these therefore: he must acquire superior knowledge in his profession, and superior industry in the exercise of it. He must be patient in labour, resolute in danger, and firm in distress. These talents he must bring into public view, by the difficulty, importance, and, at the same time, good judgment of his undertakings, and by the severe and unrelenting application with which he pursues them. Probity and prudence, generosity and frankness, must characterize his behaviour upon all ordinary occasions; and he must, at the same time, be forward to engage in all those situations, in which it requires the greatest talents and virtues to act with propriety, but in which the greatest applause is to be acquired by those who can acquit themselves with honour. (TMS I.iii.2.5)

Smith's catalogue of character qualities is striking for several reasons. First it reveals his commitment to normative moralism; in recommending the prudent path as a surer means to distinction than either aristocratic dilettantism or unrestrained political ambition, Smith clearly intends to capture the attention of his students, many of whom would find quite pleasing the thought that, "in all governments," the highest offices are occupied by those "educated in the middle and inferior ranks of life, who have been carried forward by their own industry and abilities" – indeed carried beyond their superiors by birth, and who "regarded them first with contempt," but now must before them "truckle with the same abject meanness with which they desire that the rest of mankind should behave to themselves" (TMS I.iii.2.5). Beyond this splendid concession to bourgeois resentment, Smith also makes two important substantive points. First and most obviously, the virtues essential to the rising private man are precisely those on which the success of the commercial system described in WN rests. Second, these same traits form the point of departure for Smith's study of the character of virtue in TMS VI.

With regard to the former claim, it is largely recognized today that the model citizen of Smith's commercial society resembles less an interest-maximizing caricature of *homo economicus* (or even a desperate poor man's son) than the more moderate, sober prudent man described in TMS.[15] In this sense, the virtues of the commercial world of WN bear the stamp of the familiar set of virtues Benjamin Franklin sought to inculcate through his autobiography, teaching "industry and frugality, as the means of procuring wealth and thereby securing virtue."[16] One indeed can hardly take a step in any direction in WN without being reminded of the utility of these virtues. The dangers of indolence are impressed on readers through reminders of the lassitude of those rendered "slothful and lazy" by their "sauntering" and "indolent careless application" (WN I.i.7). Industry and perseverance are encouraged via reminders that those talents that require longer to develop are more esteemed and their products considered more valuable (WN I.vi.3). Frugality is shown to bring not just one-time gain but to establish a "perpetual fund" for growth and continued employment of productive labor (WN II.iii.19), whereas a prodigal, "by feeding the idle with the bread of the industrious, tends not only to beggar himself, but to impoverish his country" (WN II.iii.20; see also WN II.iii.25). Franklinian too is the claim that "order, economy and attention" not only promote business but are in turn

---

[15] For helpful illustrations, see Griswold, *Smith and the Virtues of Enlightenment*, 206; Brown, *Smith's Discourse*, 50; Macfie, *Individual in Society*, 75; Heilbroner, "Socialization of the Individual in Smith," 122–24; Phillipson, "Smith as Civic Moralist," 179ff.; Mehta, "Self-Interest and Other Interests," in *Cambridge Companion*, 259–65; Fitzgibbons, *Smith's System of Liberty, Wealth, and Virtue*, 61; and Montes, *Smith in Context*, 88.

[16] Franklin, *Autobiography*, in *Benjamin Franklin, Writings*, ed. J. A. Leo Lemay (New York: Library of America, 1987), 1397.

reaffirmed and further encouraged by it (WN III.iv.3). And commercial life itself, and particularly banking, depends, we are told, on confidence in not only the fortune but also the "probity, and prudence" of potential lenders (WN I.x.b.20; WN II.ii.28); probity and punctuality are indeed "the principal virtues of a commercial nation" (LJB 328). Smith knows well that the transient nature of international relations frequently gives diplomats incentives to duplicity, but "wherever dealings are frequent," as in commercial markets, it is in the advantage of all to cultivate virtues that best promote efficient and sustainable repeated interactions (LJB 326–28) – an observation that anticipates Robert Axelrod and other contemporary game theorists who study the emergence of norms of cooperation via iterated prisoner's dilemmas.[17]

Smith's recommendation of the utility of industry, frugality, probity, and patience is thus unmistakable, and indeed brings his ethics within the ambit of Franklin's. Yet at the same time it would be a mistake to infer that Smith's recommendation of the useful virtues is best taken as evidence of his commitment to utilitarianism, or even as evidence of his conception of commerce as an extension of Machiavellianism. In recommending the commercial virtues under the general aegis of prudence, Smith's aim in TMS VI.i is not simply to equip the acquisitive with more efficient tools for the instrumental attainment of their desires. Rather, recognizing both the material advantages of acquisitiveness as well as its potential ills, Smith seeks less to teach us the means by which our desires might be best pursued than to shape our desires themselves. In this sense, his account of prudence aims to substitute for an emphasis on short-term self-interest an appreciation of what Tocqueville would later call self-interest rightly understood.[18] Put differently, Smith's account aims to prompt reconsideration of the very ends and desires of the self by fostering a renewed appreciation of interests that lie beyond more immediate and familiar, but less fundamental, interests. His definition of prudence in TMS IV reveals this aim. Responding to Hume's understanding of utility, he explains that

the qualities most useful to ourselves are, first of all, superior reason and understanding, by which we are capable of discerning the remote consequences of all our actions, and of foreseeing the advantage or detriment which is likely to result from

---

[17] See Axelrod, *The Evolution of Cooperation* (New York: Basic Books, 1984). For specifically Smithean accounts of this phenomenon, see Vernon L. Smith, "The Two Faces of Adam Smith," *Southern Economic Journal* 65 (1998): esp. 10–11 and 16–18; and Otteson, *Marketplace of Life*, 246.

[18] See esp. Tocqueville, *Democracy in America*, II.ii.8–9.

them: and secondly, self-command, by which we are enabled to abstain from present pleasure or to endure present pain, in order to obtain a greater pleasure or to avoid a greater pain in some future time. In the union of those two qualities consists the virtue of prudence, of all the virtues that which is most useful to the individual. (TMS IV.2.6)

Smith's vision is striking, not least because it explicitly subsumes self-command within prudence itself, providing further evidence for regarding self-command less as a separate virtue in Smith's system than as a category that promotes each virtue's "principal lustre" (TMS VI.iii.11).[19] But equally important is his claim that the utility of prudence lies in the fact that both of its discrete components, rational foresight and self-command, are united in privileging the future over the present and encouraging us to "abstain from present pleasure, in order to secure greater pleasure to come" (TMS IV.2.8).[20] This shift from present to future is important for reasons both moral and economic. First Smith argues that such a shift provides a safer road to the gratification of the love of recognition; thus his emphasis on "that eminent esteem with which all men naturally regard a steady perseverance in the practice of frugality, industry, and application," even when directed to wealth accumulation. To use Hume's language, this prudence is agreeable to others, as "the resolute firmness" of the one who sacrifices present pleasures "in order to obtain a great though remote advantage" always "necessarily commands our approbation" and will lead us to "admire" and "think it worthy of a considerable degree of applause" (TMS IV.2.8). But there are also excellent economic reasons for the admiration of prudence. Prudent men are sensitive to "the unavoidable obstructions which the natural course of things opposes to the immediate or speedy establishment of a better system" and know that such "natural obstructions" can only be transcended by "a long course of frugality and industry" (WN I.xi.l.3). In this, the prudent man distinguishes himself from all those, from the man of system to the poor man's son, who are deluded or seduced by an "absurd presumption in their own good fortune" (WN I.x.b.26; cf. WN IV.vii.a.18; WN V.iii.33; WN I.x.b.28; WN I.x.b.32). Smith knows well that such overweening faith in

---

[19] See also Chapter Five, Note 36 (this volume). The specific place of self-command within prudence has been helpfully noted in Sen, "Adam Smith's Prudence," in *Theory and Reality in Development*, ed. Sanjay Lal and Francis Stewart (London: Macmillan, 1986), 31.

[20] See Gordon Davis's excellent account of how this point separates Smith from Hume and the prevailing luxury argument, as well as his explanations of the centrality of frugality and resistance to time preferences in Smith's conception of prudence ("Philosophical Psychology and Economic Psychology in David Hume and Adam Smith," *History of Political Economy* 35 (2003): esp. 272–77 and 291–99).

fortune, coupled with frustration at a recognition that the "natural course of things, is necessarily both slow and uncertain," constitutes the volatile mixture of resentment and pride that, with vanity, frequently drives human endeavor. Yet his claim is that this trap is endemic neither to our nature nor to commercial culture, hinting to ambitious young men who might otherwise follow the path of the poor man's son that another option yet remains:

A young man, who, instead of applying to trade or to some profession, should employ a capital of two or three thousand pounds in the purchase and cultivation of a small piece of land, might indeed expect to live very happily, and very independently, but must bid adieu, forever, to all hope of either great fortune or great illustration, which by a different employment of his stock he might have had the same chance of acquiring with other people. (WN III.iv.19)

In offering this choice Smith suggests that economic growth and personal happiness are not necessarily incompatible, however incompatible the greedy ambition for great wealth and happiness may well be. Risky speculative investing he thus consistently disparages as a less satisfying and less sure route to the augmentation of our fortune than the "calm and dispassionate" desire to better our condition, which not only sustains the progress of the individual but also "is frequently powerful enough to maintain the natural progress of things toward improvement" in spite of all political mismanagement (WN II.iii.28; WN II.iii.31; WN II.iii.36; WN V.iii.49). Smith's account of prudence in TMS VI.i might be said to have the inculcation of this desire as its primary goal. Herein then lies the second import of Smith's sketch of the character of the rising private man in TMS I. Not only did he consider these qualities requisite for the system of natural liberty described in WN, but he also considered these qualities requisite for the amelioration of the corruptions of that system. By so doing, Smith means to show that self-interest rightly understood – the preference for long-term over short-term pleasures – not only stimulates economic growth but also ameliorates the anxiety and restlessness that would otherwise inhibit happiness.[21]

---

[21] Several commentators have noted that Smith's understanding of prudence privileges the pursuit of long-term benefits over immediate gratifications; especially helpful accounts include Campbell, *Smith's Science of Morals*, 179; Winch, "Moral Philosopher as Political Economist," 104; Lerner, "Commerce and Character," 202; Muller, *Smith in His Time and Ours*, 133; Vivenza, *Smith and the Classics*, 54–56; and Mehta, "Self-Interest and Other Interests," in *Cambridge Companion*, 260. But the attractions of prudence so conceived are only partly economic; as important (if not more so) are the psychological benefits afforded by prudence thus understood insofar as enables its possessor to withstand the predilections to anxiety, restlessness, and inauthenticity characteristic of commercial society.

The goal of TMS VI.i is thus to provoke a reconsideration of self-interest leading to a recovery of the deeper interests that lie beyond the more imme- diate interests pursued so destructively by the poor man's son, the fop, and the tyrant. In this sense, one might say that in 1790 Smith set forth a sec- ond "new-model man" to atone for the deficiencies of the first.[22] To effect this reconsideration he employs the dialectical techniques examined earlier. Particularly notable is his point of departure in TMS VI.i. Earlier we saw that Smith introduces Part VI as an exercise in training the mind's eye to recognize virtue on seeing it. But more particularly, he calls us to apprehend the virtuous character "under two different aspects; first, as it may affect his own happiness; and secondly, as it may affect that of other people" (TMS VI.intro.1). On a formal level, this indicates that his treatment will begin with a study of the self-regarding virtue of prudence and then will proceed to a consideration of the other-regarding virtue of beneficence. But Smith here also hints at the guiding movement from self to beyond the self that governs not only his ascending account of virtue as a whole but also his discrete accounts of each individual virtue. The movement of TMS VI, that is, is replicated in the movement of TMS VI.i; just as the inquiry into the character of virtue begins by considering prudence, the virtue most directly concerned with the self, the inquiry into prudence begins by considering the most pressing and immediate forms of self-concern.

The significance of this departure point is evident if we compare it to that of Rousseau. Two similarities emerge from so doing. The first is method- ological. Rousseau's *Second Discourse* offers a conjectural anthropology, or nonhistorical investigation of man's true nature. But Smith seeks to do the same in TMS VI, and particularly in TMS VI.i. To be sure, Smith's account is couched in terms of the moral and intellectual development of the individual rather than the species; one might say that Smith domesticates within the trajectory of the moral development of the individual precisely the trajectory of the moral degeneration of the species Rousseau describes. But substan- tively Rousseau and Smith share a certain view of the substance of natural self-love. Both Rousseau and Smith take as their departure point the belief that vanity is not primary in human nature, and that our natural self-interest is limited to a concern for self-preservation. In this respect Smith's point of departure replicates the fundamental assumptions of the first part of the *Second Discourse*: "the preservation and healthful state of the body seem to be the objects which Nature first recommends to the care of every individual." Man is, on both accounts, by nature a creature of "appetites" implanted in

---

[22] The term is again Lerner's; see Chapter One, Note 14 (this volume).

him for the sake of reinforcing a "principal object": teaching the individual "how to keep out of harm's way" (TMS VI.i.1). Furthermore, like Rousseau's natural savage, Smith's natural man is dedicated solely to "providing the means of gratifying those natural appetites" – "procuring pleasure and avoiding pain" are his principal objects, and his "care and foresight" are restricted solely to procuring the goods that promote his "external fortune" (TMS VI.i.2). Thus Smith begins Part VI with a clear codification of a doctrine running throughout his works and which lies at the heart of his synthesis of Stoic and Epicurean and modern natural law perspectives: namely the view that human beings are constituted by a natural solicitude for their self-preservation, and that this natural solicitude for the satisfaction of the needs of our own bodies is more immediate than our solicitude for the well-being of others (TMS I.i.4.8; TMS II.ii.2.1; TMS VI.ii.1.1; TMS VI.ii.2.2).

Yet neither Smith nor Rousseau thinks that the simple state of nature is destined to last long. Herein lies another important similarity in their conjectural anthropologies: both trace to the advent of social life the emergence of a new form of self-love. In the *Second Discourse*, the introduction of civil society is clearly envisioned as a nonnatural or contingent accident, and the passion that it engenders, *amour-propre*, is no less clearly an artificial imposition on natural man. Smith is much more circumspect on the question of whether love of esteem is properly understood as "natural"; his translation of Rousseau's social anthropology of the species into a story of the psychological development of the individual absolves him from having to take a definitive stand on this fundamental question. Yet his account follows Rousseau's in two decisive respects: first, it traces the love of esteem to sociability, whether natural or adventitious; and second, it identifies the corruption of this love as the main obstacle to individual happiness and civic flourishing:

> Though it is in order to supply the necessities and conveniences of the body, that the advantages of external fortune are originally recommended to us, yet we cannot live long in the world without perceiving that the respect of our equals, our credit and rank in the society we live in, depend very much upon the degree in which we possess, or are supposed to possess, those advantages. The desire of becoming the proper objects of this respect, of deserving and obtaining this credit and rank among our equals, is, perhaps, the strongest of all our desires, and our anxiety to obtain the advantages of fortune is accordingly much more excited and irritated by this desire, than by that of supplying all the necessities and conveniences of the body, which are always very easily supplied. (TMS VI.i.3)

The influence of Rousseau evidently remains quite strong on Smith in 1790. Not only does he share Rousseau's conjecture that the desire for esteem may be "the strongest of all our desires," but he also clearly defines the central problems it induces: restlessness (here suggested by Smith's reference to the "anxiety" that is "excited and irritated" by it) and duplicity (here suggested by his equivocation on the difference between "the degree in which we possess" and that to which we "are supposed to possess" external advantages that elicit esteem). At the same time, Smith does not, of course, advocate the excision of this desire. As he repeatedly notes, the earlier described concern for rank and esteem is not only one of the strongest but also one of the most potentially beneficial of our natural dispositions – hence his several invocations of the social and individual advantages of the concern to maintain one's rank and status, and his several claims that the maintenance of rank is a "natural right" properly defended under a system of positive law (LJA i.24; LJA ii.93; LJA ii.135; LJB 7–8; cf. TMS I.iii.2.8). In light of the advantages that a regard for rank brings – from the moral benefits of self-approbation in TMS, to political stability in LJ, and to wealth creation in WN – Smith is less concerned to excise it than to educate it in such a way as to maximize its benefits and minimize its ills. In this respect, Smith might again be said to agree with Rousseau, insisting that the way in which the love of esteem is expressed is what distinguishes "the present misery and depravity of the world" from "the natural and ordinary state of mankind" (TMS I.iii.1.7) and, furthermore, that the rehabilitation of this love is the first and most pressing task of moral education.

To achieve this end, Smith sets forth a new conception of self-interest. The main aim of this new conception is to preempt the problems of restlessness and duplicity, thereby preempting the individually destructive and socially pernicious tragedies of the lives of the poor man's son, the dilettante fop, and the would-be tyrant. Yet Smith's optimism on this front is hardly the hope of a Pollyanna. So, far from attempting to disabuse others of their self-interest, he takes a specifically realist approach; rather than appeal to softer sentiments or amiable virtues, he appeals to our long-term interest in preservation and prosperity as a means of restraining short-term self-interest and the desire for immediate pleasures. Smith's strategy in this respect is similar to that of Hobbes. In *Leviathan*, Hobbes famously argues that the only means of enticing men to cede any portion of their absolute freedom is to appeal to their deepest desires for self-preservation, which Hobbes calls the sum of natural right.[23] Smith's own strategy for mitigating the pernicious effects of self-interest in his practical moralism takes a similar approach. Hence, although prudence is the virtue concerned with "the care of the health, of the fortune, of the rank and reputation of the individual" (TMS VI.i.5), its

---

[23] Hobbes, *Leviathan*, ch. 14, para. 4.

principal end is to minimize anxiety and restlessness by encouraging us to reconsider our fundamental desires, enabling us to see that preservation is more valuable to our happiness than acquisition:

Security, therefore, is the first and the principal object of prudence. It is averse to expose our health, our fortune, our rank, or reputation, to any sort of hazard. It is rather cautious than enterprising, and more anxious to preserve the advantages which we already possess, than forward to prompt us to the acquisition of still greater advantages. The methods of improving our fortune, which it principally recommends to us, are those which expose to no loss or hazard; real knowledge and skill in our trade or profession, assiduity and industry in the exercise of it, frugality, and even some degree of parsimony, in all our expences. (TMS VI.i.6)

Smith's argument here is more complex than a conventional assertion of the utilitarian benefits of the bourgeois virtues for the ambitious and acquisitive. In sharp contrast, the endorsement of the useful commercial virtues here is grounded not in a privileging of the love of acquisition but in a desire to minimize anxiety and therefore promote tranquility. In keeping with his (quite Hobbesian) view that "man is an anxious animal" (LJB 231), Smith thus regards the first proper end of prudence to be the minimization of this anxiety through the establishment of security in the face of fortune. In this, he explicitly follows the Epicureans, particularly their vision of prudence as reducing anxiety by attention to long-term self-interest (TMS VII.ii.2.4; TMS VII.ii.4.7). Prudence is thus intended in part to provide modern men with a recovery of the blessings afforded by the infant's ignorance, namely "an antidote against fear and anxiety, the great tormentors of the human breast" (TMS I.i.1.12).

Smith's emphasis on the need to substitute long-term for short-term self-interest to manage anxiety becomes even more pronounced as his inquiry develops in Part VI. The concept of the impartial spectator is introduced in this context. Impartial spectators, we are here told, are indifferent to "the importunate calls of their present appetites" and moreover regard "their present, and what is likely to be their future situation" as "very nearly the same." What makes the prudent man admirable, therefore, is not simply that he adopts the standpoint of the impartial spectator, but that he adopts in his orientation to his own interests the impartial spectator's capacity to regard present and future interests as equal. This approach is the key to managing the anxiety that commerce induces. The prudent man is distinguished by "the steadiness of his industry and frugality, in his steadily sacrificing the ease and enjoyment of the present moment for the probable expectation of the still greater ease and enjoyment of a more distant but more lasting period of time." By so doing, he frees himself from the psychological discord characteristic of an exaggerated solicitude for the consumption of present pleasures, and enjoys "the entire approbation of the impartial spectator" (TMS VI.i.11). This defense of prudence thus suggests a very different foundation for a defense of the commercial virtues than one might expect. For although it is surely correct to say that Smith's prudent man is an embodiment of the ideal commercial man envisioned in *The Wealth of Nations* – and particularly the commercial man whose acquisitions are governed by "an exact attention to small savings and small gains" (WN III.ii.7) – Smith's defense of prudence as self-interest rightly understood never argues that the commercial life is either nobler or more natural than other lives. In sharp contrast, his aim is to provide those who have already chosen this life with the tools to live it with the minimum possible degree of anxiety and the maximum possible degree of tranquility. Smith shows us such a life at its best:

The man who lives within his income, is naturally contented with his situation, which, by continual, though small accumulations, is growing better and better every day. He is enabled gradually to relax, both in the rigour of his parsimony and in the severity of his application; and he feels with double satisfaction this gradual increase of ease and enjoyment, from having felt before the hardship which attended the want of them. He has no anxiety to change so comfortable a situation, and does not go in quest of new enterprises and adventures, which might endanger, but could not well increase, the secure tranquility which he actually enjoys. If he enters into any new projects or enterprises, they are likely to be well concerted and well prepared. He can never be hurried or drove into them by any necessity, but has always time and leisure to deliberate soberly and coolly concerning what are likely to be their consequences. (TMS VI.i.12)

Herein lies the superiority of the prudent man to the poor man's son, the dilettante fop, and the aspiring tyrant; the prudent man achieves his ends while avoiding their misery. Thus, the story of the poor man's son is absolved of having to carry the weight of Smith's final teaching on the possibility of happiness and commercial society. Far from proving that social opulence necessarily comes at the cost of individual misery, revisited in light of the prudent man, the story of the poor man's son seems merely a dramatic illustration of the dangers of an unregulated love of wealth and greatness exaggerated and inflamed by the imagination. And in terms of Smith's historical context, the story of the prudent man offers a response to Rousseau. Therefore, far from accepting Rousseau's reductive binary between carefree indolent poverty and miserable commercial anxiety, Smith's portrait of the prudent man means to provide citizens of commercial societies with a way to pursue self-interest, and thus opulence, with minimal restlessness.

Yet Smith's response to Rousseau is at this point still incomplete. Thus far his account of prudence has answered only half of the problem inherited from Rousseau; having explained how prudence mitigates restlessness and anxiety, it remains for him to show how prudence responds to the problem of duplicity and deceit. Smith's account in fact responds to this problem directly, and the means by which it does so are analogous to those of his response to the problem of restlessness. In the same way that Smith sought to moderate and redirect rather than extirpate the self-interest that prompts restlessness, so too he aims to moderate and redirect rather than extirpate the love of esteem that can prompt a preference for external appearances to genuine virtue. This response develops in two stages: first by encouraging prudent men to seek a different type of esteem than that sought by those prone to duplicity and deceit, and second by demonstrating that this type of esteem requires methods of pursuit both more effective and psychologically healthier than the duplicity of the vain.

To begin: Smith makes clear in several places that the prudent man is every bit as concerned as the vain man with esteem, and never does he suggest that those given to the love of external goods are likely to transcend this love. Yet the prudent man, Smith also makes clear, is considerably more discriminating than the vain in the types and sources of esteem that he solicits. The chief difference between their desires is their scope: where the vain man seeks the praises of all, the prudent man is more selective. He recognizes that our rank and credit often largely depend on what a truly virtuous man "would wish them to depend entirely": "our character and conduct, or upon the confidence, esteem, and good-will, which these naturally excite in the people we live with" (TMS VI.i.4). As a result, he disdains the vain man's indiscriminate and immoderate quest for esteem and prefers to seek the esteem of those who know him best from close, sustained, and repeated contact. In so doing, he averts what Smith considers one of the most powerful incentives to vice – the anonymity afforded by extensive societies. The intimate relationship between anonymity and egoistic corruption is a pervasive theme in Smith's corpus; thus "obscure strangers who visit foreign countries" are more likely to ruin themselves via excessive spending than those living with their peers (TMS VI.iii.37); thus even the best young man on the Grand Tour and "at a distance from the inspection and control of his parents and relations" is likely to return home conceited, unprincipled, and lazy (WN V.i.f.36; TMS VI.ii.1.10); and thus the "man of low condition" from a village often finds himself, in a great city, "sunk in obscurity and darkness," as "his conduct is observed and attended to by nobody, and he is therefore very likely to neglect it himself, and to abandon himself to every sort of low profligacy and vice" (WN V.i.g.12). Such stories suggest that our ideal and abstract spectator "requires often to be awakened and put in mind of his duty, by the presence of the real spectator" (TMS III.3.38) and indeed that education depends less on "the abstruse syllogisms of a quibbling dialectic" than on "that great discipline which Nature has established for the acquisition of this and of every other virtue; a regard to the sentiments of the real or supposed spectator of our conduct" (TMS III.3.21). The prudent man seems to know this instinctively. Where impersonal and anonymous social relations of vain men encourage their egoistic vices, he avoids these vices by locating himself in an identifiable community that provides a context for his pursuit of position and reputation. As a result, his love of esteem takes a more admirable and morally salutary form than the vain man's love of praise.

In this sense the prudent man reaps the benefits of a disposition Smith describes elsewhere. Xenophon's *Memorabilia*, he notes, offers the image of Socrates turning his companions from vanity to virtue by teaching that the noblest path to a good reputation is to become good at that for which one desires repute (TMS VII.ii.2.13).[24] It is an idea that the prudent man under-stands well. So far from seeking praise by any means possible, he restricts himself to the desire for "reputation in his profession" earned by the "solidity of his knowledge and abilities" alone (TMS VI.i.7). The consequence is that where the immoderate love of praise characteristic of the poor man's son and Rousseau's civilized man compels duplicity, the prudent man's mod-erate love of esteem guarantees that he "is always sincere, and feels horror at the very thought of exposing himself to the disgrace which attends upon the detection of falsehood" (TMS VI.i.8). Hence Smith's account of his modesty, which celebrates his authenticity and his sincerity – and indeed his freedom from the propensity to deceit and dissimulation typical of other praise-lovers:

The prudent man always studies seriously and earnestly to understand whatever he professes to understand, and not merely to persuade other people that he understands it; and though his talents may not always be very brilliant, they are always perfectly

---

[24] Rousseau, too, understood this well: "Anyone who has the courage to be what he seems to be will sooner or later become what he ought to be" (quoted in Jean Starobinski, *Jean-Jacques Rousseau: Transparency and Obstruction*, trans. Arthur Goldhammer (Chicago: University of Chicago Press, 1988), 63). Rousseau's post-1755 work provides helpful illustrations of this idea. If the basic lesson of the *Second Discourse* is that vanity corrupts, elsewhere Rousseau later clearly argues that solicitude for the opinions of spectators can be put to good effect; particularly good on this point is Zev M. Trachtenberg, *Making Citizens: Rousseau's Political Theory of Culture* (London: Routledge, 1993), 175–210.

genuine. He neither endeavours to impose upon you by the cunning devices of an artful imposter, nor by the arrogant airs of an assuming pedant, nor by the confident assertions of a superficial and imprudent pretender. He is not ostentatious even of the abilities which he really possesses. His conversation is simple and modest, and he is averse to all the quackish arts by which other people so frequently thrust themselves into public notice and reputation. (TMS VI.i.7)

The difference between this moderate love of esteem and the desire for praise endemic to vanity is clear, and turns principally on the contrast between the prudent man's sincerity and the vain man's duplicity. Furthermore, his aversion to the "quackish arts" employed by those eager to thrust themselves forward suggests his understanding of another truth: namely that "the pleasures of vanity and superiority are seldom consistent with perfect tranquility, the principle and foundation of all real and satisfactory enjoyment" (TMS III.3.31). The lover of praise, quite simply, "is never to be satisfied, is full of jealousy and suspicion that we do not esteem him so much as he desires, because he has some secret consciousness that he desires more than he deserves," and is hence "restless and impatient" and "always anxious to obtain new expressions of esteem" (TMS VII.ii.4.9). The prudent man is the opposite: rather than cultivate appearances to garner the praises of the distant world, he works to maximize genuine talents that his immediate companions cannot fail to recognize. His excellence thus goes beyond disdain for faction and public intrigue (TMS VI.i.13), or even his amiable preference for intimate circles of friends to the glamorous but corrupt world of high society (TMS VI.i.8). The prudent man is not only a practical man of affairs who prefers the esteem of his peers to recognition from society more generally; he is at once the preeminent representative of Smith's conviction that, when well directed, a desire to seem admirable can be a useful means of encouraging its possessor to become admirable, and that a moderate sensitivity to the opinions of others is not necessarily a step down the slippery slope to inauthenticity and duplicity, but the first step in moral education.

THE ADVANTAGES AND DISADVANTAGES OF PRUDENCE

To restate: Smith envisioned the virtue of prudence as an improvement on the headlong rush toward fame and fortune that characterizes the pursuit of self-interest in commercial modernity. Prudence preserves authenticity from the propensity to deceit just as it rescues tranquility from the propensity to anxiety; by reorienting these passions in a direction that optimizes both individual happiness and social welfare, Smith offers a means by which the characteristic passions of commercial modernity might be managed. Yet even these accomplishments fail to exhaust prudence's benefits. Smith's ambition is to promote not merely a reorientation of self-interest but a reconsideration of the proper ends of a human being. Of course, just as Smith's first word on ethical virtue cannot be taken as his last, neither can his first word on the ends of human life be taken as his last. Still, TMS VI.i takes an important step toward describing these ends. In particular it offers a reconsideration not simply of the way in which happiness might be pursued but of the nature of happiness itself.

In offering this reconsideration, Smith further develops a theme that lies at the heart of his normative moral project: namely the question of why one ought to be just. Smith's treatment of this question is somewhat less explicit than the treatments of some of his contemporaries and predecessors; one looks in vain in his work for a sustained inquiry akin to Hume's study of the "sensible knave" or Plato's Thrasymachus. Yet the problem of how one might reply to the egoist or moral cynic of this type is one that seems to have occupied Smith intensely. In Smith's case, the problem takes the form of the question of why an individual ought to prefer justice to power if indeed he is fundamentally animated by self-interest, as repeatedly suggested in TMS VI.i. Smith's response partakes of a side of the answer given by Socrates to Thrasymachus. In part this answer is founded on the claim that the manipulator of opinions and appearances, however clever, can never garner rewards commensurate with the magnitude of his efforts to maintain such appearances; this seems at least to be the implication of the studies of the blushing and sweating of Thrasymachus and the misery of the would-be and the actual tyrants.[25] Smith takes a similar stance when addressing his own adolescent interlocutors on this same problem. To such an audience the life of the polygamist perhaps may seem, at first glace, not to lack certain charms or advantages. But carefully examined, Smith insists, it becomes clear that "this happy man to appearance" is in fact "racked with the most tormenting jealousy." His unmanageable family affords him "no enjoyment in the exercise of the parental affections, but a great deal of anxiety, jealousy, and vexation," and his constant solicitude for his wives affords him "very little conjugal affection, but a greater share of jealousy than any other man has" (LJA iii.30–32). Smith's account of misery of the slave-master follows a similar trajectory of his account of the misery of the master of the seraglio. Here again his claim is that slavery is not only clearly "very unhappy to

---

[25] Plato, *Republic*, 350d; 577b–578b; 579a–e.

the slave himself," but that it is also "so to the masters" (LJA iii.111). Both stories reiterate the lesson of his own account of the would-be tyrant in TMS I, examined earlier: the life of aggrandizement, however happy it may appear, comes at a psychological price that precludes the attainment of genuine happiness. Clearly this answer assumes, as Smith elsewhere more explicitly suggests, that anxiety is necessarily inimical to the tranquility that happiness is founded upon – indeed, it must be admitted, Smith's account will fail to persuade any genuinely selfish knave indifferent to tranquility itself.

Smith's pessimism with regard to the relationship of aggrandizement to happiness forms a crucial context for his optimism concerning the relation of prudence to happiness. Among the most important normative claims of TMS VI.i is that the prudent man's life is in fact genuinely happier than that of the man who seemingly possesses unlimited means to gratify unlimited desires. Smith reiterates the genuineness of this modest happiness in his account of how prudence enables its possessor to recover the sweetness of ordinary life in the face of the many elements in modern commercial society which consciously or unconsciously militate against our enjoyment of this sweetness. Put differently, the value of commercial virtues lies not so much in their capacity to further our pursuit of material ends, but in their instrumental necessity to the recovery of an appreciation of common life's genuinely wonderful pleasures:

Temperance, decency, modesty, and moderation, are always amiable, and can seldom be directed to any bad end. It is from the unremitting steadiness of those gentler exertions of self-command, that the amiable virtue of chastity, that the respectable virtues of industry and frugality, derive all that sober lustre which attends them. The conduct of all those who are contented to walk in the humble paths of private and peaceable life, derives from the same principle the greater part of the beauty and grace which belong to it; a beauty and grace, which, though much less dazzling, is not always less pleasing than those which accompany the more splendid actions of the hero, the statesman, or the legislator. (TMS VI.iii.13)

So far from being valued for its capacity to promote material aggrandizement, prudence is chiefly valuable for its capacity to enable us to enjoy the pleasures of the familiar and ordinary. In TMS I Smith insists that "we can scarce express too much satisfaction in all the little occurrences of common life, in the company with which we spent the evening last night, in the entertainment that was set before us, in what was said and what was done, in all the little incidents of the present conversation" (TMS I.ii.5.2). Prudence is the virtue that enables us to recover such pleasures by foregoing the more seductive pleasures of distant and extravagant wealth and greatness; indeed prudence is the virtue most closely associated with the recovery of the moral status of common life.[26] The way in which prudence promotes this recovery is particularly reiterated in Smith's study of the prudent man's capacity for friendship. In other places Smith makes clear that upstarts are lonely, whereas those who pursue the bettering of their condition more steadily and soberly often cultivate a modesty and moderation that leads others to seek them out (TMS I.ii.5.1; cf. WN V.ii.k.73; TMS III.3.32). Smith's prudent man particularly reaps this advantage and is guided by a "steady and faithful attachment to a few well-tried and well-chosen companions; in the choice of whom he is not guided by the giddy admiration of shining accomplishments, but by the sober esteem of modesty, discretion, and good conduct" (TMS VI.i.9).

Smith's prudent man thus follows not simply a more efficient and honorable route to the pursuit of external goods – the fruit of his commitment to industry, temperance, and probity – but also a route to the attainment of several greater goods, including tranquility, authenticity, friendship, and a moderate love of ordinary life. In each of these respects he serves as the paragon of a certain type of excellence available to a citizen of commercial modernity – an excellence, furthermore, that is meant to preempt both the contemporary critique of those like Rousseau, who argue that the truth of commercial life is to be found in the condition of the poor man's son, and the later critique of those like MacIntyre, who argue that capitalism depends on a "total divorce" between success and virtue akin to a world in which "the ethics of success comes to be combined with a certain kind of relativism."[27] Smith sees success and virtue as far less opposed and much more capable of reconciliation. His faith on this front is clearly manifested in a letter he wrote to Burke. Congratulating his friend on the propriety of his conduct, he observed, "it gives me, however, great satisfaction to see, that what was so agreeable to the highest principles of honour may in the end prove not inconsistent with interest" (CAS 226). The letter may have been

---

[26] The prudent man's recovery of ordinary pleasures is itself emblematic of Smith's broader commitment to the recognition of the dignity of common life and ordinary morality and the need to preserve them from the incursions and subversions of philosophy. For comprehensive treatments of this theme, see esp. Griswold, *Smith and the Virtues of Enlightenment*, esp. 13–15, 21–22, 73–74, 141, 174, 177, 245; and Brubaker, "'A Particular Turn or Habit of the Imagination': Adam Smith on Love, Friendship, and Philosophy," in *Love and Friendship: Rethinking Politics and Affection in Modern Times*, ed. Eduardo Velásquez (Lanham, MD: Lexington Books, 2003), esp. 230, 252.

[27] MacIntyre, *Short History*, 103; MacIntyre, *After Virtue*, 139.

casually penned, yet the hope at its heart – that the useful and the honorable are reconcilable, if not the same – is, one might say, the fundamental hope upon which Smith grounds his continued attachment to commercial society in spite of his appreciation of the ethical challenges it poses. So far from a crude apology for greed, WN itself tends to point to ways in which markets foster the reconciliation of virtue and material benefit; indeed much of WN can be taken as an illustration of TMS's dictum that "the practice of virtue" is "in general so advantageous, and that of vice so contrary to our interest" (TMS VII.ii.2.13). This is particularly emphasized in the proposals made in WN concerning the well-being of the poor; hence its arguments for more generous compensation of labor, for improved work conditions, and for restrictions on the taxation of necessities often invoke notions of "common humanity" and advise the powerful to "always listen to the dictates of reason and humanity" on the grounds that attention to such dictates is not only of obvious benefit to the worker but is ultimately in the true interest of the employer and the general society alike (WN I.viii.40–45; WN I.viii.48; WN I.x.c.12; WN IV.vii.b.54; WN V.ii.k.9; cf. WN IV.vii.c.102). Put differently, the macroeconomic aim of the invisible hand – reconciliation of individual utility and collective benefit – is itself, in its obverse, the fundamental claim of Smith's microeconomics: that individual humanity promotes collective utility.

Smith's admiration of prudence and the commercial virtues more generally thus rests on his hope that interest and virtue might be reconciled. Yet Smith also recognizes the limits of this hope – and herein lies much of the sophistication of his virtue theory, for although his hope is sincere, he also offers us good reasons to temper any uncritical optimism to which we might be tempted. For Smith is aware that the otherwise happy synthesis of virtue and interest in prudence has an unexpected consequence of its own. In particular, insofar as prudence teaches its possessors a safer and more effective means of pursuing external goods, it simultaneously places more such goods within the grasp of the prudent. Insofar as it expands the instrumental capacities of the acquisitive, prudence thus has the unintended consequence of potentially reaffirming certain aspects of the egocentrism and instrumentalism that it was designed to counteract. Smith's study of prudence in fact concludes with an examination of two consequences of such increased instrumentalism: an increased propensity to individualism on the one hand and an increased propensity to mediocrity on the other. With regard to the first category, Smith explains that the capacity of prudence to expand our capacity to satisfy our bodily necessities as well as our love of recognition can, if left unmanaged, have the paradoxical effect of further narrowing the horizons of the individual and leading him to focus ever more on the attainment of the goods that prudence renders more convenient. With regard to the second category, Smith explains that an increased capacity to acquire pleasures and goods often leads to distorted estimates of their value as well as decreased capacities to appreciate other sources of value. Put differently, the virtue that enables its possessor to enjoy the ordinary pleasures of common life threatens to incapacitate him to appreciate other possibly greater goods afforded by other types of human activities.[28]

Smith presents these unexpected consequences in his descriptions of the prudent man's condition and disposition. His condition, he says, is "comfortable" (TMS VI.i.12), and his disposition is "perfectly inoffensive" (TMS VI.i.10). But herein lies prudence's ambiguity. Comfort is clearly superior to the squalor of the savage and the serf, just as inoffensiveness is clearly superior to the clamor of the vain and the great. Yet Smith is aware that solicitude for comfort and inoffensiveness necessarily precludes pursuits that are capable of affording greater goods than comfort and pleasantness. This shortcoming is made particularly clear in his account of the prudent man's inoffensiveness. At the same time that it renders the prudent man incapable of petulance and rudeness and impertinence, so too prudence renders its possessor a colossal bore: "He rarely frequents, and more rarely figures in those convivial societies which are distinguished for the jollity and gaiety of their conversation. Their way of life might too often interfere with the regularity of his temperance, might interrupt the steadiness of his industry, or break in upon the strictness of his frugality" (TMS VI.i.9). In this sense the prudent man is almost a caricature of the industrious man, a Franklinian stripped of the sociability that made Franklin lovable − a Franklinian rendered "dull."[29] Yet if the greatest failing of prudence was only deficient *joie de vivre*, there would hardly be grounds for a critique. His shortcomings are in truth more serious. The same privileging of comfort and tranquility that renders him indifferent to sociability also leads him to forego the kind of pursuit that might afford him a nobler sort of recognition than the mere

---

[28] Dickey's account helps bring this point into relief. Dickey helpfully calls attention to Smith's account of the prudent man's shortcomings, but in his account, these chiefly consist in the fact that by 1790 Smith had judged that the prudent man "had become unreliable, for he was fast succumbing to vanity and to the lure of luxury" ("Historicizing the 'Adam Smith Problem'," 598). Dickey is quite right to note these failings of the prudent man, yet we might hesitate to identify them with "vanity." The prudent man in fact seems quite good at keeping in vanity in check. His shortcomings are rather the result of his susceptibilities to mediocrity and individualism − related but ultimately distinct corruptions.

[29] Den Uyl, *Virtue of Prudence*, 264.

esteem of immediate peers – thus the problem suggested by his commitment to being at all times "perfectly inoffensive." Smith is quick to insist that it is well that he is "not a bustler in business where he has no concern; is not a meddler in other people's affairs; is not a professed counselor or advisor, who obtrudes his advice where nobody is asking it." Such a disposition particularly renders him "averse to enter into any party disputes," and, in his professed hatred of "faction," he shows himself to be precisely the embodiment of that "good temper and moderation" which Smith frequently insists is necessary to combat the faction that he repeatedly identifies as a devastating corruptor of both political orders and moral sentiments (TMS VI.i.13; WN V.i.f.40; cf. TMS III.3.43; TMS VII.ii.1.8). Yet even as he transcends the propensities to anxiety, restlessness, vanity, and duplicity that might lead him to participate in faction's intrigues, his very means of transcending such propensities renders him either deaf or indifferent to a nobler calling. The prudent man thus

is not always very forward to listen to the voice even of noble and great ambition. When distinctly called upon, he will not decline the service of his country, but he will not cabal in order to force himself into it, and would be much better pleased that the public business were well managed by some other person, than that he himself should have the trouble, and incur the responsibility, of managing it. In the bottom of his heart he would prefer the undisturbed enjoyment of secure tranquility, not only to all the vain splendour of successful ambition, but to the real and solid glory of performing the greatest and most magnanimous actions. (TMS VI.i.13)

In preferring private life to public affairs, the prudent man shares the predilections of those from Socrates to Swift who prefer liberty to ruling. Yet the prudent man, unlike Socrates and Swift, buys his private freedom at the cost of an incapacity for the freedom afforded by a cultivation of the self's nobler dispositions. Put differently, the prudent man's love of quiet esteem precludes pursuit of honor; in terms of the dialectic presented in Smith's response to Mandeville, the prudent man privileges the love of praise over the love of true glory. And herein lies both his claim to superiority over the poor man's son as well as his inferiority to the lover of true glory; his love of basic external goods renders him indifferent to desires that are "noble and great" and actions that are "the greatest and most magnanimous."

The centrality of nobility is reaffirmed in Smith's final judgment on prudence: "Prudence, in short, when directed merely to the care of the health, of the fortune, and of the rank and reputation of the individual, though it is regarded as a most respectable and even, in some degree, as an amiable and agreeable quality, yet it never is considered as one, either of the most endearing, or of the most ennobling of the virtues" (TMS VI.i.14). This last word reaffirms that prudence's capacity to ameliorate commercial anxiety and duplicity is of genuine value and is rightly admired. Yet, at the same time, prudence's very successes prompt in a discerning spectator a desire for virtues more noble and more worthy of our love. And thus Smith presents his distinction of "inferior prudence" from "superior prudence." The former is the virtue on which Part VI has until now focused and which is elsewhere identified with Epicureanism, namely the prudence dedicated to "the judicious pursuit of our own private interest and happiness, or in the proper government and direction of those selfish affections which aim solely at this end" (TMS VI.i.15; TMS VII.ii.intro.2; cf. TMS VII.ii.2.2; TMS VII.ii.2.8). Yet this inferior prudence fails for the same reason Epicureanism itself fails: each approach, in focusing on instrumentality, fails to account for the fact that "the sentiments which they naturally excite in others are the objects of a much more passionate desire or aversion than all their other consequences; that to be amiable, to be respectable, to be the proper object of esteem, is by every well-disposed mind more valued than all the ease and security which love, respect, and esteem can procure us" (TMS VII.ii.2.12; cf. TMS VII.ii.2.16–17).

Prudence is thus insufficient unto itself, though it constitutes a necessary point of departure for the development of a more complete ethical system. Smith, we have seen, believes that in rhetorical discourses, honorableness and utility are the proper appeals for a practically minded audience. The account of prudence in TMS VI.i might be seen as precisely such an initial appeal insofar as its principal concern is the regulation of that concern with esteem and interest that the *Lectures on Rhetoric* insist drives most men. It is a point suggested by Smith himself in his response to Epicurus: when men by their acts "manifestly show that the natural beauty of virtue is not like to have much effect upon them, how is it possible to move them but by representing the folly of their conduct, and how much they themselves are in the end likely to suffer by it?" (TMS VII.ii.2.13) This itself is only the obverse of a sentiment that Smith elsewhere expresses in a positive form in arguing that the claiming of external goods is "the reward most proper for encouraging industry, prudence, and circumspection" (TMS III.5.8). Yet in each case, Smith also makes clear that such claiming is not the whole of virtue, but only an introduction to it. So too in TMS VI.i, which ends with the explicit introduction of the "superior prudence" characteristic of "the Academical or Peripatetic sage" as well as "of the great general, of the great statesman, of the great legislator," and dedicated in its efforts to "greater and nobler purposes than the care of the health, the fortune, the rank and reputation of the individual" (TMS VI.i.15). Smith's treatment of this virtue is given in his treatment of magnanimity, the virtue dedicated to addressing the two problems characteristic of commercial society and exacerbated by prudence: individualism and mediocrity.

5

MAGNANIMITY, OR CLASSICAL VIRTUE

THE PROBLEMS OF PRUDENCE AND THE
THERAPY OF MAGNANIMITY

Let us restate the problem to this point. Commerce seems to depend on vanity, yet vanity induces restlessness, anxiety, duplicity, and inauthenticity. Prudence offers a palliative remedy that ameliorates these vices by redirecting, and thus mitigating, the love of esteem inseparable from commerce. Yet such a remedy engenders new ills of its own – particularly individualism and mediocrity, the consequences of prudence's reanimation of the love of acquisition – and hence Smith's dialectical approach to the study of prudence, and indeed to the study of ethical virtue more generally. Smith's balanced account of prudence testifies to his recognition that positing a practical solution to a moral or political problem often induces new problems which in turn require redress. In the case at hand, the reification of self-love encouraged by prudence intensifies the natural propensity to self-preference that it was in fact intended to ameliorate. As a consequence, Smith must now confront a new set of challenges – challenges that are both original to the corruption induced by commercial society and exacerbated by prudence. Chief among these are the ills of self-preference, or individualism, and mediocrity, or an indifference to excellence and nobility. Remedying these two ills is the task of his account of magnanimity.

Stating the problem in these terms is likely to prompt at least two objections, one skeptical of this description of the problem, another skeptical of the solution. The former concerns the claim that Smith sought to limit self-preference. Smith has been labeled a champion of self-interest by his partisans and detractors alike, and those invested in this view are likely to question the claim that he in fact sought to encourage ethical agents to transcend self-preference. And this view is held not only by crude versions of economic laissez-faire which reduce his conception of self-love to an endorsement of self-interest; a more sophisticated version of the view is held by social theorists who regard Smith's postulation of a natural desire for the sympathy of others as evidence of his intention to create a self-regulating and autonomous moral sphere in which the desire for sympathy and esteem compels individuals to conform to norms generated by the reiterated judgments of a community of spectators – a view that finds its fullest development in the claim that Smith's is an ethics of social construction.[1] Each of these conceptions of his project is in some measure in the right insofar as it is based on his foundational principles of self-interest and sympathy. Yet one might also object that these views are partial and fail to account for the principal theme of TMS VI (and the sixth edition more generally): the encouraging of individuals ambitious for excellence to transcend the individualistic self-preference leading to mediocrity and conformism endemic to commercial modernity. A complete account of Smith's project thus requires attention to the role of magnanimity and nobility.

The second objection is more skeptical of the remedy than of the diagnosis. While granting that the problems of conformity and mediocrity are in fact real dangers, such an objection is likely to resist the language of magnanimity or nobility to describe Smith's intentions, as such language sits uncomfortably with certain received conceptions of Smith as a champion of commercial liberalism's middling virtues or as a practitioner of an incipient version of value-neutral social science.[2] Yet here again the problem is how to reconcile such views with Smith's texts. In TMS VI, and indeed across the sixth edition, his discussions of virtue consistently embrace the categories of the honorable, the noble, and the magnanimous – categories unavailable in the languages of liberalism or social science. Readers then must either explain away such textual inconveniences or explain how Smith's commitment to them might be reconciled with his more familiar commitments. In taking the latter route our inquiry seeks to take seriously his efforts to reconcile the peak virtue of the ancients with the characteristic dispositions of the moderns.[3]

---

[1] The most important of these studies include those cited in this chapter, Notes 19–23.

[2] See, e.g., Macfie's claim that, in invoking the categories of the noble and the honorable, TMS III.3.4 ends "on what is surely a false note" (*Individual in Society*, 97; cf. 113n25).

[3] On the challenges inherent to such a project, see esp. Manent, *City of Man*, 200–3; and Donald Livingston, *Philosophical Melancholy and Delirium: Hume's Pathology of Philosophy* (Chicago: University of Chicago Press, 1998), 49–50 and 141–42. Related discussions focusing on the tensions between self-perfection and social cooperation in Smith can be found in Den Uyl and Griswold, "Smith on Friendship and Love," 613–15; Den Uyl, *Virtue of Prudence*, 128 and 140; cf. Macfie, *Individual in Society*, 125.

This study of Smith's conception of magnanimity thus has two goals beyond demonstrating that this conception offers a response to the corruptions of commercial society exacerbated by prudence. The first is backward-looking and the second forward-looking. The first goal is to demonstrate that Smith's embrace of magnanimity constitutes a useful defense against a familiar argument against liberalism. Among the most prevalent and influential claims against liberalism is that it elevates self-preservation and material comfort as primary ends of human aspiration and, consequently, substitutes the individualistic or bourgeois virtues that promote peace and prosperity for nobler virtues characteristic of the ancient polis.[4] Procedural liberalism of the Kantian or Rawlsian sort inevitably seems both attenuated and unsatisfying from such a perspective. Yet Smith's position suggests that magnanimity is not merely the province of antiliberal reactionaries, but rather that a robust liberalism can accommodate – indeed perhaps requires – magnanimity.[5] In this sense Smith's vision of magnanimity represents an effort to remedy one of liberalism's chief ills as well as an effort to recover an understanding of self-perfection informed by antiquity. His vision thus points to another mechanism for the "preservation of desirable aspects of ancient thought" within modernity and to further evidence for the suggestion that "there is more antiquity in modernity than is commonly suspected."[6] The second, forward-looking goal is to encourage a reconsideration of the context of Smith's moral philosophy. In his efforts to combat the individualism that is at once the birth of mediocrity and the death of nobility, some may hear, in addition to echoes of Aristotle, anticipations of a tradition that extends from Tocqueville to Mill to Nietzsche. However unfamiliar such a context might seem for the Smith we have come to know, this tradition's vision of excellence and nobility is anticipated by Smith's study of magnanimity in the sixth edition, and particularly in his encouragement of the

---

[4] See, e.g., MacIntyre, *After Virtue*, 181–203; Manent, *City of Man*, 17–31 and 46–49. My view is closer to that of Fleischacker, who sees Smith's liberalism as "distinct from, and indeed a challenge to, the liberalism of those who would maintain that human excellence is something we need to sacrifice for the sake of freedom" (*Smith's Wealth of Nations*, 102).

[5] Smith's efforts to recover magnanimity within liberalism anticipate, in some sense, certain more recent treatments of magnanimity from scholars working in a neo-Aristotelian tradition that might be understood as broadly sympathetic to liberalism's core aims; see, e.g., Mary Keys, *Aquinas, Aristotle, and the Promise of the Common Good* (Cambridge: Cambridge University Press, 2006), 143–72; Collins, *Aristotle and the Rediscovery of Citizenship*, 61–66; and Gabriel Richardson Lear, *Happy Lives and the Highest Good: An Essay on Aristotle's Nicomachean Ethics* (Princeton: Princeton University Press, 2004), 168–74.

[6] Griswold, *Smith and the Virtues of Enlightenment*, 7; Berkowitz, *Virtue and Modern Liberalism*, 22.

self-love, self-approbation, and self-sufficiency that enables one to act independently of the norms that emerge from the collective agreement of a moral community.

UP FROM INDIVIDUALISM: DESERT, PRAISEWORTHINESS, CONSCIENCE

Smith's overcoming of self-preference via his recovery of magnanimity in Part VI is predicated on a series of specific moves in Part III. Smith signals the relation of Parts VI and III in the Advertisement to the sixth edition, in which he explains that his major revisions include not only the addition of Part VI but also alterations to "the last Chapter of the third Section of Part First," as well as "the four first Chapters of Part Third" (TMS Advertisement.1). These revisions to Part III are in fact central to his virtue theory, particularly to the challenges inherited from his treatment of prudence, because their fundamental aim is to encourage transcendence of self-preference.[7] By so doing, these revisions advance Smith's projects to recover the love of nobility in the face of a growing love of esteem, and to recover love of self-sufficiency and genuine ethical independence in the face of pervasive conformism. Individualism and mediocrity are thus linked, and nobility is inextricable from each; overcoming the self is itself noble to Smith. Collectively these revisions thus constitute a preparative for the examination of self-preference in TMS VI. Three stages of this preparative demand our particular attention: the distinction between claiming and deserving in TMS III.1, the distinction between praise and praiseworthiness in TMS III.2, and the distinction of two types of self-love in TMS III.3.[8]

The departure point for the first of these distinctions is the now-familiar concept of anxiety. Smith's previous discussions of praise and esteem, as we have seen, typically begin with the anxiety that the love of praise and esteem prompts; thus, the main virtue of the esteem-seeker, prudence, is conceived in part as a means of minimizing unnecessary anxiety. A similar movement governs Smith's treatment of the desire to deserve or be worthy of praises, which suggests that the social anxiety of the citizen of modern commercial society may be more complex than has been assumed. The anxiety of the poor man's son and Rousseau's civilized man is easily understood: their

---

[7] I am indebted here to Lauren Brubaker for encouraging me to attend more carefully to the relationship between Parts III and VI.

[8] III.2 and III.3 are again largely (though not wholly) original to the sixth edition, and III.1 is largely (though not wholly) carried over from previous editions. The specific revisions are detailed at Chapter 3, Note 1 (this volume).

debased capacity to appreciate self-worth renders them anxious to solicit the esteem of others. But in Part III, Smith extends this diagnosis and in so doing shows us another side of modern man's social anxiety, one that goes well beyond the familiar game of reciprocal spectatorship culminating in disapproval and disapprobation for some and approval and esteem for others. His aim is to show us that even after this game ends, esteem-seekers cannot find tranquility but are in fact beset by new anxieties. So, far from resting satisfied or content with possession of long-sought approval, a new concern emerges: "we become anxious to know how far our appearance deserves either their blame or approbation" (TMS III.1.4). The mere possession of praise cannot satisfy us, for even (and perhaps especially) when we succeed at praise-claiming, we "become anxious to know how far we deserve their censure or applause, and whether to them we must necessarily appear those agreeable or disagreeable creatures which they represent us" (TMS III.1.5).

Here Smith introduces the central concept of his theory of moral judgment – the impartial spectator. The intention of this mechanism is to enable the person principally concerned to become a self-spectator and thereby promote the development of conscience.[9] But here Smith's account of moral judgment and his theory of virtue interestingly overlap. The goals of both his impartial spectator and his distinction between claiming and deserving are first, to encourage our equality with others by teaching us to transcend self-preference, and second, to prompt us to reconsider the sort of goods our happiness requires. The latter is an especially prominent theme of TMS III.1, in which it is argued, "to be amiable and to be meritorious; that is, to deserve love and to deserve reward, are the great characters of virtue." Herein of course lies our central concern, the "character of virtue." But even more striking is the fact that Smith's understanding of the character

---

[9] Several influential discussions have done much to illuminate this aim of the impartial spectator and have been especially helpful in tracing the growth and significance of this concept in the second and sixth edition revisions; see esp. Raphael, "The Impartial Spectator," in *Essays on Adam Smith*, 83–99; Hope, "Smith's Demigod," in *Philosophers of the Scottish Enlightenment*, 157–67; and Valihora, "Judgement of Judgement," esp. 140–41, 148–49 (particularly helpful in calling attention to Smith's movement from an ethics of propriety to an ethics of "heroic virtue"). To these one might add that Smith's shift from intersubjectivity to self-sufficiency may itself suggest less a "tension" in his thought than a specific recognition: namely that the morality of commercial society, so far from being a unified monolith, encompasses multiple dimensions, and that different dimensions require differing emphases depending on the relative state of corruption within a given commercial society. In any case, in light of these comprehensive treatments, as noted in the introduction, my focus is less the impartial spectator than Smith's theory of virtue and the way in which it furthers the overcoming of self-preference that is often associated exclusively with this device.

of virtue, as expressed here, also provides an answer to the rhetorical question that concludes the section: "What so great happiness as to be beloved, and to know that we deserve to be beloved?" (TMS III.1.7) If indeed both happiness and the character of virtue are defined by the love of deserved love rather than by the mere love of being loved or need to be loved, we can expect that a similar recognition of desert's primacy will animate the fuller treatment of the character of virtue in Part VI.[10] Furthermore, Smith's recognition of the strength of our desire to deserve praise is the linchpin of his faith in the continued capacity of even sympathetic men to transcend the solicitude for the opinions of others which might otherwise promote conformity and homogeneity. Only those convinced of their worth are capable of transcending the pressures induced by solicitude to conform to group norms, for "we can be more indifferent about the applause, and, in some measure, despise the censure of the world; secure that, however misunderstood or misrepresented, we are the natural and proper objects of approbation" (TMS III.1.5). Finally, our anxiety to deserve praise is also important insofar as it affords a new vantage point from which to assess commercial society. To this point our inquiry has largely been governed by terms and concepts inherited from Rousseau and his legacy; "duplicity" or "authenticity" have helped us capture a distinction between commercial society and its alternatives as it was envisioned by Rousseau and, to some degree, shared by Smith. Yet in establishing a new category between the anxiety to claim esteem, characteristic of Rousseau's civilized man, and a self-sufficient indifference to esteem, characteristic of Rousseau's savage or solitary walker, Smith points us to a new horizon. Against the reductive suggestion that man is necessarily either natural or artificial, Smith's recognition of the persistence of our anxiety to deserve praise suggests a different vision – one that, like Rousseau's *Emile*, aims to identify and cultivate an element of our natures that persists in civilized society.[11]

---

[10] Even though Smith's use of the phrase "character of virtue" in both TMS VI and here in TMS III.1 are from the sixth edition, it should be noted that Smith's use of the phrase dates back both to the 1759 draft revision in the letter to Gilbert Elliot (see CAS 40, p. 52; ultimately TMS III.1.7), and, significantly, to his discussions of Hutcheson from the first edition onward; see, e.g., TMS VII.ii.intro.3–4 and TMS VII.ii.3.7, 9, 10, 13.

[11] At the same time, the savage also held some attractions for Smith; for helpful studies of how his study of native North Americans in TMS V represents a "counternarrative" to accounts of commercial progress and an anticipation of his impartial spectator, see Harkin, "Natives and Nostalgia: The Problem of the 'North American Savage' in Smith's Historiography," *Scottish Studies Review* 3 (2001): 21–32; and "Smith's Missing History," esp. 433, 436–40, 442–3. Also Rousseau himself understood praiseworthiness well. Laurence Cooper helpfully distinguishes between two forms of *amour-propre* in Rousseau, pride and vanity,

Smith's distinction between praise and praiseworthiness in TMS III.2 reaffirms his belief that the concern for desert is an element of our natures. Smith is often assumed to have regarded the bodily necessities related to self-preservation and physical survival as the most fundamental elements of our natures; our treatment of prudence earlier noted the role of such claims in TMS VI.i. Yet in retrospect it can be seen that even Smith's strongest statements on this front are carefully qualified; revisiting TMS VI.i, one sees that preservation of the body and its health merely "seem" to be the first concerns of nature (TMS VI.i.1). The significance of this qualification becomes clearer in TMS III.2, which provides a more comprehensive treatment of human nature – one that goes well beyond the ostensible primacy of self-preservation or material gratification:

Man naturally desires, not only to be loved, but to be lovely; or to be that thing which is the natural and proper object of love. He naturally dreads, not only to be hated, but to be hateful; or to be that thing which is the natural and proper object of hatred. He desires, not only praise, but praise-worthiness; or to be that thing which, though it should be praised by nobody, is, however, the natural and proper object of praise. He dreads, not only blame, but blame-worthiness; or to be that thing which, though it should be blamed by nobody, is, however, the natural and proper object of blame. (TMS III.2.1)

Smith's familiar distinction between praise and praiseworthiness thus has a remarkable though underemphasized intention at its heart: namely to set forth a new conception of human nature that considers the love of desert as essential to our natures as the love of claiming external goods. This intention offers a useful window into the difficult question of Smith's conception of the genealogy of normative values. Smith's consistent assumption here and elsewhere is that we are naturally attached to certain values and ideals; these are, in a very real sense, part of our beings by nature. This assumption itself has an important consequence for his project. Rather than lead him to further investigate the provenance of our love of praiseworthiness or even

and explains that Rousseau himself was hardly indifferent to the distinction between the love of praise and the love of praiseworthiness; for where vanity seeks praise at any cost, the proud seek to "*deserve* praise," for "what pride most wants, even more than praise, is praiseworthiness" (*Rousseau, Nature, and the Good Life*, 164). On praiseworthiness and desert in *Emile*, see N. J. H. Dent and Timothy O'Hagan, "Rousseau on 'Amour-Propre'," *Proceedings of the Aristotelian Society* 99 (1999): 93, which quotes the tutor's hope that Emile will come not simply to proclaim "'I rejoice because they approve of me'," but rather, "'I rejoice because they approve of what I have done that is good'" (*Emile*, 339). An excellent account of this passage and a comparison to Smith's understanding of praise and praiseworthiness is offered in France, "Rousseau, Smith and the Education of the Self," in *Moy Qui Me Voy*, ed. Craig and McGowan, 49.

the criteria for praiseworthiness itself, it seems to have compelled him to pursue a different, urgent task: not to seek to define or discover far-off ideals, but to seek to recover and redirect our natural longing for the good in light of the constraints and corruptions of our commercial culture.

The recovery of this side of our nature is central to Smith's response to the ethical ills of commercial society. First it reveals the vulgarity of the love of praise independent of desert. TMS III.2 thus offers a reconsideration of vanity in light of the clarity afforded by an appreciation of praiseworthiness; in its light, the desire to claim unmerited praises is hardly esteemed for its utility but rather strikes us as evidence of "the most superficial levity and weakness," a mere "illusion of the imagination" and "superficial weakness and trivial folly" (TMS III.2.4), a "contemptible" disposition, fit only for "the most frivolous and superficial of mankind" (TMS III.2.8, 11), a "false and delusive light" in which only a "weak man" regards himself (TMS III.2.15). Thus his reconsideration: vanity is perfectly admissible as an animating force of the moral education of those whose age or ignorance forbids access to a more elevated disposition, but those who have come to understand the difference between deserving and claiming praise are expected to see vanity for what it is. Yet this recognition of vanity's vulgarity is only the first step in a broader process. In emphasizing the persistence of our natural love of praiseworthiness, Smith means to recover within commercial society a respect for this truer nature that itself may mitigate the corruption encouraged by commercial society's exacerbation of the more familiar and elemental desires of our nature. Smith makes this point twice in TMS III.2. In the first instance he notes that "Nature, when she formed man for society, endowed him with an original desire to please, and an original aversion to offend his brethren," and taught him to take pleasure in the approbation and pain in the disapprobation of others (TMS III.2.6). Were Smith to have left matters here, his position might have been taken as an endorsement of the horizons of the esteem-loving prudent man. But Smith tempers this implication in what follows. The love of praise and fear of shame alone are insufficient foundations on which to erect a social order, he insists, and hence nature took care not to rest here. Anticipating precisely the worst corruptions described by Rousseau, nature also took care to invest man with another love:

But this desire of the approbation, and this aversion to the disapprobation of his brethren, would not alone have rendered him fit for that society for which he was made. Nature, accordingly, has endowed him, not only with a desire of being approved of, but with a desire of being what ought to be approved of; or of being what he himself approves of in other men. The first desire could only have made him wish to appear to be fit for society. The second was necessary in order to render him anxious to be really fit. The first could only have prompted him to the affectation of virtue, and to the concealment of vice. The second was necessary in order to inspire him with the real love of virtue, and with the real abhorrence of vice. (TMS III.2.7)

Smith's argument here is crucial in two respects. First, his distinction testifies to the persistence of his concern with one of the aspects of commercial society that Rousseau, as we have seen, found most troubling: its propensity to separate concern for appearances from concern for character, *paraître* from *être*. Smith's solution to this problem rests on his postulation of a love of praiseworthiness both logically and temporally prior to a love of praise, the former being necessary to mitigate the excesses of the latter. Herein lies Smith's Rousseauan solution to the characteristically Rousseauan problem identified earlier. Having already established that individuals in commercial societies are uniquely sensitive to the opinions of others, Smith now makes the Rousseauan claim that nature in its wisdom antecedently invested man with a love of praiseworthiness capable of withstanding and mitigating civilization's corruptions (cf. TMS I.iii.3.7).[12]

Smith reaffirms this distinction in a second set of paragraphs later in the section. These begin by restating the utility of our natural predisposition to value the opinions of others, insisting that "the all-wise Author of Nature" has "taught man to respect the sentiments and judgments of his brethren; to be more or less pleased when they approve of his conduct, and to be more or less hurt when they disapprove of it," and that man has been taught by nature to be "humbled and mortified" by censure and "elated" by applause to better maintain social order (TMS III.2.31). Yet Smith immediately qualifies this in what follows. Our solicitude for the judgments of our peers holds "only in the first instance," for beyond such intersubjective judgments men have access to "a much higher tribunal, to the tribunal of their own consciences, to that of the supposed impartial and well-informed spectator, to that of the man within the breast, the great judge and arbiter of their conduct" (TMS III.2.32). Here again Smith's language invites consideration of this passage from both the perspective of virtue as well as from that of moral judgment. Two crucial steps toward answering the question concerning the nature of virtue are in fact being made here. First, Smith reaffirms the necessity of transcending our distorting self-preference. Smith is well

---

[12] Insofar as the love of praiseworthiness is natural, it deserves to be regarded as another of the sentiments that nature has implanted in the human breast for the sake of promoting happiness (see TMS II.iii.3.2). For an excellent treatment of the complexity of this phenomenon in Smith's work, see esp. Brubaker, "Does the 'Wisdom of Nature' Need Help?" in *New Voices*, ed. Montes and Schliesser, esp. 176–81.

aware that too keen a sensitivity to the judgments of others corrupts insofar as it is anxiety-inducing; those overly solicitous for the opinions of others are "astonished and confounded by the vehemence and clamour" of detractors, whose "violence and loudness" not only "stupify and benumb our natural sense of praise-worthiness and blame-worthiness" but also destroy "the tranquility of the mind." Insofar as happiness requires tranquility, happiness itself requires our cultivating an indifference to external judgments of our worth; the encouragement of vanity in educating the young is again only a starting point which the mature individual is expected to transcend. But this account also takes a second step toward the explanation of virtue by introducing a new category. To this point the horizon for moral judgment has been the judgments of actual spectators. But here, Smith suggests that this horizon is to be transcended and a new horizon introduced – and not simply that of the "supposed" impartial spectator. In the midst of some of his most pointed statements on the necessity of transcending vanity and a sensitivity to praise and blame, Smith no less pointedly reminds his reader that the all-wise author of nature "has, in this respect, as in many others, created him after his own image," and that this same creator has invested the individual with an "immortal" and "divine" side – and indeed that the very fact of the natural love of praiseworthiness attests to the capacity to transcend the "connexion with mortality" that is characteristic of man's merely human side, and "act suitably to his divine extraction" (TMS III.2.31–32). So far from mere rhetorical flourish, Smith introduces a concept that does crucial work in his theory of virtue. In suggesting that ethical activity is not limited to the sphere of mere intersubjective human judgments but is rather grounded in a plane that ultimately transcends human judgment, Smith testifies to his belief that the consideration of ethical activity is inseparable from consideration of what lies beyond human action. Thus, although it is surely right to say that in this passage Smith presents "two different conceptions of nature," he has grand ambitions in so doing.[13] His practical ambition is to mitigate a specific side of commercial corruption. His philosophic ambition is to extend the horizon of ethical inquiry beyond the horizon of ethical action. To put it in terms that have been applied to Aristotle, Smith's recognition of the possibility of "something divine in man" is evidence of

---

[13] Dickey, "Historicizing the 'Adam Smith Problem'," 602–6. Griswold also notes the importance of Smith's grounding of the love of praiseworthiness in nature, and especially the development of a concept of "second nature" (*Smith and the Virtues of Enlightenment*, 130–31).

his awareness of "the ultimate dependence of morality upon a trans-moral good."[14]

Smith's interest in such transcendent goods can be found elsewhere in TMS III.2 as well. That resistance to an excessive love of praise and blame requires recourse to the divine is a point also made in his often-repeated claim that religion is the "only" effective way of consoling "disgraced and insulted innocence" – "religion can alone afford them any effectual comfort," "she alone" can convince the misunderstood that the judgments of men pale in comparison to the judgments of "the all-seeing Judge of the world," "she alone" can provide the just with the hope that their virtue will be rewarded in an afterlife (TMS III.2.12). The claim is repeated elsewhere: the "only" effective consolation of a "humbled and afflicted man" is to appeal to "the all-seeing Judge of the world," as faith in this tribunal can "alone" save one from despondency. The line of argument culminates in a defense of the anthropological foundations of religion, particularly of belief in an afterlife. To be clear: Smith's claim is not to prove the truth of the afterlife or of religion. His goal is at once more modest and more ambitious: rather to show that the belief in the afterlife is, to use a term more commonly applied to Hume, a natural belief. He explains this necessity as an effect of both our natural love of justice and our natural desire for happiness:

Our happiness in this life is thus, upon many occasions, dependent upon the humble hope and expectation of a life to come: a hope and expectation deeply rooted in human nature; which can alone support its lofty ideas of its own dignity; can alone illumine the dreary prospect of its continually approaching mortality, and maintain its cheerfulness under all the heaviest calamities to which, from the disorders of this life, it may sometimes be exposed. (TMS III.2.33)

Herein lies the core of what has been called Smith's argument for religion's "psychic utility."[15] Elsewhere Smith claims that religion is "so well fitted to soothe the natural feelings of the human breast" (LJB 133). Here he explains this is so because it satisfies the psychological longing for a just

[14] Jaffa, *Thomism and Aristotelianism*, 120 and 143. Among Smith scholars, one of the few to emphasize the import of Smith's insistence on man's creation in God's image is Otteson; see *Marketplace of Life*, 59–60 and 255–56.

[15] Evensky, *Smith's Moral Philosophy*, 107. We know very little about the substance of Smith's lectures on natural theology at Glasgow, but Millar's comment as reported in Stewart's commemorative "Account of the Life and Writings of Adam Smith, LL.D." that they focused in part on "those principles of the human mind upon which religion is founded" seems commensurate with Smith's explicit interest in this same theme across his published works (see EPS 274). I examine Smith's account of these epistemological principles in "Skepticism and Naturalism in Smith," in *Essays on Smith's Philosophy*, ed. Brown and Fleischacker.

distribution of rewards by merit and desert – hence our faith in an afterlife "where that modest, silent, and unknown merit, will be placed upon a level, and sometimes above those who, in this world, had enjoyed the highest reputation" (TMS III.2.33); hence "Nature teaches us to hope, and religion, we suppose, authorises us to expect" that injustice will be "punished, even in a life to come" (TMS II.ii.3.12); hence if we "despair of finding any force upon earth which can check the triumph of injustice, we naturally appeal to heaven" in the hope that "the great Author of our nature" will "complete the plan which he himself has thus taught us to begin; and will, in a life to come, render to every one according to the works which he has performed in this world." But importantly, it is not only the fallibility familiar to most of us but also the love of justice characteristic of the best among and within us that draws us to religion: "We are led to the belief of a future state, not only by the weaknesses, by the hopes and fears of human nature, but by the noblest and best principles which belong to it, by the love of virtue, and by the abhorrence of vice and injustice" (TMS III.5.10). Here and elsewhere Smith offers an apologia for belief; without claiming that faith is a universal necessity, he defends religious longings as manifestations of the best and noblest elements of our souls.[16] Thus, although religion clearly serves as a source of "consolation" that goes beyond the solace afforded by the impartial spectator, the source of this solace is not our craven cowardliness, but rather "a still nobler and more generous principle," namely "a firm reliance upon, and a reverential submission to, that benevolent wisdom which directs all the events of human life, and which, we may be assured, would never have suffered those misfortunes to happen, had they not been indispensably necessary for the good of the whole" (TMS VII.ii.1.45). The noble and the pious are thus intimately connected: an argument remarkable not least because it questions the equation of faith in the divine with humility and faith in the self with hubris. Smith also suggests this connection manifests itself in a second way. Religion benefits virtue as it encourages not only mortification of self-love but also transcendence of the narrow concern with the self characteristic of both our natures and politics. Religion provides the

---

[16] Smith's relationship with Hume is of central import here. Smith's eulogy to Hume's deathbed Stoicism has often been celebrated as evidence of his belief that religion is unnecessary for virtue. But in the lines here quoted, Smith's aim is quite different: not, with Hume, to demonstrate that faith is optional for the philosopher, but rather, contra Hume, to demonstrate that our religious longings stem from what is best rather than from what is worst within us. The most thorough account of Smith's eulogy in his letter to Strahan can be found in Schliesser, "The Obituary of a Vain Philosopher: Adam Smith's Reflections on Hume's Life," *Hume Studies* 29 (2003): 327–62.

longing for self-transcendence with an object and is thus an important ally in efforts to overcome self-preference. In this respect, Smith's interest in religion is of vital concern not only to his economics, as recent discussions of his theology have emphasized, but also to his theory of virtue.[17] In sum, natural religion is needed to supplement our commitment to natural liberty if we hope to sustain our natural longing for natural justice.

Smith's discussions of religion reiterate the necessity of transcending opinion and self-preference that is the focus of TMS III. Yet this concern, unto itself, is hardly new to the sixth edition. Smith's response to Gilbert Elliot's objection in the second and following editions of TMS – a response that would in time develop into TMS III.2.31–32 – provides another window into this concern. In response to Elliot, Smith explained that he sought a resource by which individuals could avoid becoming "slaves of the world" – that is, from becoming precisely the slaves to opinion he and Rousseau alike feared.[18] He makes this concern clear in his cover letter to Elliot, in which he described his response as an effort to "make virtue sufficiently independent of popular opinion," and thereby show that although "our judgements concerning our own conduct have always a reference to the sentiments of some other being," it yet remains true that "real magnanimity and conscious virtue can support itself under the disapprobation of all mankind" (CAS 40). This formulation is revealing on several levels. First, it demonstrates Smith's association of magnanimity with consciousness of desert, itself the crucial category in the liberation from dependence on others' opinions. Second, it clearly lays out Smith's principal problem with regard to the concept of magnanimity, an appreciation of which helps explain the often heroic language that he uses to describe the love of virtue independent of opinion in TMS III. His fear is that, lacking a capacity to resist public opinion, men are necessarily rendered mediocre and conformist. Self-consciousness of merit, however, enables transcendence of the anxiety for praiseworthiness that was our departure point; hence Smith's reiteration of the three-stage ascent of self-love characteristic of his response to Mandeville, separating three distinct orientations to praise – the "contemptible vanity" of seeking praise "where

---

[17] The most important of these include A. M. C. Waterman, "Economics as Theology: Adam Smith's *Wealth of Nations*," *Southern Economic Journal* 68 (2002): 907–21; Hill, "The Hidden Theology of Adam Smith," *European Journal of the History of Economic Thought* 8 (2001): 1–29; Alvey, "The Secret, Natural Theological Foundation of Adam Smith's Work," *Journal of Markets and Morality* 7 (2004): 335–61. A guide to the scholarship emphasizing this "new view" of Smith can be found in Alvey, "The 'New View' of Adam Smith," esp. 67–69.

[18] The quotation is from the original draft response to Elliot, published in TMS, with slight changes, in editions 2–5, and reprinted in the Glasgow edition as a note to pp. 128–30 (quote at 130).

no praise is due," the "love of just fame, of true glory" when praise "is really due," and the superior orientation of self-approbation that "stands in need of no confirmation from the approbation of other men," and which regards self-approbation as "if not the only . . . at least the principal object" about which one "can or ought to be anxious" (TMS III.2.8; cf. TMS III.2.7). Indeed this inverse relationship of faith in the rectitude of judgments of our conscience to the need for the supporting judgments of others is perhaps the main animating force of TMS III.2 (see, e.g., TMS III.2.16–17; TMS III.2.21–24).

The aim of TMS III.2 is thus to demonstrate that the recovery of our natural love of praiseworthiness is needed to mitigate tendencies to both mediocrity and conformism characteristic of sympathetic beings in commercial society. This intention itself mitigates a possible objection to Smith's system as a whole. Its emphasis on the role of sympathy in constructing ethical norms has rightly led several commentators to emphasize that its treatment of moral judgment leads to a view of morality as "a social phenomenon" that is "intersubjectively produced" via a process of iterated reciprocal social interactions.[19] Put differently, insofar as sympathy is natural, Smith suggests that it is natural for our natures to be shaped by convention. But the same observation has led less charitable critics to reject Smith tout court. In Smith's day, the objection was most directly expressed by the successor to his Chair of Moral Philosophy at Glasgow, Thomas Reid. In support of his contention that Smith's system is a mere "refinement of the selfish system," Reid argued that in Smith "there is no fixed standard of virtue at all," that his "ultimate measure and standard of right and wrong in human conduct" is "the variable opinions and passions of men," and hence that Smith's system can ultimately account merely "for men's putting on the appearance of virtue than for their being really

---

[19] See, e.g., Berry, "Smith and the Virtues of Commerce," in *NOMOS XXXIV: Virtue*, 79; Martin, "Utility and Morality," 118-19; Forman-Barzilai, "Sympathy in Space(s)," 190; Fleischacker, *Third Concept of Liberty*, 51; Jerrold Seigel, *The Idea of the Self* (Cambridge: Cambridge University Press, 2005), 144–45; Dwyer, "Ethics and Economics," 665, 668–69. A provocative reading of the intersubjectivity of Smith's ethics through a Hegelian lens is offered in Kalyvas and Katznelson, "Rhetoric of the Market," 558, 560–61; cf. Todorov, "Living Alone Together," 8–14. The intersubjective side of Smith's ethics has been further developed recently and helpfully in the claims that for Smith "the only source of normativity becomes the approval or disapproval of the people who matter to one," that Smith understands conscience to be merely "the internalization of respect," and that what is worthy of being praised is merely "that which has been praised and admired enough to be presumed so by the group"; Alexander Welsh, *What is Honor? A Question of Moral Imperatives* (New Haven: Yale University Press, 2008), 173, 176, 179.

virtuous."[20] The same objection has persisted into our own day, in which an extended study of Smith's theory of virtue argues that the "main idea" of the Scottish moralists was that "morality, and more particularly virtue, depends on a consensus" regarding reciprocal pleasures and pains.[21] Yet Smith himself clearly foresaw the consequence of such an ethics if pursued to its conclusion: namely that an individual shaped by the morality of intersubjective sympathy would be "preeminently a slave to the strong need that men have for the approbation of their fellows."[22] In this sense his emphasis on praiseworthiness and the magnanimity that supports it takes an important step toward resolving one of the central problems Smith inherited from Rousseau. Rousseau's account of the genesis of civilized corruption in the *Second Discourse* seems to point to two paths for its remedy: either an abandonment of civilization altogether and a retreat to nature (a remedy that Rousseau repeatedly denies advocating), or a transformation of society into a wholly artificial construct suitable to the corruptions already present in our natures (as Rousseau seems to advocate in the *Social Contract*). But to claim, as Smith does, that the loves of praise and praiseworthiness are each essential features of human nature is to point in a different direction. On this view, the proper aim is neither to excise the love of praise (that is, to return us to the natural goodness of the savage) or to inculcate a thoroughgoing enthusiasm for praiseworthiness (that is, to encourage the production of the sort of citizen found in Rousseau's political writings), but to restore the balance between the two loves that had been established by nature but threatened by commercial society.

The discussions of desert and praiseworthiness in TMS III.1–2, it can now be said, establish both the problem to be solved (self-preference) and the solution (the recovery of a transethical horizon). But to put the question thusly is to raise another question: how does Smith think that this transethical horizon is to be either apprehended or achieved? At first glace, there is reason to be skeptical that Smith's epistemology has the resources to apprehend such

---

[20] Reid to Henry Home, Lord Kames, 30 October 1778, in John Reeder, ed., *On Moral Sentiments: Contemporary Responses to Adam Smith* (Bristol: Thoemmes Press, 1997), 66; and Reid, "A Sketch of Dr Smith's Theory of Morals," in Reeder, ed., *On Moral Sentiments*, 77, 81.

[21] Hope, *Virtue by Consensus*, 2, 102, 113.

[22] See especially Cropsey, *Polity and Economy*, 15–16, 19–20; and Cropsey, *Political Philosophy and the Issues of Politics* (Chicago: University of Chicago Press, 1977), 87 (where the quotation can be found). See also Justman on conformism and the possible inability of commercial man to "oppose the opinions of society" (*Autonomous Male*, 90); cf. Griswold, *Smith and the Virtues of Enlightenment*, 94; and Haakonssen and Winch, "Legacy of Smith," in *Cambridge Companion*, 386.

a horizon. Recent studies have tended to emphasize both Smith's antirealism and his skepticism; if indeed Smith is truly a skeptic or an antirealist, this would seem fatal to his capacity – and the capacity of those working in his tradition – to claim to speak of such a horizon, however much he relies on the language of providentialism or final causes.[23] At the same time Smith's formulation of this transmoral horizon might circumvent this debate. Put differently: even if Smith demonstrably subscribes to a form of mitigated skepticism that forbids the attainment of ontological truths, such skepticism – perhaps better called skeptical realism, if a label must be given – is hardly fatal to his project of recovering a different sort of transethical horizon. Perhaps the most developed of his accounts of this horizon comes in his account of the relationship of nobility to self-love in TMS III.3.

Among the most important elements of TMS III.3 is its distinction between two types of self-love. The purpose of such a distinction is to show how an elevated form of self-love, itself coincident with the love of nobility, restrains self-preference and enables a transcendence of individualism and mediocrity. Smith draws this distinction in the course of his well-known account of the reaction of a humane and sympathetic European to the news of a devastating earthquake in China.[24] In his story, the reaction of the decent European is one of relative indifference: a moment of compassion quickly followed by a drop in sympathy as the vision fades from his imagination. On one level, this story illustrates a seeming truism: that sympathy has its limits and ought to be neither expected nor encouraged to pass beyond the requirements of propinquity imposed on it by nature.[25] But here again, Smith's account not only bears on his theory of judgment but also on his theory of virtue itself. The problem at the heart of the story of the Chinese earthquake is in fact the problem of self-preference which we have been tracking. Smith introduces his account as a further illustration of the distortions to which the "natural eye of the mind" is prone if not corrected by a regard for perspective (TMS III.3.2). The story of the Chinese earthquake

---

[23] In this vein, see Griswold's revealing discussions of Smith's "sophisticated emotivism," his theory of the "constructed or projected nature of value," his claim that "ultimately morality must be understood as arising 'from us,' not as established by nature or the divine," his "self-consciously nonfoundationalist" perspective, his faith in moral poiesis, his suggestion that the concept of nature's unity is "an 'invention of the imagination'," and his insistence that "in some sense or another, morality is of our making" (*Smith and the Virtues of Enlightenment*, 130, 146, 161, 165, 310, 339, 361). See also Haakonssen, "Introduction" to TMS, xvii; Haakonssen, "What Might Properly Be Called Natural Jurisprudence?" 205; and Cropsey, *Polity and Economy*, 23, cf. McKenna, *Rhetoric of Propriety*, 117.

[24] This is of course a response to Hume; see, e.g., Fleischacker, *Third Concept of Liberty*, 42–43.

[25] For a helpful treatment, see Forman-Barzilai, "Sympathy in Space(s)," 201–3.

merely translates this claim from epistemology to ethics, suggesting that the phenomena of ethics that are closest to us – our interests – are distorted by the natural eye of the mind in precisely the same manner that our perception of nearby physical objects is distorted. Thus Smith observes that "to the selfish and original passions of human nature, the loss or gain of a very small interest of our own" appears of vastly greater import to us than "the greatest concern of another with whom we have no particular connexion" (TMS III.3.3). Yet this raises a significant problem. So far from merely assuming a harmony of mutual self-interests or a spontaneous order of aggregate pursuits, Smith foresees a more dire consequence. The interests of others, so long as they are regarded from our selfish perspective, "can never be put into the balance with our own, can never restrain us from doing whatever may tend to promote our own, how ruinous soever to him" (TMS III.3.3). Smith is thus well aware of the potential degeneration of self-interest into a state of dire conflict. And in stating the problem as a struggle between self-interest and justice, Smith invites the consideration of a liberal political solution commensurate with this description of the quintessential liberal political predicament, and as a proper liberal Smith appeals to "those sacred rules, upon the tolerable observation of which depend the whole security and peace of human society" (TMS III.3.6). Like Hobbes, Smith appeals to our deepest self-interest – our desire for peace and security, itself the product of the primacy of self-preservation established by natural law – to mitigate the chaos of self-interest run amok.

Yet Smith also proposes a second solution to the problem of self-preference. This solution is moral or ethical rather than political, and points in a far different direction than the liberal solution. In particular, this solution points Smith away from Hobbes. Hobbes, as we have seen, teaches that collective rationality alone can overcome the catastrophe of universal selfishness – hence the social contract, itself merely the embodiment of a rational appeal to man's most selfish desire for self-preservation in order to restrain his immediate selfish passions. Smith, we have argued, offers a structurally analogous argument in his conception of prudence, in which the selfish desire for long-term utility maximization is employed to overcome impetuous short-term desires. What distances Smith from Hobbes, however, is his decidedly un-Hobbesian insistence that the love of self-preservation and of claiming external goods fails to exhaust the whole of our loves.[26] In particular, it fails to account for a persistent love of nobility, and it is

---

[26] Cf. Cropsey, *Polity and Economy*, x, 3–5, 32–34, 115–16; cf. esp. the responses in Werhane, *Smith and Modern Capitalism*, 4–7, 23–25; and Fleischacker, *Smith's Wealth of Nations*, 100–3.

this decidedly un-Hobbesian love that Smith commends in the story of the Chinese earthquake in order to overcome selfishness.

Smith's novel solution rests on his conviction that "nature" must be "corrected" – a locution that he uses in at least three discrete instances in TMS III.3.3–4.[27] But in so doing he has a specific conception of what it is that requires redress. His claim is that we must transcend and "correct" our propensity to prefer immediate first-order desires to the no-less-natural love of praiseworthiness. Both political stability and individual virtue require transcending such vulgar preferences; thus we must "change our position" (TMS III.3.3). Smith initially presents his explanation of why this is so as a phenomenological inquiry into a lacuna not sufficiently explained by the selfish system of morality: "When our passive feelings are almost always so sordid and so selfish, how comes it that our active principles should often be so generous and so noble?" If it is indeed true that we are "always so much more deeply affected by whatever concerns ourselves, than by whatever concerns other men," what "prompts the generous, upon all occasions, and the mean upon many, to sacrifice their own interests to the greater interests of others?" To suggest that we owe this happy effect to the workings of a benevolence equally as natural as self-interest – a commonplace of mid-eighteenth-century British moralism – is simply insufficient: "it is not the soft power of humanity, it is not that feeble spark of benevolence which Nature has lighted up in the human heart, that is thus capable of counteracting the strongest impulses of self-love." So far from accepting a conventional distinction of egoism and altruism, or self-directed and other-directed passions, Smith suggests that the remedy for this form of self-love is to be found rather in "a stronger power, a more forcible motive, which exerts itself upon such occasions":

It is not the love of our neighbour, it is not the love of mankind, which upon many occasions prompts us to the practice of those divine virtues. It is a stronger love, a more powerful affection, which generally takes place upon such occasions; the love of what is honourable and noble, of the grandeur, and dignity, and superiority of our own characters. (TMS III.3.4)

Smith's striking claim will seem incongruous to some readers, yet it does important work in his theory of virtue as a whole, and thus requires careful attention. First, it conveys his clearest explanation of the importance of the love of the noble. Respect for nobility – or, alternatively, for the natural

---

[27] Smith's recognition of the need for human agency to assist in the remedying of nature's deficiencies has been most thoroughly developed by Brubaker in "Does the 'Wisdom of Nature' Need Help?" in *New Voices*, ed. Montes and Schliesser, esp. 171, 181, 187.

love of praiseworthiness – is alone capable of enabling us to transcend the pettier forms of self-preference and thereby manage the central ethical ill of commercial society. Second, in positing a higher or nobler self-love as the proper way of managing the lower form of self-preference, Smith reveals his dedication to recovering a classical, and particularly Aristotelian, distinction as a means of responding to a modern problem.[28] Put slightly differently, the conclusion to TMS III.3.4 challenges the familiar claim that Smith privileges modern self-interest at the expense of a classical solicitude for genuine excellence or nobility.[29] Third, the result of this solicitude is itself crucial. Smith appropriates a classical idea here, but he hardly does so for reasons that would be familiar to the ancient champions of pride. His purpose in appealing to noble self-love is to overcome self-preference; this is what he means when he says that the end of noble self-love is "astonishing the most presumptuous of our passions" and thereby overcoming "the natural misrepresentations of self-love," reinforcing one lesson above all: "That we are but one of the multitude, in no respect better than any other in it" (TMS III.3.4).[30] So far from bolstering pride, the natural object of such self-love is the encouragement of a disposition necessary for justice itself: the recognition of one's equality with others.[31]

[28] I treat Aristotle's distinction between two types of self-love more fully in "Aristotle on the Greatness of Greatness of Soul," *History of Political Thought* 23 (2002): 1–20, esp. pp. 18–19; and "Smith, Aristotle and Virtue Ethics," esp. pp. 24–25.

[29] See Cropsey: "The self-love which is the desire for self-preservation was meant by nature to prevail over the self-love which is self-respect and which corresponds to the requirements of dignity" (*Polity and Economy*, 61). Among Cropsey's principal themes is this "conflict" or "tension" between self-preservation and virtue (43, 115–16), or nature and nobility (46), or love and honor (60–61).

[30] See Susan Wolf: "The moral point of view, we might say, is the point of view one takes up insofar as one takes the recognition of the fact that one is just one person among others equally real and deserving of the good things in life as a fact with practical consequences, a fact the recognition of which demands expression in one's actions and in the form of one's practical deliberations" ("Moral Saints," in *Virtue Ethics*, ed. Crisp and Slote, 95–96). See also Hope: "The most important moral discovery one can make . . . is of one's insignificance in the eyes of others" (*Virtue By Consensus*, 85).

[31] For helpful studies of the relationship of Smith's egalitarianism to the argument for universal justice, see esp. James Buchanan, "Equality, Hierarchy, and Global Justice," *Social Philosophy and Policy* 23 (2006): 255–65; see also Buchanan, "The Justice of Natural Liberty," *Journal of Legal Studies* 5 (1976): 1–16. Also very much worth noting in this vein is the reading of TMS III.3.4 offered by David Levy and Sandra Peart. Where I focus on the role of nobility in this passage, they focus on the role of generosity and its place in Smith's response to Hume's selfish knave and "other rational species" problems. But ultimately we reach the same conclusion: namely that Smith's intention in TMS III.3.4 is to provide a mechanism for promoting respect for the dignity of equals, thereby overcoming the propensity to domination that Hobbes and Hume thought inescapable ("Sympathy and Approbation

MODERNITY, ANTIQUITY, AND MAGNANIMITY

Smith's conception of self-love is striking unto itself, but more so when compared to the conceptions of his contemporaries and predecessors – a comparison Smith himself invites. His most obvious interlocutors in this debate are Hutcheson and Mandeville, and his distance from the latter is particularly clear. Mandeville's moral rigorism insists that self-love and virtue are inimical; if nothing else, TMS III.3.4 is meant as a refutation of this reductive view and a reaffirmation of Smith's claim that in fact "self-love may frequently be a virtuous motive of action" (TMS VII.ii.4.8). But this claim applies equally well as a response to Mandeville's adversary (and Smith's teacher), Hutcheson. For all their differences, Hutcheson is said (unfairly, I think) to share with Mandeville the belief that self-love "could never be virtuous in any degree or in any direction" (TMS VII.ii.3.12). Hutcheson and Smith share considerable ground, but on this point Smith feels compelled to part ways. They agree on the need to discover a mechanism "to check the injustice of self-love" (TMS VII.ii.3.14). They also agree that the optimal mechanism promotes transcendence of self-preference, and, in describing Hutcheson's own remedy as "submitting all inferior affections to the desire of the general happiness of mankind, in regarding one's self but as one of the many," Smith testifies to the source of his own thrice-repeated insistence that individuals must come to recognize that they are but one among many, no better than others (TMS VII.ii.3.11; cf. TMS III.3.4; TMS VI.ii.2.2; TMS II.ii.2.1). But Smith rejects Hutcheson's claim that benevolence is the best or most effective means of checking self-love. In both TMS III and TMS VII he thus explicitly denies that "pure and disinterested benevolence" alone marks the "character of virtue," and that "regard to the pleasure of self-approbation" necessarily diminishes "the merit of a benevolent action" (TMS VII.ii.3.13). Smith's awareness of the ephemerality and inefficacy of sentimental benevolence and compassion compels him to try to recover nobility via lofty self-love.

Smith's conception of self-love thus leads him to engage noncontemporaries as well. This is first evident in his differentiation of his position from Stoic and Christian teachings. Immediately after offering noble self-love as a solution to the problem of self-preference, Smith turns to two other solutions for the achievement of "this hardest of all the lessons of morality," the overcoming of "the inequalities of our passive feelings": that of those

in Hume and Smith: A Solution to the Other Rational Species Problem," *Economics and Philosophy* 20 (2004): esp. 337–39, 346–48).

Christian moralists who "have laboured to increase our sensibility to the interests of others," and that of those Stoics who have sought "to diminish that to our own" (TMS III.3.7–8). Smith shares their ambition to establish an equilibrium between regard for self and regard for others, yet each of their proposals on this front strikes him as unnatural. The former, in encouraging "extreme sympathy" with distant others, promotes an "artificial commiseration" both "absurd" and "unattainable," achievement of which would at any rate be "perfectly useless" and "produce only anxiety to ourselves, without any manner of advantage to them" (TMS III.3.9). The misguidedness of such artificial compassion is rivaled only by the "unnatural indifference" encouraged by the Stoics (TMS III.3.13). So far from tempering self-love, we are told, "stoical apathy" in fact "can seldom serve any other purpose than to blow up the hard insensibility of a coxcomb to ten times its native impertinence" (TMS III.3.14).

Having distanced his own position from Stoic and Christian positions – as well as from Mandeville's and Hutcheson's positions – Smith invites us to wonder how best to classify his conception of self-love. His treatment of ancient systems of propriety further invites us to so wonder. In TMS VII he offers his well-known review of four "different accounts which have been given of the nature of virtue" (TMS VII.ii.intro.1): systems of propriety, those of prudence, those of benevolence, and "licentious systems." His study of the fourth presents his critique of Mandeville, and his study of the third presents his critique of Hutcheson. The limitations of the second category have been made clear in his study of prudence. Yet the systems of the first category, even as they fail to present a conception of virtue fully satisfactory to Smith, afford him with several crucial elements of his own conception of the honorable and noble. But here we must be careful. Earlier we saw that Smith takes care to distinguish virtue from propriety when he speaks in his own name; again, "virtue is excellence, something uncommonly great and beautiful," whereas mere propriety requires only the "common and ordinary degree of sensibility or self-command" characteristic of "the most worthless of mankind" (TMS I.i.5.6–7). But his study in TMS VII of "systems which make virtue consist in propriety" draws on a concept of propriety different from that which he employs in his own system. In discussing the ancient propriety theorists in TMS VII.ii.1 – Plato, Aristotle, and Zeno – Smith uses the term to refer to the management of the spirited part of the soul and its redirection toward the pursuit of the noble and honorable.

Ancient systems of propriety "seem chiefly to recommend the great, the awful, and the respectable virtues, the virtues of self-government and self-command; fortitude, magnanimity, independency upon fortune, the contempt of all outward accidents, of pain, poverty, exile, and death" (TMS VII.ii.4.2). What is striking in Smith's treatment of the ancient theorists of propriety is the degree to which their doctrines anticipate his own teachings on nobility and magnanimity. His study of Plato begins with an invocation of the concept of the tripartite soul, and suggests that magnanimity or propriety is the virtue concerned with "the irascible part of the soul" and characterized by a propensity toward ambition, superiority, honor, and the love of victory (TMS VII.ii.1.4). When the passions of this part "had that degree of strength and firmness, which enabled them, under the direction of reason, to despise all dangers in the pursuit of what was honourable and noble; it constituted the virtue of fortitude and magnanimity" (TMS VII.ii.1.7). But this view of spiritedness is precisely replicated by Smith, who also praises in his own name those exercises of fortitude and magnanimity directed to honorable and noble purposes. Furthermore, Smith explicitly endorses another claim here attributed to Plato: that just as nature has imbued us with pleasure-loving or concupiscent passions in order to stimulate us "to provide for the support and necessities of the body," the passions that trace their origin to *thymos* are best "considered as necessary parts of human nature," given to us to "defend us against injuries, to assert our rank and dignity in the world, to make us aim at what is noble and honourable, and to make us distinguish those who act in the same manner" (TMS VII.ii.1.5). Smith's own teachings on self-command find a premonition also in the story of Leontius, an illustration of how "the love of pleasure prompts to do what we disapprove of; and the irascible part of our nature is in this manner called in to assist the rational against the concupiscible" (TMS VII.ii.1.7).[32] A slightly different lesson is found in Aristotle, yet one also commensurate with another aspect of Smith's teaching. On Aristotle's account, magnanimity "lies in a middle between the excess of arrogance and the defect of pusillanimity, of which the one consists in too extravagant, the other in too weak a sentiment of our own worth and dignity" (TMS VII.ii.1.12). Where Platonic magnanimity speaks to a desire for nobility, Smith interprets Aristotle as focusing on the cultivation of our conception of self-worth – a concept which, as we have seen, could be said to represent the other half of noble self-love. Finally, Smith's account of Zeno and the Stoics as propriety theorists isolates a third discrete aspect of his theory of magnanimity and noble self-love. Smith suggests that, of the three systems, the idea of magnanimity was most central to the Stoics; indeed the "general tendency" of the system as a whole, for all its shortcomings, is to animate adherents "to actions of the most heroic

---

[32] Plato, *Republic*, 439d–440b.

magnanimity and most extensive benevolence" (TMS VII.ii.1.47).[33] This Stoic conception of magnanimity contributes a third unique aspect to Smith's conception of nobility. For the Stoics, magnanimity is closely identified with self-command, and the chief benefit of self-command is not simply that it enables us to withstand challenges but rather that its exercise is pleasurable; a magnanimous man "exults" in dangers that "afford an opportunity of exercising that heroic intrepidity, whose exertion gives the exalted delight which flows from the consciousness of superior propriety and deserved admiration" (TMS VII.ii.1.23). The exercise of magnanimity enables him to achieve "the complete approbation of his own breast" from the knowledge that "how untoward soever things might be without, all was calm and peace and concord within" (TMS VII.i.1.28). Stoic magnanimity thus affords its possessor the pleasure that comes from a conscious sense of self-worth and desert or merit.

Smith's study of the three ancient systems of propriety thus calls attention to three discrete aspects of magnanimity: first, its capacity to steer *thymos* toward the noble and honorable (Plato); second, its capacity for moderate and accurate self-assessment free of both arrogance and undue humility (Aristotle); and third, its capacity to afford a tranquil self-sufficiency, necessary to preserve happiness in the face of adverse external opinion and fortune (Zeno). Smith's account of noble self-love in TMS III.3.4 draws on each of these themes, but his fullest development of their interrelationships comes in his study of magnanimous self-command in TMS VI, itself perhaps best regarded as an attempt to synthesize these discrete elements of the Platonic, Aristotelian, and Stoic accounts, and thereby to recover them within modernity. Smith regarded these accounts as "one of the most instructive, as well as one of the most interesting remains of antiquity," and insisted that the "spirit and manhood" of such teachings "make a wonderful contrast with the

---

[33] This summary judgment, new to the sixth edition, seems to indicate a change of heart. Here Smith claims that in encouraging "actions of the heroic magnanimity and most extensive benevolence," Stoicism has in fact "very great influence upon the character and conduct of its followers" (TMS VII.ii.1.47). This would seem, however, to contrast sharply with the summary judgment on Stoicism in editions 1–5, which concludes that although it affords "the noblest lessons of magnanimity," Stoics are yet susceptible to that "honourable" objection that "they teach us to aim at a perfection altogether beyond the reach of human nature" (TMS, p. 60). But ultimately one suspects that this revision reflects less his change of heart on Stoicism than Smith's reconsideration of the value of aiming at perfection – a reading supported by the fact that, in the sixth edition, Smith's only use of this same locution was employed to *deny* that heroic or "magnanimous resignation" to God's will is "in any respect beyond the reach of human nature" (TMS VI.ii.3.4), a point then reiterated in similar terms in a second passage on the "good soldier," also new to the sixth edition (see TMS III.3.5).

desponding, plaintive, and whining tone of some modern systems" (TMS VII.ii.1.29). Smith of course found much to disagree with in the ancient systems, yet in light of his striking claims that Plato's account "coincides in every respect" and Aristotle's account "corresponds too pretty exactly" with his own account of propriety (TMS VII.ii.1.11–12), we are obligated to trace out these specific points of agreement, particularly as developed in TMS VI.

Yet turning from TMS III and VII to VI, we are confronted with an immediate dilemma. Smith's chapter headings suggest that TMS VI.iii is devoted to self-command in the same way that TMS VI.i is devoted to prudence. In light of his ready association of self-command with magnanimity (see, e.g., TMS V.2.9), Smith's readers are likely to expect to find his clearest account of magnanimity in TMS VI.iii. But if so, how ought we account for TMS VI.ii? TMS VI.ii is not immediately recognizable as a treatment of a specific virtue in the same way that the chapters that directly precede or follow it are; its title instead suggests that it is dedicated to the way in which the individual "can affect the happiness of other people." Yet TMS VI.ii is nevertheless a crucial preparative for the treatment of magnanimity in VI.iii as it forms a bridge between this treatment and the central themes of TMS III, examined earlier. Two aspects of this bridge are particularly crucial: first, its reaffirmation of the necessity of ascending from the selfish individualism of prudence; and second, its identification of nobility as the aim of such transcendence.

On both fronts TMS VI.ii picks up where TMS III.3.4 left off. As in the previous discussion, Smith here aims to find a mechanism capable of enabling us to transcend the most vulgar forms of self-preference. Also, as before, Smith's remedy for self-preference hardly relies on conventional exhortations to benevolence, but calls for the cultivation of a nobler form of self-love. Smith reiterates these claims in the course of describing the differing degrees of "natural affection" that individuals possess for people, objects, and ends of varying types (TMS VI.ii.1.14). He begins with the now-familiar claim that our most natural and immediate preference is for the self and its needs (TMS VI.ii.1.1). But, consistent with his concern to transcend self-preference, he quickly turns to a study of our concern for the effects of our actions on others. As others have detailed, Smith organizes these concerns in a set of concentric circles radiating out from the self, beginning with children and immediate household members (TMS VI.ii.1.2–5), then business partners and associates (TMS VI.ii.1.15), and ultimately neighbors (TMS VI.ii.1.16). Recognition of this movement has prompted an important debate concerning Smith's understanding of the nature of our capacity to empathize with distant others, pitting those who regard him as an advocate of cosmopolitan universalism against those who emphasize his awareness of the limits of our capacity for meaningful sympathetic engagement with far-removed peoples.[34] This question is central to an appreciation of Smith's politics, yet his account here is also central to his conception of virtue, and we need to take care not to lose sight of his original contributions on this front amidst engagement with the question of his relevance to contemporary concerns with regard to ethical universalism. The most striking aspect of his argument in this respect lies in the standard he posits to determine the circles in which we classify our interests. The proper determining standard, he explains, lies in a person's capacity to replicate or approximate for another the degree of concern that approaches "to what he feels for himself" (TMS VI.ii.1.2). Distance, of course, influences the potential for such approximation (see, e.g., TMS VI.ii.1.6–7). Yet physical proximity alone is not constitutive of our sympathetic attachments; more important than "physical" connections are "moral" connections (TMS VI.ii.1.14) – the former are in fact important only insofar as they exacerbate or diminish the latter, itself a representation of the degree to which our attachment to others replicates our original love of ourselves.

Smith highlights the centrality of self-love to our sympathetic attachments in two discrete instances in the account that follows. One comes at the end of his account, in which he claims that our debts to our benefactors trump all others. Here Smith argues that, of all those to whom our beneficence is owed, "there are none to whom it seems more properly directed than to those whose beneficence we have ourselves already experienced" (TMS VI.ii.1.19). Such a conception of gratitude as founded on reciprocal obligations is itself striking, but what is most important here is the claim that reciprocal beneficence is grounded in our attachment to that which promotes the interests prompted by self-love. The same point is reiterated in Smith's discussion of patriotism in the following chapter. Smith's formal aim here is to defend patriotism by distinguishing the "mean principle of national prejudice" from the "noble one of the love of our own country" (TMS VI.ii.2.3). At the heart of the latter lies a refined self-love. Smith offers a glimpse into this self-love in describing the psychological attachment that binds individuals to social groups. This attachment is itself born in

---

[34] See esp. Luc Boltanski, *Distant Suffering: Morality, Media and Politics*, trans. Graham Burchell (Cambridge: Cambridge University Press, 1999), 35–55; Forman-Barzilai, "Smith on 'Connexion,' Culture, and Judgement," in *New Voices*, ed. Montes and Schliesser, 89–114; and Jennifer Pitts, *A Turn to Empire: The Rise of Imperial Liberalism in Britain and France* (Princeton: Princeton University Press, 2005), 43–52.

egocentric dispositions: "Every individual is naturally more attached to his own particular order or society, than to any other" as "his own interest, his own vanity, the interest and vanity of many of his friends and companions, are commonly a good deal connected with it" (TMS VI.ii.2.7). Yet Smith's consistent interest in moral education is the turning of the more vulgar forms of self-love – and vanity in particular – from ignoble to noble objects, and his conception of patriotism here seeks to encourage this transformation as well. Paralleling Rousseau's well-known account of patriotism as redirected *amour-propre*, Smith thus argues that patriots identify with their country for a simple reason: "The state or sovereignty in which we have been born and educated" commonly encompasses the largest sphere on which "our good or bad conduct can have much influence," as well as the sphere in which "all the objects of our kindest affections" are included. Consequently our state (or nation; Smith uses the terms interchangeably), is

endeared to us, not only by all our selfish, but by all our private benevolent affections. Upon account of our own connexion with it, its prosperity and glory seem to reflect some sort of honour upon ourselves. When we compare it with other societies of the same kind, we are proud of its superiority, and mortified in some degree, if it appears in any respect below them. (TMS VI.ii.2.2)

Like Rousseau, Smith believes patriotism can redirect ignoble and vulgar forms of self-love to greater objects, thereby ennobling the passion itself and potentially encouraging salutary political effects. Like Rousseau, Smith's aim might be described as an attempt to use a well-directed self-love to open up the self to loves beyond the self.[35]

Smith's conception of patriotism captures his proposed remedy for mediocrity as well as his remedy for individualism. Indeed in his account of patriotism Smith offers us a glimpse into the substantive greatness of the genuinely magnanimous man as well as an argument for the necessity of transcending individualism. This former goal is a main aim of his portrait of the "heroic virtue" of the patriot. What distinguishes a patriot is not his devotion to the whole, but his capacity to regard himself "as but one of the multitude, in the eye of that equitable judge, of no more consequence than any other in it, but bound at all times to sacrifice and devote himself to the safety, to the service, and even to the glory of the greater number" (TMS VI.ii.2.2). Smith's language here is a direct replication of the language used at TMS III.3.4 to describe the noble self-love that restrains vulgar self-preference. The patriot's greatness itself consists in the fact that he, as a noble

[35] On Rousseau's conception of patriotism, see especially Shklar, *Men and Citizens: A Study of Rousseau's Social Theory* (Cambridge: Cambridge University Press, 1969), 187–88.

self-lover, is able to transcend self-preference – a point dramatically reiterated in Smith's account of his opposite, the traitor, whose desire to "promote his own little interest" at the expense of public good is evidence that he "prefers himself, in this respect so shamefully and so basely, to all those with whom he has any connexion," on which grounds Smith is led to condemn him as "of all villains the most detestable" (TMS VI.ii.2.2).

TMS VI.ii thus reiterates TMS III's insistence on overcoming individualism and achieving nobility. But Smith's most sustained exposition of overcoming self-preference is provided in his account of self-command in TMS VI.iii. Smith introduces this account by invoking a theme central to his study of Plato and Aristotle. In TMS VII he notes that, where Plato calls virtue "a species of science," Aristotle argued that "good morals arose not from knowledge but from action" (TMS VII.ii.1.14). Smith suggests in TMS VI that both approaches need to be synthesized, because the "most perfect knowledge" of virtue's rules cannot lead to virtue in practice without "the most perfect self-command" (TMS VI.iii.1). The objects of self-command are properly the "passions," and these Smith divides into two groups: those difficult to restrain for a moment, and those difficult to restrain over the course of a lifetime (TMS VI.iii.2). The latter category includes "love of ease, of pleasure, of applause, and of many other selfish gratifications," dispositions the ancients sought to command by "temperance, decency, modesty, and moderation" (TMS VI.iii.3). Smith's own account of prudence replicates this approach, suggesting that the same virtues should be used to manage similar vices – an association reinforced a few pages later in the suggestion that the "unremitting steadiness of those gentler exertions of self-command" associated with the "amiable virtue of chastity" and the "respectable virtues of industry and frugality" are what make possible the happiness of all those "contented to walk in the humble paths of private and peaceable life." Put differently, Smith's account of prudence is itself an account of a species of self-command.[36]

---

[36] Smith's explicit identification of prudence and magnanimity as forms of self-command reveals the insufficiency of the conventional canon of Smithean "cardinal virtues" (see Chapter 3, Notes 26–27, this volume). Smith's account of self-command in TMS VI.iii suggests that self-command is less an autonomous virtue than a disposition that manifests itself in both a lower form of prudence (focused on the control of selfish desires for necessaries and conveniences) and a nobler form of magnanimity (focused on the control of fear and anxiety resulting in a lofty sense of self-worth). Helpful in this regard is the observation by Montes that "self-command is not only literally beyond the other Smithean virtues, it is also behind them, underpinning the moral value of actions" (*Smith in Context*, 85, cf. 78); and the observation by Den Uyl that the amiable virtues too require self-command lest we be "led away from our duty by the siren's song of pleasant

Yet Smith's primary interest here is not the self-command of the prudent private man but the self-command characteristic of "the more splendid
actions of the hero, the statesman, or the legislator" (TMS VI.iii.13). This
self-command concerns itself not with easy pleasures but with the more
furious and immediate "fear and anger" that the ancients managed via "fortitude, manhood, and strength of mind" (TMS VI.iii.2–3). Now, Smith's
identification here of ancient prudence as the control of anger replicates
his comments on Plato, Aristotle, and Zeno in TMS VII and, given that
his own conception of this form of self-command is similarly dedicated to
the management of fear and anger, it testifies to his indebtedness to the
classical vision of self-command as dedicated to the management of *thymos*.
Smith's explanation of the way in which self-command enables its possessor
to overcome the fear of death has a particularly classical orientation. Nam-
ing Socrates alongside such other martyrs as More, Raleigh, and Sidney,
Smith testifies to the essential virtues of "the heroes of ancient and modern
history":

The man who, in danger, in torture, upon the approach of death, preserves his
tranquility unaltered, and suffers no word, no gesture to escape him which does
not perfectly accord with the feelings of the most indifferent spectator, necessarily
commands a very high degree of admiration. If he suffers in the cause of liberty
and justice, for the sake of humanity and the love of his country, the most tender
compassion for his sufferings, the strongest indignation against the injustice of his
persecutors, the warmest sympathetic gratitude for his beneficent intentions, the
highest sense of his merit, all join and mix themselves with the admiration of his
magnanimity. (TMS VI.iii.5)

Repeatedly Smith returns to this vision and holds up for our admiration
the "habitual contempt of danger and death which ennobles the profession of a soldier, and bestows upon it, in the natural apprehensions of
mankind, a rank and dignity superior to that of any other profession" (TMS
VI.iii.7). Such visions, of course, offer portraits more than arguments. Consistent with his commitment to recovering the love of nobility, Smith is
less concerned to explain why such a disposition is in fact noble than to
persuade his audience that such an image is worthy of its admiration and

sentiment" (*Virtue of Prudence*, 127–28; but cf. 138). To reclassify Smith's virtues as prudence,
magnanimity, and beneficence as I have done is thus not to obviate self-command, but to
recognize that it is present in varying degrees in each of these three virtues – in prudence,
as a command of one's desire for short-term pleasures; in magnanimity, as a command
of one's reactions to external fortune; in beneficence, as a command of one's sentimental
compassion or pity.

emulation.[37] Thus his main aim is to impassion his auditors to cherish the nobility of the one who "suffers in the cause of liberty and justice" for all (TMS VI.iii.5), and thereby encourage them to claim such nobility for their own; hence his repeated claim that command of anger is "generous and noble," and his invocations of "noble propriety," the "nobleness of pardoning," the "nobleness of the restraint," and the "great and noble powers" of the man of self-command (TMS VI.iii.9–10, 12). Smith's discourse at times threatens to degenerate into a riot of the noble, but this fact alone is perhaps sufficient to mark the degree of his concern to recover it as an animating principle of the imagination and of action.

Smith's specific aim here is then to inflame the imaginations of those disposed toward politics, particularly those attracted to the life of true glory characteristic of the hero, the statesman, or the legislator. Three separate exemplars of such a life have at their core the magnanimous man's transcendence of vulgar selfishness for the noble glory that comes from service to the whole. In each case his dedication to magnanimity marks him as worthy of the superlatives Smith attributes to him. Hence Smith claims that "the greatest and noblest of all characters" seeks to "re-establish and improve the constitution, and from the very doubtful and ambiguous character of the leader of a party, he may assume the greatest and noblest of all characters, that of the reformer and legislator of a great state; and, by the wisdom of his institutions, secure the internal tranquility and happiness of his fellow-citizens for many succeeding generations" (TMS VI.ii.2.14). Just as a noble man transcends the love of pleasures, bringing stability to the soul, so too a noble politics transcends jarring domestic interests, bringing peace and tranquility. The same movement from strife to concord is to be found in his vision of external political life, or international relations: "The most extensive public benevolence which can commonly be exerted with any considerable effect, is that of the statesmen, who project and form alliances among neighbouring or not very distant nations, for the preservation either of, what is called, the balance of power, or of the general peace and tranquility of the states within the circle of their negotiations" (TMS VI.ii.2.6). Genuine magnanimous action in international relations thus requires the transcendence of private attachments. And so too in domestic politics: "When the public interest requires that the most mortal enemies should unite for the discharge of some important

---

[37] My formulation of this point is greatly indebted to the studies of Aristotelian magnanimity in Tessitore, *Reading Aristotle's Ethics*, 28ff.; and Rousseau's legislator in Kelly, "'To Persuade Without Convincing'."

duty, the man who can cast away all animosity, and act with confidence and cordiality towards the person who had most grievously offended him, seems justly to merit our highest admiration" (TMS VI.iii.9). In each case, the lesson is the same: nobility comes from transcendence of the partial and individual, and the replacement of such attachments with a love of the whole. This love of the whole is expressed in the policies of this best statesman. Thus, in a passage that militates against a laissez-faire reading of Smith, we are told,

The civil magistrate is entrusted with the power not only of preserving the public peace by restraining injustice, but of promoting the prosperity of the commonwealth, by establishing good discipline, and by discouraging every sort of vice and impropriety; he may prescribe rules, therefore, which not only prohibit mutual injuries among fellow-citizens, but command mutual good offices to a certain degree.

Smith is quick to add that this duty is hardly the province of a common magistrate or bureaucrat, but rather, "of all the duties of a law-giver," is the one "which it requires the greatest delicacy and reserve to execute with propriety and judgment." And herein lies Smith's remarkable claim: not only does he recognize the necessity of a necessarily rare and exceptional capacity for statesmanlike judgment, but he also insists that the classical ideal of the legislator dedicated to the regulation and preservation of morals is a necessity even in a modern liberal state, for "to neglect it altogether exposes the commonwealth to many gross disorders and shocking enormities" – even as "to push it too far is destructive of all liberty, security, and justice" (TMS II.ii.1.8; cf. TMS IV.2.1).[38]

Smith's striking view of political greatness deserves the attention of students of modernity. Smith has himself been accused alternately of hastening the demise of magnanimity and heroism, or, only slightly more charitably, as describing the "going-down of those ideals in a sort of sentimental twilight or last-light."[39] His conscious development of this ideal – coupled with the

---

[38] Citing Smith as inspiration, Samuel Bowles has recently suggested that contemporary public policy should attempt to maximize "public-spirited" and "other-regarding motives," and not merely self-regarding motives ("Policies Designed for Self-Interested Citizens May Undermine 'The Moral Sentiments': Evidence from Economic Experiments," *Science* 320 (2008): 1605–9); see also the introductory essay in Bowles et al., eds., *Moral Sentiments and Material Interests: The Foundations of Cooperation in Economic Life* (Cambridge, MA: MIT Press, 2005), esp. 3–4, 31–33.

[39] Justman, *Autonomous Male*, 40. See also Cropsey's claims that Smith describes "the field whereon honor was defeated by the virtues that flow from the requirements of preservation" and that Smith is "denying the possibility of that excellence which justifies pride" (*Polity and Economy*, 61, 57–58).

important role it plays in his effort to stave off commercial corruption –
suggests a very different view, however – one much more receptive to the
need to sustain magnanimity within modernity. At the very least it is clear
that Smith deserves to be seen by students of modernity as a key ally in
responding to two primary problems of contemporary political life: first,
the failure to take the problem of *thymos* seriously; and second, the separation of claiming honor and esteem from deserving it.[40] Smith's responses
to those challenges demand attention from those concerned to discover in
modernity the resources to ameliorate its greatest ills, and particularly those
who, like Tocqueville, believe that recovery of nobility is indispensable to
the preservation of modern democratic – and, by extension, commercial –
societies.[41]

THE DANGERS OF MAGNANIMITY

At this point we can reach a provisional conclusion. Smith introduced his
study of magnanimity as a remedy for the ills of commercial society that prudence exacerbates. His conscious efforts to recover nobility seek to respond
to the moral mediocrity endemic to commercial modernity, and his efforts to

---

[40] On the first point, see Harvey Mansfield, *Manliness* (New Haven: Yale University
Press, 2006); and "How to Understand Politics: What the Humanities Can Say to
Science," 2007 National Endowment for the Humanities Jefferson Lecture, at http://www.
neh.gov/whoweare/Mansfield/HMlecture.html. On the second problem, see Pangle, "The
Classical and Modern Liberal Understandings of Honor," in *The Noblest Minds: Fame, Honor,
and the American Founding*, ed. McNamara (Lanham, MD: Rowman and Littlefield, 1999),
211; and MacIntyre, *After Virtue*, 232.

[41] For Tocqueville's claim, see this work's epigraph. And on this point lies my difference from
Griswold. With Griswold, I agree that Smith is concerned to set forth both a "diagnosis of
and therapy for the modern age" (20). I further agree with Griswold that the chief problem
or "omnipresent theme" in TMS is self-love (see, e.g., 81, 91, 134, 138, 144, and 269n15),
and that Smith was a "critic" of the ancient sort (65), committed to moral education (see
esp. 210–17). But Griswold's ultimate claim is that the core of Smith's remedy lies in the
"recognition of our imperfection" (see, e.g., 261, 265, and 302), whereas I want to argue
precisely the opposite: so far from encouraging our embrace of the ordinary in the world,
our acceptance of imperfection in the self, and our capitulation to the imagination's efforts
to make our cave comfortable (247), Smith's remedy calls for (and indeed requires) the
transcendence of the common via a recovery of the beautiful and the noble. I also address
Griswold's Smith in my review essay "Language, Literature, and Imagination," *Adam Smith
Review* 4 (2008): 221–30. In a related vein, Carrasco notes the place of eudaimonistic and
teleological categories in Smith, especially in his account of the wise and virtuous man, but
ultimately concludes that these elements pale before Smith's "pessimism and recognition
of human weakness," which leads him to focus on a "pseudo-eudaimonia" founded on
the "imagination's delusions" and the necessity of "permanent dissatisfaction" ("Smith's
Reconstruction of Practical Reason," 108–12).

recover self-approbation and self-sufficiency seek to respond to commercial modernity's encouragement of individualistic self-preference. Yet are these remedies successful? And even if these remedies are sufficient to cure the ills for which they were intended, what new challenges might they bring? Herein lies the second stage of Smith's dialectical account of ethical virtue, for even in presenting the advantages of magnanimity, Smith also presents the new challenges that this remedy introduces. This dialectical approach is reflected in the organization of his study of self-command. The account of noble self-command at TMS VI.iii.5–13, as we have seen, includes many of Smith's most breathless praises of heroic virtue. Yet these praises are limited to the odd-numbered paragraphs; each of the even-numbered paragraphs, by contrast, presents a no-less-breathless critique of the political and psychological dangers of magnanimous self-command. The effect of this approach is subtle: at the same time that Smith inflames a love of the noble in those disposed to claim it for themselves, he at once presents those skeptical toward the superiority of the life of noble activity with good reasons for such skepticism – as well as incentive to seek an altogether different life for themselves. This higher life – the subject of our final chapter – is thus conceived as a remedy for the shortcomings of magnanimity, just as magnanimity was conceived as a remedy for the shortcomings of prudence.

Smith's account of magnanimity's iniquities begins with a reassessment of its characteristic sphere of activity. Earlier Smith presented the magnanimous man as an ideal political man. But in what immediately follows he gives us good reasons to doubt that political life can admit such a type. His realistic reassessment of the possibilities of politics can be glimpsed in another of his letters to Burke. On 6 July 1782, Smith wrote Burke to express an admiration of his conduct in the wake of the ascension of Shelburne to prime minister on the death of the second Marquis of Rockingham the week before; along with Cavendish and others, Burke had since resigned from office. Smith's letter interestingly begins by expressing approval for Burke's resignation on the grounds that "when honour is not only perfectly and completely saved, but acquired and augmented, all other losses are insignificant." Smith is well aware that he is addressing a gentleman, one to whom honor and true glory are the greatest of all possible goods. This awareness itself shapes his expression of his lament that "it must afflict every good citizen that any circumstance should occur which could make men of their probity, prudence and moderation judge it proper in these times to withdraw from the service of their country" (CAS 217). Such consolation is sincere, yet Smith's own portraits of political life elsewhere would suggest that Burke's situation is anything but anomalous. Readers of TMS in fact are given more than enough reasons to hesitate to join the political fray, from the story of Lucullus, who sees his glory stolen out from beneath him, to the story of loyal Parmenio, whose services to Philip and Alexander failed to prevent the latter from torturing and executing him on "groundless suspicions," to the recounting of the story of Borgia's slaughter at Senigallia, originally told by Machiavelli (TMS II.iii.3.2; TMS VI.iii.32; TMS VI.i.16). Burke was himself a careful reader and genuine admirer of TMS, yet one suspects his attention was drawn to elements other than these stories, which present a vivid conception of politics as driven by almost unmitigated self-interest.[42] Smith's general reflections on the structure of political life reinforce this view and might prompt lovers of justice to wonder whether in fact politics is the realm in which justice is most likely to be realized. His critique of international law is especially pronounced. The most atrocious crimes against humanity – from pillage to enslavement to murder – are frequently committed "in the most perfect conformity to what are called the laws of nations" (TMS III.3.42). These laws are, in any case, wholly inefficacious to prevent such crimes, as the very acceptance of international law by state actors "is often very little more than mere pretence and profession," indeed "from the smallest interest, upon the slightest provocation, we see those rules every day, either evaded or directly violated without shame or remorse" (TMS VI.ii.2.3). Both war and diplomacy are consequently bad businesses in which

the laws of justice are very seldom observed. Truth and fair dealing are almost totally disregarded. Treaties are violated; and the violation, if some advantage is gained by it, sheds scarce any dishonour upon the violator. The ambassador who dupes the minister of a foreign nation, is admired and applauded. The just man who disdains either to take or to give any advantage, but who would think it less dishonourable to give than to take one; the man who, in all private transactions, would be the most beloved and the most esteemed; in those public transactions is regarded as a fool and an idiot.

In politics, quite simply, the just finish last, and Smith would have none go into politics who fails to realize at the outset that his good intentions and honorable actions will reap "always the contempt, and sometimes even the detestation of his fellow-citizens" (TMS III.3.42). And the conduct of actors in domestic politics, Smith continues, is often "still more atrocious" than that of diplomats. Those few men capable of sober judgment are, by virtue of their very moderation, often excluded from any significant role in

---

[42] See Burke's review, as published in the *Annual Register* 2 (1759): 484–89; and reprinted in Reeder, ed., *On Moral Sentiments*, 51–57.

their party. The wisest man is necessarily "upon that very account, one of the most insignificant men in the society," destined to be held in "contempt and derision, frequently in detestation, by the furious zealots of both parties" (TMS III.3.43). The sum total of Smith's portrait of political life thus presents a realm of unmitigated self-interest even more vicious than the most exaggerated caricature of his conception of commercial markets might suggest. But herein lies the principal irony of the magnanimous man's predicament. His quest to transcend the self-preference characteristic of the vain leads him to renounce attempts to better his condition through the pursuit of wealth or rank alone. At the same time, his very quest for transcendence leads him to submit himself to a world characterized even more thoroughly by self-preference.

An analogous irony is to be found in the psychological effects of this context on the magnanimous man. The magnanimous man, we remember, sought to overcome self-preference by coming to value self-approbation over the praises of others. Yet as Smith continues he explains that this move toward a self-sufficient self-approbation – though originally conceived as a means of transcending self-preference – is prone to degenerate into a more destructive form of self-preference. Smith makes this clear in his discussion of the relationship of "self-approbation" to "excessive self-admiration," which begins at TMS VI.iii.27. Here again the organization of TMS VI is important, because the account of "excessive self-admiration" forms a clear parallel to the earlier account of magnanimity; indeed just as vanity is the corruption of a disposition regulated by prudence, excessive self-admiration is the corruption of a disposition regulated by magnanimity.[43] But the central import of this account is to reinforce the claim that the problem at the heart of the magnanimous man is a corruption of self-love. Smith makes this clear in his description of the chief vice of the glory-lover.[44] The principal attention of glory-lovers is commonly directed to comparing themselves with

[43] TMS VI in fact comprises five parts, with sections on prudence (pp. 212–17), magnanimity (pp. 218–42); wisdom and virtue (pp. 242–49); excessive self-admiration (pp. 249–55); and pride and vanity (pp. 255–64). Taken as a whole, these five parts describe a bell-shaped curve that proceeds from an account of the lowest ethical virtue, to the nobler ethical virtue, to the peak of ethical virtue, to the grandest ethical vice, to the frivolous ethical vices. Moreover, the categories on each side of the peak match up; the vice of excessive self-admiration represents a corrupt form (or absence) of the virtue of magnanimity, as vanity and pride represent corrupt forms (or absence) of the virtue of prudence. For the more standard division of TMS VI into "three categories," see, e.g., Raphael, "Adam Smith 1790," in *Adam Smith Reviewed*, ed. Jones, 104.

[44] On the greatness and the tragedy of the glory-lover, see also the helpful account in Brubaker, "'Particular Turn or Habit'," in *Love and Friendship*, ed. Velásquez, 246–49.

others – with the result that "they have little sense of their own weaknesses and imperfections; they have little modesty; are often assuming, arrogant, and presumptuous; great admirers of themselves, and great contemners of other people" (TMS VI.iii.27). Glory-lovers thus suffer from a degree of self-concern greater than even that of mere prudent praise-lovers. Smith partly excuses this propensity; his own sober realism has taught him that "great success in the world, great authority over the sentiments and opinions of mankind, have very seldom been acquired without some degree of this excessive self-admiration," and it is precisely to such self-admiration that we owe our greatest warriors, statesmen, and legislators (TMS VI.iii.28). Yet at the same time Smith is also keen to show the tremendous costs at which such greatness is bought.

In the first place, these costs are psychological. In profiling three of the greatest self-admirers – Caesar, Alexander, and Socrates – Smith explains that their combination of considerable external success with their excessive self-admiration deluded them into a belief in apotheosis; thus, he argues that "when crowned with success" their "presumption has often betrayed them into a vanity that approached almost to insanity and folly."[45] In continuing he explains that the self-delusion that results from combining success and self-admiration not only incapacitates individuals to judge their own merit, but it also leads them to misjudge their capacities and consequently carries them "into many rash and sometimes ruinous adventures." On these grounds Smith celebrates the "characteristic almost peculiar to the great Duke of Marlborough," that he was able to avoid folly amidst success; more often great abilities coupled with great enterprise "have frequently encouraged to undertakings which necessarily led to bankruptcy and ruin in the end" (TMS VI.iii.28–29). The love of true glory and the magnanimity that sustains it are thus double-edged swords; at the same time that the magnanimous man's imagination transports him "to perform actions which seem almost beyond the reach of human nature," it blinds him to his all-too-human limits (TMS III.2.5).

This observation forms the core of perhaps the most frequently repeated claim of TMS VI: namely that the magnanimous man's endeavors are often as pernicious as they are beneficial. Smith's account of the man of system perhaps provides his clearest view of the political dangers of excessive

---

[45] Smith uses this same argument against the Neoplatonic "Eclectics," who posit benevolence as the peak ethical virtue on the grounds that the benevolent man's imitation of God through works of charity and love would enable him to arrive "at that immediate converse and communication with the Deity to which it was the great object of this philosophy to raise us" (TMS VII.ii.3.2).

self-admiration. The man of system has attracted a great deal of attention from those prone to regard him as the embodiment of a particularly pernicious sort of meddlesome economic progressive.[46] Smith himself presents the man of system as the product of a mixture of a "spirit of system" and "that public spirit which is founded upon the love of humanity, upon a real fellow-feeling with the inconveniences and distresses to which some of our fellow-citizens may be exposed" (TMS VI.ii.2.15). Taken separately, each of these dispositions is both natural and desirable in Smith's view, which is clearly demonstrated by his comments on the utility of system-love in the *History of Astronomy* and his account of sympathy in TMS. The problem lies in that their indiscriminate combination prompts "the madness of fanaticism" of a man of system (TMS VI.ii.2.15). This fanaticism is itself exacerbated by the excessive self-estimation and self-preference characteristic of the man of system, who is "very wise in his own conceit; and is often so enamoured with the supposed beauty of his own ideal plan of government, that he cannot suffer the smallest deviation from any part of it" (TMS VI.ii.2.17). The man of system thus suffers from a peculiarly acute form of self-love, or love of his own, which is itself the result of a certain form of self-preference:

Some general, and even systematical, idea of the perfection of policy and law, may no doubt be necessary for directing the views of the statesman. But to insist upon establishing, and upon establishing all at once, and in spite of all opposition, every thing which that idea may seem to require, must often be the highest degree of arrogance. It is to erect his own judgment into the supreme standard of right and wrong. It is to fancy himself the only wise and worthy man in the commonwealth, and that his fellow-citizens should accommodate themselves to him and not he to them.

The fault of the man of system is thus precisely the "arrogance" of those who "entertain no doubt of the immense superiority of their own judgment," and consequently "consider the state as made for themselves, not themselves for the state" (TMS VI.ii.2.18). And the proper remedy for this problem is consequently psychological rather than political – not a reorientation of policies, but the reorientation of self-conception via recognition of the limits of human political efficacy (see, e.g., TMS VI.ii.2.16; WN IV.v.b.53;

---

[46] F. A. Hayek, "Adam Smith's Message in Today's Language," in *New Studies in Philosophy, Politics, Economics and the History of Ideas* (Chicago: University of Chicago Press, 1978), 267–69; Milton Friedman, "Adam Smith's Relevance for 1976," in *Adam Smith and the Wealth of Nations*, ed. Fred R. Glahe (Boulder: Colorado Associated University Press, 1978), 7–20. An excellent study of the man of system's epistemological hubris that accords with the position developed here can be found in Otteson, *Marketplace of Life*, 210–15.

WN IV.ii.10; WN IV.ii.39).[47] Many have noted that Smith endorses episte-mological skepticism as a means of restraining the hubris of the ambitious legislator.[48] Yet his interest is less to induce skepticism than to induce the humility skepticism encourages; only an admission of imperfection leading to an acceptance of self-restraint enables a politician to transcend the "innu-merable delusions" consequent to excessive self-admiration (WN IV.ix.51).

Smith's account of the devastating effects of excessive self-estimation cul-minates in a study of its effects on our capacities for judgment. Here Smith explains that not only does excessive self-estimation lead to destructive action, it also frequently corrupts neutral observers, especially their ability to distinguish noble from pernicious self-command. Smith introduces this theme in his discussion of the man of system, noting that frequently his admirers are "intoxicated with the imaginary beauty" of a system "of which they have no experience, but which has been represented to them in all the most dazzling colours in which the eloquence of their leaders could paint it" (TMS VI.ii.2.15). This seduction of the "dazzling" is repeatedly empha-sized in the sixth edition.[49] In developing it Smith develops his account of the propensity of men to worship the wealthy and ignore the virtu-ous. In TMS I.iii.3 Smith thus emphasizes our natural fascination with the "gaudy and glittering" appearances of "the rich and the great" who force themselves "upon the notice of every wandering eye," whereas the beauty of wisdom and virtue attract "scarce any body but the most studious and careful observer" (TMS I.iii.3.2). His study of the ill-conceived but all-too-common reverence for political glory replicates this claim. In describing the common reaction to the "splendour of great actions" that "dazzle and trans-port," Smith observes that "the superiority of virtues and talents" has less effect than "the superiority of achievements" (TMS II.iii.2.3). Elsewhere he explains parenthetically that daring success "has a great tendency to attract our admiration and applause" (LRBL ii.100), and that the "undiscerning eye of giddy ambition" is often seduced by "dazzling splendor" (WN IV.vii.c.85)

---

[47] I treat these themes at greater length in my "Enlightened Nation Building," esp. 230–31.

[48] On the political benefits of this skepticism, see esp. Griswold, *Smith and the Virtues of Enlightenment*, 301–10; Fleischacker, *Smith's Wealth of Nations*, 166–69; Haakonssen, *Science of a Legislator*, esp. 92; and Craig Smith, *Smith's Political Philosophy*, esp. 66.

[49] With one exception (see TMS, p. 58), all of Smith's references to the "dazzling" date to the sixth edition; see TMS I.iii.2.9; I.iii.3.8; III.2.33; VI.ii.2.15; VI.iii.5; VI.iii.13; VI.conc.7; cf. Hume's observation that "the glory of a conqueror is so dazzling to the vulgar"; *History of England*, ed. William Todd (Indianapolis: Liberty Fund, 1983), vol. 2, p. 272. And to be clear: excessive self-admiration and extreme self-command Smith considers separate ethical phenomena that deserve different measures of approbation. Yet in his discussions of how these are in fact received in the world, he is prone to elide them together.

that leads "the great mob of mankind" to regard conquerors with "a wondering, though, no doubt, with a very weak and foolish admiration" (TMS VI.ii.1.20; TMS VI.iii.30). But these parenthetical observations become a principal theme of TMS III and VI. Were "dazzling splendour" the sole property of the virtuous, we would have little cause for concern, he suggests here (TMS VI.iii.5); there would be little to fear if our natural tendency to "sympathize with the excessive self-estimation of those splendid characters in which we observe a great and distinguished superiority above the common level of mankind" led us always and only to honor men genuinely "spirited, magnanimous, and high-minded" (TMS VI.iii.33). But in truth,

those great objects of self-interest, of which the loss or acquisition quite changes the rank of the person, are the objects of the passion properly called ambition; a passion, which when it keeps within the bounds of prudence and justice, is always admired in the world, and has even sometimes a certain irregular greatness, which dazzles the imagination, when it passes the limits of both these virtues, and is not only unjust but extravagant. Hence the general admiration for heroes and conquerors, and even for statesmen, whose projects have been very daring and extensive, though altogether devoid of justice. (TMS III.6.7)

Herein lies the problem: the beauty of self-command disarms reason and renders both the acute and undiscerning alike unable to distinguish its appearances from its effects; indeed knaves, Smith notes, have "been often much admired by many people of no contemptible judgment" – including Davila, Clarendon, Locke, and Cicero (TMS VI.iii.12). Too often "even the man of sober judgment" who is "much superior to the multitude" abandons himself to uncritical admiration of conquerors' "excessive presumption, founded upon their own excessive self-admiration" that "dazzles the multitude" and those "much superior to the multitude" alike (TMS VI.iii.27).

What is particularly difficult for both good and bad judges alike to distinguish is the difference between genuine magnanimity and a pernicious self-command. At several points Smith reminds us that self-command is a neutral disposition: a claim most directly conveyed in the final lines of TMS VI, which ends by reminding us that "the most heroic valour may be employed indifferently in the cause either of justice or of injustice," as its "splendid and dazzling quality" renders its effect "too often but too little regarded" (TMS VI.conc.7). Herein lies perhaps the most frequently reiterated point in TMS VI: that "great warlike exploit, though undertaken contrary to every principle of justice, and carried on without any regard to humanity" often "commands even some degree of a certain sort of esteem for the very worthless characters which conduct it"; that "intrepid valour may be employed in the cause of the greatest injustice" which, while sometimes useful, "is at least equally liable to be excessively pernicious"; that "the violence and injustice of great conquerors," however destructive, "often pass for deeds of the most heroic magnanimity"; that magnanimity will not "give lustre only to the characters of innocent and virtuous men," but also to "the greatest criminals"; that the success of conquerors covers "the great injustice of their enterprises," and that only on their failure does "what was before heroic magnanimity" again resume "its proper appellation of extravagant rashness and folly" and "avidity and injustice" (TMS VI.iii.8; TMS VI.iii.12; TMS VI.i.16; TMS VI.iii.6; TMS VI.iii.30). The tragedy of magnanimity lies in the fact that the dazzle of its display renders both its possessor and its spectator unable to assess worth – an ironic failing given that the turn to magnanimity was itself justified as an attempt to recover the concept of moral worth from its vulgarization by the rich and the great. At least one of Smith's aims in his account of magnanimity is to reintroduce this category, both by training spectators to distinguish true magnanimity from false and by insisting that true magnanimity must be grounded in the virtues that constitute worth and desert; hence his qualification of "just" magnanimity at TMS III.6.11, and his insistence in TMS VI that self-command must be "directed by justice and benevolence" (TMS VI.iii.12).

Magnanimity, we can thus conclude, appeals to a natural human psychological propensity. In the words of one of Smith's scribes: "Men generally are more desirous of being thought great than good, and are more afraid of being thought despicable than of being thought wicked" (LRBL ii.103). The love of nobility at the heart of magnanimity encourages this propensity, and in so doing threatens to transform our decent and natural regard to reputation and rank into an exclusive concern with superiority and domination at any cost. One of Smith's most consistent claims is that "the pride of man makes him love to domineer" (WN III.ii.10). This observation dominates the moral psychology of his economic and jurisprudential writings in particular, which frequently emphasize our "love of domination and tyrannizing," our "love of dominion and authority over others," and that "the love of domination and authority over others" is "natural to mankind" (LJA iii.114, 117, 130). This recognition does important work on several fronts. Smith knows that men prefer to use force rather than persuasion (LJA iii.130; WN III.ii.10; WN V.i.g.19). His own defense of commerce, famously founded on the substitution of persuasion for force (see TMS VII.iv.25; WN I.ii.1; LJA vi.57), is grounded in the recognition of the necessity of managing the lover of force and injustice. But this same concern also does important work in Smith's moral theory, because it constitutes his final argument in favor of ascending from the virtue of magnanimity to a higher virtue. Smith rejects the belief that greatness and domination are necessarily connected. But in what then must greatness be grounded to prevent it from devolving into the violent struggle for superiority characteristic of lovers of glory? Put differently: what vision of excellence can Smith provide to gratify our natural desires for personal superiority and greatness on the one hand, and for justice and humanity on the other?

The last question is important because it precludes Smith from embracing the classical solution to the problem of magnanimity. Plato and Aristotle of course anticipate Smith's critique of self-command in their studies of the advantages and disadvantages of *thymos* and *megalopsychia*. To tar with a broad brush: Plato and Aristotle, on the heels of these studies, each claim that the life superior to these flawed political lives is the philosophical life. Smith rejects this claim, as is well known; his skepticism toward intellectual virtue and philosophy has been well canvassed.[50] But what explains his skepticism? And more pointedly: given Smith's self-identification as a philosopher – a self-identification evident even from the original title page of TMS – what vision of the philosophical life did Smith embrace for himself, and how does this conception differ from the classical conception he consciously rejected? Smith's answer lies in his conviction that the classical conception of the philosophical life, albeit noble, suffers from the same ills as the dazzling political life: namely a propensity toward excessive self-admiration and, if not an outright indifference to justice and humanity, at least a subordination of such concerns.

Smith's treatments of Socrates as the embodiment of "dazzling splendour" and "excessive self-admiration" attests to this association of the classical philosophical life with the ills of magnanimity (TMS VI.iii.5; TMS VI.iii.28). Yet his fullest development of this critique is set forth in his response to the

---

[50] See Cropsey, *Polity and Economy*, 8; and Griswold, *Smith and the Virtues of Enlightenment*, esp. 23–24, 154–55, 257n34, 344–49. Schliesser has developed the most thorough explication of Smith's attractions to and justifications of the philosophical life in contrast to the consensus view that tends to emphasize Smith's skepticism toward philosophy and the intellectual virtues; see "Adam Smith's Theoretical Endorsement of Deception," *Adam Smith Review* 2 (2006): esp. 212–14; and also his further development of this position in "Smith's Conception of Philosophy," which calls helpful attention to Smith's shift from Hume's emphasis on "fundamental skepticism about possible knowledge of nature" to his embrace of perplexity as giving rise to a "*research problem*" (330; italics original).

Stoics. His response is blunt: "The plan and system which Nature has sketched out for our conduct, seems to be altogether different from that of the Stoical philosophy" (TMS VII.ii.1.43). By this Smith means in the first place, of course, that Stoicism denies our natural self-loving tendencies to attend to "every thing which Nature has prescribed to us as the proper business and occupation of our lives" (TMS VII.ii.1.46). Their endorsement of suicide provides the most obvious point of contention; in light of his insistence on the first-order duties of self-preservation, Smith can hardly but consider such an endorsement as "a refinement of philosophy" and "perhaps the highest exertion of human vanity and impertinence" – the fruit of a "species of melancholy" foreign to "Nature, in her sound and healthful state" (TMS VII.ii.i.33–34). But Smith's argument here is hardly limited to the Stoic's failure to attend to the duties of self-preservation; he also worries that the Stoic's cosmopolitan desire for "the greatest possible happiness of all rational and sensible beings" leads him to prefer the distant and unrealizable to our naturally primary concern, "the events which immediately affect that little department in which we ourselves have some little management and direction" (TMS VII.ii.1.21, 44).[51] Smith's claim then is not that the Stoic's attempt to transcend self-preference is unnatural – Smith himself encourages precisely this transcendence, as we have seen – but rather that, in attempting to transcend vulgar self-love, the Stoic wise man comes to embrace an even more problematic self-love: one which, like that of the magnanimous man, renders him simultaneously prone to excessive self-admiration and deficient in respect for the dignity and well-being of others. Thus, although Smith

---

[51] Smith's utilitarian formulation is reminiscent of Hutcheson and likely directly indebted; Smith himself interestingly and repeatedly remarks that Hutcheson, like the Stoics, prefers the distant and universal to the local (see TMS VII.ii.3.8 and TMS VII.ii.3.10). Smith's critique of the Stoics for their zero–sum insistence with regard to virtue that "as in shooting at a mark, the man who missed it by an inch had equally missed it with him who had done so by a hundred yards" (TMS VII.ii.1.40–41) is similarly replicated in his argument not only against Mandeville's moral rigorism but also against Hutcheson's claim that benevolence "alone" is praiseworthy (TMS VII.ii.3.2; TMS VII.ii.3.6; TMS VII.ii.3.7). Here too lies the significance of Smith's incorporation, in VII.ii.1.21, of the material ostensibly withdrawn from the earlier versions of VII.ii.1.17. The sixth edition version of the passage retains the original observation on the Stoical wise man's indifference to "his own happiness" and follows this with a new sentence that claims "all his affections were absorbed and swallowed up in two great affections; in that for the discharge of his own duty, and in that for the greatest possible happiness of all rational and sensible beings" (TMS VII.ii.1.21). In its final form, the passage thus reaffirms an argument set forth earlier, as Smith's rejection of Stoicism on the grounds of its indifference to eudaimonism and its concomitant prioritizing of deontological and utilitarian concerns is in keeping with his attachment to a virtue ethical perspective.

endorses the Stoic's efforts to transcend partial perspectives and see himself from the perspective of "that divine Being" and consider "himself as an atom, a particle, of an immense and infinite system" (TMS VII.ii.1.20), he cannot countenance the extremism with which this project is embraced. Paradoxically, the effect of the Stoic's attempt to see himself as a part of the whole is not a renewed appreciation of the interdependence of the cosmos, but its exact opposite: a renewed encouragement of the self-sufficient tendency to "consider ourselves as separated and detached from all other things" (TMS VII.ii.1.19).

Hence the problem of *ataraxia* and *apatheia*: "To the Stoical wise man, all the events of human life must be in a great measure indifferent." The Stoic transcendence of the fear of death comes at the cost of a detachment from the goods of life – the effect of a view of life as a "game," the stakes of which are hardly worth the anxiety they elicit (TMS VII.ii.1.21–24; cf. TMS II.i.5.10; TMS I.i.1.13). But this is problematic in the first instance because it promotes an unnatural indifference to the "success or disappointment" of the Stoic's practical endeavors (TMS VII.ii.1.21) and, hence, an embrace of the belief that the stretching of a finger is "an action in every respect as meritorious, as worthy of praise and admiration, as when he laid down his life for the service of his country" (TMS VII.ii.1.39). As did the magnanimous man, the Stoic misunderstands moral worth. But the Stoic also replicates a second, and perhaps more serious, failing of the magnanimous man. Magnanimous men, smitten with nobility, are indifferent to justice and humanity. But so too the Stoic philosopher, and hence Smith's critique of Marcus Aurelius and his contemplation of the "prosperity of the universe": "The most sublime speculation of the contemplative philosopher can scarce compensate the neglect of the smallest active duty" (TMS VI.ii.3.6). Here, in this closing line of TMS VI.ii, Smith clearly states the dilemma that the ethical virtue that succeeds magnanimity in TMS VI.iii must address: the same love of nobility necessary for self-transcendence threatens to obviate the persistence of the love of decency and justice that also animates the best men.

On the basis of the foregoing, Smith cannot simply be called a critic of philosophy or the excellence of the philosophical life. One finds in his works no critique of the life dedicated to the search for truth; the closest he comes to addressing the relations between philosophy and happiness – his account in the *History of Astronomy* – in fact praises the genuine gratification and tranquility that such a search brings (even if only temporarily). Smith's goal then is not simply to displace this life, but rather to displace one particular vision of it; in this sense, his critique of the classical conception of the philosophical life might be said to parallel, in several crucial respects,

Hume's critique of what he calls "false philosophy."[52] Smith's aim, we might say, is not simply to reject the philosophical life but to describe an alternative life that transcends the specific ills of the magnanimous man and the false philosopher alike.

---

[52] In this vein see especially Brubaker's excellent discussion of Smith's distinction between true philosophy and false philosophy ("'Particular Turn or Habit'," in *Love and Friendship*, ed. Velásquez, 254–58). On the pleasures and rewards of astronomical and natural philosophic inquiry more generally, see Schliesser, "Wonder in the Face of Scientific Revolutions," esp. 699–702, 715–18, 726–27.

6

BENEFICENCE, OR CHRISTIAN VIRTUE

BETWEEN CARE AND *CARITAS*

Smith's remedy for the shortcomings of magnanimity – itself a remedy for the ills of prudence – is to be found in his treatment of beneficence. The specific shortcomings it seeks to address are twofold. First, it aims to ameliorate the potential consequences of the love of nobility and glory that magnanimity encourages. As we have seen, magnanimity encourages transcendence of vulgar self-preference and thereby the pursuit of a greatness and self-sufficiency unavailable to the prudent man. Yet Smith is also keenly aware that self-sufficiency is prone to degenerate into the excessive self-estimation that promotes hubris and injustice. Smith's principal challenge on the heels of this inquiry is thus to set forth a remedy for the possible inhibition of sympathy and concern for justice encouraged by commerce and exacerbated by magnanimity. Yet this only captures half of the aim of his treatment of beneficence. Smith's study of magnanimity revealed not only a problem in the relationship between the individual and commercial society but also a problem in the excellent person's soul – and in particular, a tension between the conflicting loves of individual superiority and of humanity. Smith's account of beneficence seeks to reconcile these opposed longings and thereby set forth a path to the achievement of both greatness and goodness.

In turning to the virtue of beneficence as the necessary remedy for the problems just described, Smith appeals to a very different ethical tradition than those examined thus far. In contrast to the commercial and classical virtues examined earlier, Smith's main category is now Christian virtue. By this I mean something very specific. In Smith's system, the formal role of the Christian virtues is to supplement the virtues of the commercial and classical traditions; but its more substantive role is to afford a bridge between what might be called the virtues of *caritas* and the virtues of care.[1] The former term refers to the Apostolic teaching, later reaffirmed and systematized by the Church Fathers and Aquinas, on the highest theological virtue: the whole-hearted love of God and the extension of such love to all of God's Creation, manifesting itself ultimately in the love of one's neighbor as one's self. The latter is a category in contemporary ethics that seeks to reclaim and reestablish the benefits of compassion, pity, and additional other-regarding sentiments.[2] Smith's own system bears traces of concepts associated with each system; one hears echoes of *caritas* in his reformulation of "the great law of Christianity" (e.g., TMS I.i.5.5) and intimations of the virtues of care in his praises of generosity and humanity (e.g., TMS IV.2.10). Yet neither category captures his notion of beneficence. His treatment shares with the former a belief in the primacy of neighbor-love, yet is largely silent on its foundations in revealed religion; so too it shares with the latter a respect for other-directed passions, yet differs in clearly insisting that passions are not virtues.[3] Smith's own conception thus presents a synthesis rather than a repetition or reformulation of an extant position; yet insofar as the categories of this position are, as a matter of historical and intellectual provenance, inherited from Christian moral thought – and from the influence of Hutcheson in particular – his treatment deserves consideration from this perspective.[4]

To speak of Smith's conception of the third and highest stage of ethical virtue in the context of the Christian virtues has an additional advantage. The central question that Smith's treatment of beneficence addresses is that

[1] Smith's synthesis of Christian and classical virtues is often noted but rarely developed. For suggestive hints in this vein, see esp. Raphael's claim that Smith sought to harmonize Stoic and Christian virtues, as set forth in *Adam Smith*, 33 and 44; his editorial introduction to the Glasgow edition of TMS (with A. L. Macfie), 6–7; and his *Impartial Spectator*, esp. 67.

[2] On the former, see esp. Josef Pieper, *Faith, Hope, Love* (San Francisco: Ignatius Press, 1997). On the latter, see esp. Held, "Ethics of Care," in *Oxford Handbook*, ed. Copp.

[3] The author of *The Theory of Moral Sentiments* himself might be said to know that "sentiment, unguided by reason, becomes sentimentality and sentimentality is a sign of moral failure"; MacIntyre, *Dependent Rational Animals: Why Human Beings Need the Virtues* (Chicago: Open Court, 1999), 124–26.

[4] To be clear: I do not wish to claim that Smith reconciles (or even aspires to reconcile) the many obvious tensions that separate Christian ethics from its classical or commercial alternatives; synthesis must never be confused with reconciliation. Nor do I aspire to demonstrate that he embraces or accepts revealed religion (though his receptivity to a number of Christian tenets may lead one to think that his and his system's hostility to religion has been at times overemphasized; see, e.g., Minowitz, *Profits, Priests, and Princes*, 139ff., 188ff., 215–16). I similarly hesitate to accept McCloskey's claim that in Smith "there is no room for faith and hope" (*Bourgeois Virtues*, 307; see also McCloskey "Adam Smith, the Last of the Former Virtue Ethicists," 65–66).

of the best way of life available to those who aspire to the highest excellence. His inquiry thus far has specifically examined, and indeed rejected, each of the three categories considered by Plato and Aristotle: the life devoted to the accumulation of external goods (TMS VI.i.14), the life devoted to the achievement of honor and glory (TMS VI.iii.27), and the life devoted to speculative contemplation (TMS VI.ii.3.6). Smith's dismissal of each of these possibilities – the commercial life, the political life, and the philosophical life – naturally prompts one to ask what further categories might be available. In this respect, the turn to religion is of particular help. Christianity is distinct in postulating an additional category, that of the saint, as a candidate for the best human life. In it, the saint, among his or her other qualifications, is the perfection of human ethical virtue to the highest possible degree, realized in the character of the saint's disposition to both self and to others. Yet Christianity, of course, is hardly exclusive in such a belief; most of the major world religions posit a similar form of virtue in which, speaking broadly, transcendent excellence consists in reconciliation of proper orientation to divinity with proper orientation to fellow men.[5] Smith himself does not speak of the saint, of course, but his portrait of the peak of ethical virtue, "the wise and virtuous man," turns on the question of the way in which our disposition toward ourselves and toward what lies beyond ourselves shapes our disposition to others. It also speaks to the question of whether and how the form of excellence conventionally associated with contemplation might be harmonized or reconciled with the form of excellence conventionally associated with practical ethical activity. For these reasons, Smith's

---

[5] Without going too far into the study of comparative religion, one might point to the similarities – in spite of certain profound differences – between Smith's position and the Christian conception of *caritas*, the Jewish conception of *tzedakah*, and certain Confucian ideas. On the first, I have found especially helpful Timothy P. Jackson, *The Priority of Love: Christian Charity and Social Justice* (Princeton: Princeton University Press, 2003), 1–27; on the second, Jonathan Sacks, *The Dignity of Difference* (London: Continuum, 2002), 113–24; cf. Lerner, *Maimonides' Empire of Light: Popular Enlightenment in an Age of Belief* (Chicago: University of Chicago Press, 2000), 74–76. A useful introduction to how Smith's system comports with Catholic social thought, for example, can be found in Lawrence R. Cima and Thomas L. Schubeck, "Self-Interest, Love, and Economic Justice: A Dialogue between Classical Economic Liberalism and Catholic Social Teaching," *Journal of Business Ethics* 30 (2001): esp. 218–21. For an introduction to how Smith's conception of comfort might compare to Chinese ethical traditions, see the comments on Confucius and Mencius in Wei-Ben Zhang, *On Adam Smith and Confucius: The Theory of Moral Sentiments and the Analects* (New York: Nova Science, 2000), 13, 67, 85–86; as well as the parallels between Mencius and Smith briefly suggested or alluded to in McCloskey, "Adam Smith, the Last of the Former Virtue Ethicists," 49; and Solomon, "Free Enterprise, Sympathy, and Virtue," in *Moral Markets*, ed. Zak, 16.

portrait deserves to be regarded as a contribution to the ancient debate over the best life for a human being – as well as an apologia for Smith's own life.[6]

BENEVOLENCE AND BENEFICENCE AND THE HUMAN *TELOS*

Smith's study of the best life is presented as an inquiry into the nature of desert. As such it hearkens back to the typography described in Smith's response to Mandeville, in which he described three lives – one concerned to claim without deserving, one concerned to claim and to deserve, and one concerned merely to deserve without claiming. The first two characters are of course the lovers of praise and of true glory, and our studies of the prudent man and the magnanimous man sought to demonstrate that the excellence of each is vitiated by his dependence on the acquisition of external goods; the highest and happiest life is rather marked by indifference to claiming, and exclusive interest in deserving. Yet this prompts an obvious question: in what does desert consist? Smith's answer to this question is presented in TMS II, which serves as a preparative for the study of the wise and virtuous man in TMS VI in the same way that TMS III serves as a preparative for the study of the magnanimous lover of true glory in TMS VI, and in the same way that TMS IV serves as a preparative for the study of the prudent lover of praise in TMS VI. TMS II thus presents itself as a study of "merit and demerit, the qualities of deserving reward, and of deserving punishment" (TMS II.i.intro.1). And its conception of the nature of merit or desert is clear: "Actions of a beneficent tendency, which proceed from proper motives, seem alone to require reward; because such alone are the approved objects of gratitude, or excite the sympathetic gratitude of the spectator" (TMS II.ii.1.1).

---

[6] Cf. Griswold: "When Smith refers to 'men of virtue,' he does not mean philosophers. He has in mind what Aristotle would have called 'gentlemen,' persons of outstanding moral virtue for whom theoretical matters are of comparatively little consequence" (*Smith and the Virtues of Enlightenment*, 154); and see also his claim that "for reasons of humanity, Smith reins in the urge to transcendence so that it stays within the circle of sympathy, within the dialectic of recognition" (*Smith and the Virtues of Enlightenment*, 155). A similar claim is made by McCloskey, who argues that "Adam Smith's error was the error, and the glory, of the Enlightenment, trying to liberate us from transcendence" ("Adam Smith, the Last of the Former Virtue Ethicists," 67–68). My view is closer to that of Firth, who writes, contra T. J. Hochstrasser, that "Smith's understanding of the moral world failed to escape a transcendental understanding of human nature" ("Adam Smith's Moral Philosophy as Ethical Self-Formation," in *New Perspectives*, ed. Cockfield et al., 106).

Smith's formulation contains not only his substantive definition of desert but also the heart of his argument for why desert consists in beneficence. With regard to the first issue, the formulation presents a theme reiterated several times in Part II: that beneficent actions "appear to deserve the highest reward," for "by being productive of the greatest good, they are the natural and approved objects of the liveliest gratitude" (TMS II.ii.1.9). But although Smith's regard for beneficence is clear, the reasons for his preference are less so. His argument tends to focus on the impartial spectator's admiration of beneficence; hence "he, therefore, appears to deserve reward, who, to some person or persons, is the natural object of a gratitude which every human heart is disposed to beat time to, and thereby applaud: and he, on the other hand, appears to deserve punishment, who in the same manner is to some person or persons the natural object of a resentment which the breast of every reasonable man is ready to adopt and sympathize with" (TMS II.i.2.3). This formulation has the advantage of reminding us of the connection between justice and beneficence that animates TMS II; Smith's understanding of beneficence and merit is founded on the same mechanism of the impartial spectator's judgment that has been shown to lie at the heart of his jurisprudence.[7] Yet as an explanation of beneficence, this argument seems wanting, particularly given its dependence on a concept of universal assent to "natural" objects of gratitude – a concept that Smith's own study of custom in TMS V provides reasons to question. Thus one wonders: does his argument for beneficence's superiority have a firmer foundation than simply his wish for it to be so?

As Part II progresses, Smith in fact develops another argument for the primacy of beneficence. The development of this argument follows a characteristically Smithean trajectory. Its point of departure is not beneficence per se, but rather the sentiment of gratitude that often prompts beneficent actions.[8] Smith begins with gratitude because of its familiarity and its intimate association with our self-interest. Gratitude, that is, is the passion that we feel toward our benefactors who have promoted our interests through their actions. Smith's treatment of gratitude thus begins from the same departure point as his treatments of prudence and magnanimity, namely immediate

---

[7] See Haakonssen, *Science of a Legislator*, esp. chapters 5 and 6; and Haakonssen, "What Might Properly Be Called Natural Jurisprudence?" 208, 214–15.

[8] Here Smith himself might be poised to contribute to contemporary debates. Contemporary psychologists classify gratitude as a virtue (see, e.g., Peterson and Seligman, *Character Strengths and Virtues*, 553–68), whereas Smith calls it a "sentiment" (TMS II.i.1.2) that must be steered if it is to be cultivated into the virtue of beneficence.

needs and desires. Put differently, his initial discussion of beneficence focuses not on a noble disinterestedness but on its opposite; what drives reciprocity in beneficence is precisely the compelling psychological need to return like for like, and our awareness that until our benefactor is "recompensed," "till we ourselves have been instrumental in promoting his happiness, we feel ourselves still loaded with that debt which his past services have laid upon us" (TMS II.i.1.5). Smith reiterates this in what follows, reminding us that to be benefited is to be "still loaded with that debt" and thus compelled to make a "proportionable recompense" to a benefactor (TMS II.i.1.5; TMS II.i.3.2). Any relationship built on such foundations, of course, would partake of that "mercenary exchange of good offices according to an agreed valuation" which, as we have seen, Smith associates with commercial society (TMS II.ii.3.2).

Yet this is hardly the only conception of beneficence that Smith develops. Indeed in TMS II he sets forth a distinction between two concepts of beneficence alongside his far better known distinction between justice and beneficence. The aim of this alternative conception is again to encourage the transcendence of self-interest. Thus the distinction between the two concepts: where reciprocal beneficence is a duty or compulsion, another type of beneficence refuses to be governed by the law of *quid pro quo*, preferring the "proper and noble beneficence" or "high-spirited generosity" characteristic of "proper and beneficent greatness of mind" and which leads us to be "naturally transported" to love those who exhibit it (TMS II.i.5.3). What marks this higher beneficence is that it is "always free." In defining it, Smith thus distinguishes the "duties of beneficence" characteristic of gratitude, which impose on us "a perfect and complete obligation," from something higher: "What friendship, what generosity, what charity, would prompt us to do with universal approbation, is still more free, and can still less be extorted by force than the duties of gratitude. We talk of the debt of gratitude, not of charity, or generosity, nor even of friendship" (TMS II.ii.1.3). In contrast to those seeking to discharge the debt of gratitude, this conception of beneficence is not self-regarding. Disdaining a calculus of interest, its actions are performed without regard for self-interest in any conventional sense.

Smith's conception of the noble beneficence exhibited in charity and generosity and friendship is intimately related to the larger project of overcoming self-preference and thereby elevating self-love that unites his understanding of virtue. His study of Hutcheson's system of benevolence, emphasizes that, in spite of its incompleteness, it served "to check the injustice of self-love" (even as it went too far, Smith thinks, in trying to extirpate it altogether;

TMS VII.ii.3.14). But this same claim forms a central element of TMS II, which also notes the dangers of "the natural preference which every man has for his own happiness above that of other people":

Though every man may, according to the proverb, be the whole world to himself, to the rest of mankind he is a most insignificant part of it. Though his own happiness may be of more importance to him than that of all the world besides, to every other person it is of no more consequence than that of any other man. Though it may be true, therefore, that every individual, in his own breast, naturally prefers himself to all mankind, yet he dares not look mankind in the face, and avow that he acts according to this principle. He feels that in this preference they can never go along with him, and that how natural soever it may be to him, it must always appear excessive and extravagant to them. When he views himself in the light in which he is conscious that others will view him, he sees that to them he is but one of the multitude in no respect better than any other in it. If he would act so as that the impartial spectator may enter into the principles of his conduct, which is what of all things he has the greatest desire to do, he must, upon this, as upon all other occasions, humble the arrogance of his self-love, and bring it down to something which other men can go along with. (TMS II.ii.2.1)

Thus Smith gives his third explicit insistence on the necessity of the individual's overcoming of self-preference by coming to regard himself as but one among many. But this locution has an additional significance here. As elsewhere, Smith emphasizes the illegitimacy of injustice arising from self-preference, but here the treatment also explains the illegitimacy of a failure to execute positive works of beneficence. Put differently, both unjust action and the failure to act beneficently are the effects of misguided self-love. Smith develops this point further in what follows. We admire our benefactor, we are told, because he holds us in equal esteem with himself: "What most of all charms us in our benefactor, is the concord between his sentiments and our own, with regard to what interests us so nearly as the worth of our own character, and the esteem that is due to us. We are delighted to find a person who values us as we value ourselves, and distinguishes us from the rest of mankind, with an attention not unlike that with which we distinguish ourselves" (TMS II.iii.1.4). The opposite is true of a detractor, who we despise because of "the little account which he seems to make of us, the unreasonable preference which he gives to himself above us, and that absurd self-love, by which he seems to imagine, that other people may be sacrificed at any time, to his conveniency or his humour" (TMS II.iii.1.5). The indispensable element in the creation of a liberal political order and the realization of genuine excellence is thus, interestingly, one: the transcendence of self-preference.

Smith's account of benefaction is thus more complex than it appears. TMS II tends to be regarded as our exoneration from the duties of benefi- cence; in insisting that justice is the "pillar" that supports the social edifice and beneficence only the "ornament" that adorns it, Smith often has been taken as a partisan of the liberal primacy of justice. It is, of course, true that Smith thinks justice indispensable to social stability. Yet it is no less true that he thinks a life dedicated to justice but indifferent to beneficence is second-rate. He offers some hint of this in arguing that as "retaliation seems to be the great law which is dictated to us by Nature," beneficence and generosity are due to the beneficent and generous. Even more crucially, he argues that "those whose hearts never open to the feelings of humanity, should, we think, be shut out, in the same manner, from the affections of all their fellow-creatures, and be allowed to live in the midst of society, as in a great desert where there is nobody to care for them, or to inquire after them" (TMS II.ii.1.10). For a sympathetic, esteem-seeking social animal, this is of course the worst of fates, and such an expression seems meant to give pause to the self-interested praise-seekers who have assumed that wealth and greatness are the surest or sufficient routes to recognition.

In this respect, Smith provides what might be called a self-interested justi- fication of beneficence. Yet his conception of the way in which beneficence is in our self-interest is considerably more complex than the mere suggestion that it helps us win esteem. Beneficence is rather in our interest insofar as it furthers interests that are intrinsic to our nature but occasionally obscured by the encouragement of more visceral interests. These fundamental interests are suggested in the opening line of TMS: "How selfish soever man may be supposed, there are evidently some principles in his nature, which interest him in the fortune of others, and render their happiness necessary to him, though he derives nothing from it except the pleasure of seeing it" (TMS I.i.1.1). This opening has rightly been seen as a reproach to advocates of the selfish system of morals, from Hobbes to Mandeville, and as a partial endorsement of the resistance voiced by Shaftesbury and Hutcheson. But another aspect of this opening line deserves pause. Its claim is not simply that men are other-regarding as well as self-regarding, but rather that by "nature" they have an "interest" in promoting the well-being of others: to suggest that the well-being of others is "necessary" to us is to suggest that the champions of the selfish system, for all their obsession with self-interest, failed to under- stand our genuine interests. In this respect, the first line of TMS intimates the claim that ultimately forms the motivating center of the work as a whole: that nature has endowed us with interests that are at once less apparent and more fundamental than our all-too-familiar physical and psychological needs.

This claim receives its fullest expression in Smith's most direct statement of our natural end or *telos*:

Man was made for action, and to promote by the exertion of his faculties such changes in the external circumstances both of himself and others, as may seem most favourable to the happiness of all. He must not be satisfied with indolent benevolence, nor fancy himself the friend of mankind, because in his heart he wishes well to the prosperity of the world. That he may call forth the whole vigour of his soul, and strain every nerve, in order to produce those ends which it is the purpose of his being to advance, Nature has taught him, that neither himself nor mankind can be fully satisfied with his conduct, nor bestow upon it the full measure of applause, unless he has actually produced them. He is made to know, that the praise of good intentions, without the merit of good offices, will be but of little avail to excite either the loudest acclamations of the world, or even the highest degree of self-applause. (TMS II.iii.3.3).

Smith's statement is arresting – all the more so when we recall the reputation of its author. The celebrated image of the champion of self-interest is difficult to reconcile with the claim here that we discover our natural ends in the promotion of the well-being of others, and indeed that only in beneficent activity do we find our fullest flourishing as a unified being, purposefully at work in promoting the ends for which we have been made. But this passage not only obviates a crude view of Smith as the apostle of greed; it also challenges a more sophisticated view of Smith as inimical to teleology.[9] In insisting that "man was made for action," Smith provides the

---

[9] One commentator has gone so far as to argue, in the course of comparing Smith to Aristotle, that "Smith's doctrine has no telos of which to speak; he relies on habit and experience, thereby leaving his account of virtue open to the charge of moral relativity and nihilism"; Richard Temple-Smith, "Adam Smith's Treatment of the Greeks in *The Theory of Moral Sentiments*: The Case of Aristotle," in *New Perspectives*, ed. Cockfield et al., 43; for further development of the view that Smith's system lacks a teleology, see MacIntyre, *After Virtue*, 54–56, 234–26; Cropsey, *Polity and Economy*, 20–21; and Calkins and Werhane, "Smith, Aristotle and the Virtues of Commerce," 50–51, 55. For the related but distinct view that Smith's teleological language is an unnecessary apparatus with which readers can dispense, see Coase, "Smith's View of Man," 541; Campbell, *Smith's Science of Morals*, 60–61, 70; and Haakonssen, *Science of a Legislator*, 77; and, from a different perspective, Fleischacker, *Third Concept of Liberty*, 147–51 (cf. Evensky, *Smith's Moral Philosophy*, 23); a helpful review of this "consensus" position that Smith's "teleological explanations serve no real purpose" can be found in Otteson, *Marketplace of Life*, 240–44. Others see Smith as reliant on or longing for a teleology for which he may prove unable to account fully; see Berns, "Aristotle and Smith on Justice," 86n17; Werhane, *Smith and Modern Capitalism*, 49–51; Griswold, *Smith and the Virtues of Enlightenment*, 332–33. Yet a growing group of scholars is beginning to make a more developed case that teleology is fundamental to his thought, thereby reviving Viner's mature view in *The Role of Providence in the Social Order* (Philadelphia: American Philosophical Society, 1972), 81–82; alongside Otteson's

clearest and most direct statement to be found in his corpus of his conception of the natural and intended end of human beings – a statement, moreover, that brings him in accord with the conception of the human *telos* that is similarly, and equally forthrightly, developed by several other leading thinkers of the Scottish Enlightenment, who, like Smith, also argue that man's nature is such that his happiness requires his active regard for the well-being of others.[10] Although it will strike us to find so many Scots subscribing explicitly to teleology, that they chose this substantive understanding for their teleology is less surprising; this vision of the human being is itself commensurate with their understanding of the interdependence that defines commercial modernity. And this claim, moreover, brings us back directly to the question concerning commercial corruption that lies at the heart of our present inquiry. Earlier we saw that among magnanimity's chief ills is that it exacerbates a potentially disastrous preference for the noble over the decent, thereby reaffirming in a new idiom the individualism and indifference characteristic of commercial society. Smith's discussion of the relationship of beneficent action to the achievement of the human *telos* is itself a direct response to this problem insofar as it seeks to recover the ends of human nature as a means of mitigating corruptions of that nature.

Smith's striking statement is also important for a second reason. Not only does it provide his most forthright statement of his conception of human ends as other-directed rather than self-directed, but it also argues that these ends are to be pursued in a specific way. The statement in fact introduces itself as a critique of "mere good inclinations and kind wishes" (TMS II.iii.3.3).

excellent discussion of transcendent standards (*Marketplace of Life*, 255–57) and the works cited at Chapter 5, Note 17, this volume; see esp. Richard Kleer, "Final Causes in Adam Smith's *Theory of Moral Sentiments*," *Journal of the History of Philosophy* 33 (1995): 275–300; McKenna, *Rhetoric of Propriety*, 147; Alvey, "The 'New View' of Adam Smith," in *New Perspectives*, ed. Cockfield, et al., 71; and especially Alvey, *Adam Smith: Optimist or Pessimist?*, by far the most sustained treatment of the topic.

[10] See esp. Hutcheson, *Philosophiae Moralis Institutio Compendiaria/ Short Introduction to Moral Philosophy*, ed. Luigi Turco (Indianapolis: Liberty Fund, 2007), I.i.10, p. 34; Ferguson, *Essay on the History of Civil Society*, I.8 (pp. 51–56 in the Cambridge edition, ed. Fania Oz-Salzberger); Ferguson, *Principles of Moral and Political Science* (Edinburgh, 1792; reprint Hildesheim/New York: Georg Olms Verlag, 1975), I.ii.16, vol. 1, pp. 185–86; and Kames, *Loose Hints Upon Education*, 2nd ed. (Edinburgh, 1782), 282–85. I treat these passages in my forthcoming "Social Science and Human Flourishing." On Smith's understanding of the teleological ends of human nature, see esp. Alvey's account in chapter 2 of his *Adam Smith: Optimist or Pessimist?* which, in contrast to the account given here, emphasizes that the teleological element in this account lies in its emphasis on the way in which "our natural gregariousness serves the goal of self-preservation without us consciously aiming at it" (37).

In so doing, Smith further develops, and indeed sharpens, his distinction between mere "passive feelings" and "active principles" at TMS III.3.4, examined earlier. Developing this here, Smith distinguishes actual good-doing from mere well-wishing – a distinction fundamental to his account of human excellence. He tends to convey the distinction via the Latinized terms of "benevolence" and "beneficence." The former he associates with a well-meaning but inefficacious disposition, whereas the latter connotes successful activity on behalf of others. Smith's several critiques of compassion and pity frequently emphasize this same distinction.[11] Indeed for all his fame as advocate or expositor of sympathy, Smith hardly considers all forms of other-directedness equally valuable – hence his critique of that "illusive sympathy" that leads us to shed "sympathetic tears" which are "but a small part of the duty" we owe the afflicted. Much better than such "indolent and passive fellow-feeling" is the "more vigorous and active sentiment" that leads us to approve of positive exertions (TMS II.i.2.5; cf. TMS II.i.5.11). Elsewhere Smith further develops this critique with regard to pity in particular; insofar as pity fails to actuate or to sustain positive exertions capable of alleviating the suffering that prompts the spectator's sentiment, it necessarily pales before active exertions of beneficence that "being productive of the greatest good" thus "deserve the highest reward" (TMS II.ii.1.9; cf. TMS I.i.4.3; TMS III.3.9; TMS VI.iii.15).[12] And here Smith provides one of his most

[11] On the difference between compassion and charity, see Leon R. Kass, "Charity and the Confines of Compassion," in *The Perfect Gift: The Philanthropic Imagination in Poetry and Prose*, ed. Amy A. Kass (Bloomington: Indiana University Press, 2002), esp. 269–71; and, in the same volume, Clifford Orwin, "Princess Diana and Mother Theresa: Compassion and Christian Charity," 88–101. I am also deeply indebted to Orwin's other excellent studies of the difference between compassion and Christian charity ("Compassion and the Softening of Mores," *Journal of Democracy* 11 (2000): esp. 144–45) and of Rousseau's presentation of compassion as a relative sentiment that emerges from *amour-propre* ("Rousseau and the Discovery of Political Compassion," in *Legacy of Rousseau*, ed. Orwin and Tarcov, esp. 304–6). In a similar vein, see also Richard Boyd, "Pity's Pathologies Portrayed: Rousseau and the Limits of Democratic Compassion," *Political Theory* 32 (2004): 519–46.

[12] Montes provides an excellent summary of the distinction between benevolence and beneficence in Smith's (and in Hutcheson's and Bentham's) thought in *Smith in Context*, 106n14. The same distinction is important in contemporary moral philosophy. Thus, William Frankena explains that "benevolence is a matter of intention, not of outcome; beneficence is one of outcome, not intention, though it may be intentional." Frankena does, however, qualify this claim in a way that would have been unfamiliar to Smith, insisting that benevolence should be distinguished "from mere well-*wishing* or *meaning*-well," as benevolence means *willing*, and genuinely trying to do or bring about good and not evil" ("Beneficence/Benevolence," *Social Philosophy and Policy* 4 (1987): 2); the point is further developed in Yuval Livnat, "On the Nature of Benevolence," *Journal of Social Philosophy* 35 (2004): 309–10.

interesting invisible-hand explanations. In preferring good-doing to mere well-wishing, we better fulfill nature's intentions, which command not the "artificial commiseration" or "artificial sympathy" of extensive compassion ("always the slightest and most transitory imaginable") but rather command us to embrace that degree of fellow-feeling "necessary to prompt us to relieve them" (TMS III.3.9; TMS I.iii.1.12). Our greater approbation of good effects than of good intentions is likewise in keeping with nature's intentions. One of Smith's most frequently reiterated claims in this section is that, even if one believes, as Hutcheson does, that intentions are or should be the essence of merit, it remains the case that consequences in fact shape our conceptions of merit and demerit to a great extent in practice (see TMS II.iii.intro.3–5); "the world judges by the event, and not by the design" (TMS II.iii.3.1), and "a plan does not, even to the most intelligent, give the same pleasure as a noble and magnificent building" (TMS II.iii.2.2–3). In each of these claims, Smith reaffirms the insistence of his correspondent Pierre-Samuel Dupont de Nemours: "Il est encore plus important de bien faire que de bien dire" (CAS 277).

Smith's conviction thus runs deep that "compassion even when strongest is but a short lived passion" (LRBL ii.241). Yet if pity and compassion are too feeble to lead us to virtue, what stronger motive ought to be substituted in their place? In particular, what sentiment or disposition is needed to translate fellow-feeling into "proper beneficence"?

In responding to this challenge, Smith gives us some reason to wonder whether in fact justice and beneficence are as separate as they first appear. Two specific aspects of his argument on this front might be noted. The first concerns Smith's notion of "sympathetic indignation." This sentiment forms an explicit counter to the sympathy that he criticized earlier. Where that sympathy is indolent, illusive, and artificial, sympathetic indignation is immediate and active; not simply an unreflective sentiment passively prompted by the apprehension of suffering, it is shaped by judgments of justice and injustice and desert and merit – a point made particularly clear in his account of our response to the victims of the crimes of Borgia or Nero (TMS II.i.5.6; cf. TMS II.i.3.3; TMS II.i.5.8; TMS II.ii.2.1–4). A second argument in this vein further develops the claim that pity and compassion are not only passive but also tend to be indiscriminate in their judgments of which objects deserve our solicitude. Thus Smith's portrait of the compassionate man focuses on the tension between compassion and justice:

When the guilty is about to suffer that just retaliation, which the natural indignation of mankind tells them is due to his crimes; when the insolence of his injustice is broken and humbled by the terror of his approaching punishment; when he ceases to be an object of fear, with the generous and humane he begins to be an object of pity. The thought of what he is about to suffer extinguishes their resentment for the sufferings of others to which he has given occasion. They are disposed to pardon and forgive him, and to save him from that punishment, which in all their cool hours they had considered as the retribution due to such crimes. Here, therefore, they have occasion to call to their assistance the consideration of the general interest of society. They counterbalance the impulse of this weak and partial humanity by the dictates of a humanity that is more generous and comprehensive. They reflect that mercy to the guilty is cruelty to the innocent, and oppose to the emotions of compassion which they feel for a particular person, a more enlarged compassion which they feel for mankind. (TMS II.ii.3.7)[13]

The consequence of indiscriminate pity is often injustice. Compassion thus requires for its remedy a rational appreciation of the good of the whole, which the partial attachments of sentiment are prone to disturb. And thus Smith comes full circle. In his critique of the Stoic sage, he emphasized that its focus on the universal led the sage to neglect the particular. In his critique of the compassionate man, he claims that focus on the specific leads him to neglect the universal. Thus the challenge of the genuinely beneficent man, charged with balancing not only compassion and justice, but also the good of the whole and the good of a particular part. Herein lies proper beneficence, the central virtue of the peak figure of Smith's ethics: the wise and virtuous man.

THE CHARACTER AND PURPOSES OF THE WISE AND VIRTUOUS MAN

Smith formally introduces the wise and virtuous man in the chapter "Of Universal Benevolence" that closes TMS VI.ii. The chapter's central theme is the tension between universal benevolence and particular beneficence now familiar from TMS II. Here Smith presents this tension by noting, in the chapter's first paragraph, that "though our effectual good offices can very seldom be extended to any wider society than that of our own country; our good-will is circumscribed by no boundary, but may embrace the immensity of the universe." This is the effect of the "imagination" which prompts us to desire the happiness of all innocent, sensible beings (TMS VI.ii.3.1). Yet much of this chapter's force comes from the explicit claim, in its final paragraph, that the limits of our capacity to relieve suffering forbid the practical realization of universal good-will; rather than the duty of

[13] Cf. Rousseau, *Emile*, 252–53.

superintending to the whole, man is allotted "a much humbler department, but one much more suitable to the weakness of his powers, and to the narrowness of his comprehension," namely "the care of his own happiness, of that of his family, his friends, his country" (TMS VI.ii.3.6). Taken separately, this claim might be thought deflationary. Yet taken in conjunction with the natural desire for universal benevolence that Smith is so keen to emphasize, we are led to wonder: if benevolence's reach exceeds its grasp, what resources might be available to assist it in its project?

It is in this context that Smith introduces the wise and virtuous man. The wise and virtuous man manifests the perfection of two of the dispositions that have been our focus to now: first, a capacity for other-directed action beyond mere other-directed sentiments; and second, a willingness to subordinate his private interests to the interests of the whole. But to these dispositions he adds another:

The wise and virtuous man is at all times willing that his own private interest should be sacrificed to the public interest of his own particular order or society. He is at all times willing, too, that the interest of this order or society should be sacrificed to the greater interest of the state or sovereignty, of which it is only a subordinate part. He should, therefore, be equally willing that all those inferior interests should be sacrificed to the greater interest of the universe, to the interest of that great society of all sensible and intelligent beings, of which God himself is the immediate administrator and director. (TMS VI.ii.3.3)

The key line is the final one. Herein lies the difference between merely compassionate or benevolent well-wishers and the man prepared to sacrifice his interests for the good of the whole. His capacity for such activity is sustained not by sentiments but by his love of the whole, which is supported by his belief in the existence of God. In the terms of our inquiry, a wise and virtuous man replaces the self-transcendence of the magnanimous man, founded on self-love and the love of the noble, with a higher and surer transcendence, motivated by belief in God's "immediate" administration of the world – a faith that leads such a one to regard as necessary and beneficial even those seeming evils that would in fact reveal themselves to be what he "ought sincerely and devoutly to have wished for" had he been possessed of God's omniscience. Furthermore, here Smith points out the principal failing of universal benevolence. When severed from its original foundation in such belief, such a disposition cannot maintain its habitual cheerfulness and necessarily degenerates via "the most melancholy of all reflections": the materialist belief "that all the unknown regions of infinite and incomprehensible space may be filled with nothing but endless misery and wretchedness" (TMS VI.ii.3.2-3).

To put matters thusly is to prompt two realizations. First, TMS VI.ii.3 suggests that faith in the divine is not only inextricable from but also supportive of the ethical activity characteristic of the best life. The question of Smith's religious convictions is of course unanswerable, given the texts that we have. Yet his portrait of the relationship between ethical life and divinity suggests that he was more sensitive to the transcendent aspects of ethics than is sometimes assumed.[14] Second, this compels a reconsideration of a certain view of his project. Smith has often been regarded as a champion of the Enlightenment project to reduce human suffering and promote the relief of man's estate. Yet his portrait of the wise and virtuous man suggests a much different vision. So far from regarding suffering as an unmitigated evil, the wise and virtuous man, in light of his "habitual and thorough conviction" that a benevolent God could admit into the world "no partial evil which is not necessary for the universal good," will "consider all the misfortunes which may befall himself, his friends, his society, or his country, as necessary for the prosperity of the universe, and therefore as what he ought, not only to submit to with resignation, but as what he himself, if he had known all the connexions and dependencies of things, ought sincerely and devoutly to have wished for" (TMS VI.ii.3.3). At the same time, the acceptance of the existence of such misfortunes and partial evils hardly leads to a passive quietism. Nor does it lead to *ataraxia*, for all the "Stoic" overtones of this passage. On the contrary, the wise and virtuous man's conviction that he has been "ordered upon the forlorn station of the universe" for reasons "necessary for the good of the whole" enables him "not only with humble resignation to submit to this allotment, but to endeavour to embrace it with alacrity and joy." It is precisely this alacrity and joy, in turn, that impels the wise and virtuous man, like the good soldier, to take up arms in the cause of service to the whole and thus fulfill the duties of the "splendid and honourable station" to which he has been appointed, and thereby make "the noblest exertion which it is possible for man to make" (TMS VI.ii.3.4; cf. TMS VII.ii.1.45).

The wise and virtuous man's grounding of his other-directed dispositions thus seeks to circumvent the arbitrariness and sentimentalism to which

---

[14] On Smith's indifference to metaphysics, see, e.g., Melzer, "Anti-antifoundationalism: Is a Theory of Moral Sentiments Possible?" *Perspectives on Political Science* 30 (2001): 155; see also Hope, *Virtue by Consensus*, 83.

compassion and pity are prone. This concern is further developed in TMS VI.iii. As we have seen, TMS VI.iii opens with a discussion of the advantages and disadvantages of self-command as a means of managing *thymos*. At TMS VI.iii.14, the inquiry explicitly shifts. At this point Smith turns to an investigation into why the point of propriety is higher in the pleasant than in the unpleasant passions. But this investigation also presents another way in which the other-directed sentiments might be more firmly grounded. The inquiry begins by noting that "the disposition to the affections which tend to unite men in society, to humanity, kindness, natural affection, friendship, esteem, may sometimes be excessive." By this he means that frequently these "excessive affections" are "directed, as is too often the case, towards unworthy objects." In this way Smith reiterates his claims, examined earlier, that indiscriminate sentimental affection for others misjudges merit and perpetrates injustice, also often bringing the possessor of such generous sentiments "much real and heartfelt distress." Yet Smith is quick to make a caveat. The compassionate and humane pitier, so far from deserving our disdain, deserves "compassion" himself; thus, "a well-disposed mind regards him with the most exquisite pity, and feels the highest indignation against those who affect to despise him for his weakness and imprudence" (TMS VI.iii.15; cf. TMS I.ii.4.3; TMS II.i.3.2; TMS II.ii.3.11). Even while reminding us that some forms of beneficence are better than others and that true beneficence requires assessing the justice of the claims of its objects, Smith notes that there is something attractive even in its debased form; indiscriminate care, though hardly optimal, is less pernicious than absence of care. Thus Smith's critique of insensibility in what follows, in which he explains that the very self-command that encourages insensibility to one's self promotes insensibility to others as well; thus self-command's dark side: "The man who feels little for his own misfortunes must always feel less for those of other people, and be less disposed to relieve them. The man who has little resentment for the injuries which are done to himself, must always have less for those which are done to other people, and be less disposed either to protect or to avenge them" (TMS VI.iii.18). And this process works both ways: not only does "hardness of heart" render its possessor "insensible to the feelings and distresses of other people," it also "renders other people equally insensible to his; and, by excluding him from the friendship of all the world, excludes him from the best and most comfortable of all social enjoyments" (TMS VI.iii.15). On these grounds Smith marks the difference between a "noble firmness" founded on the consciousness of one's dignity and a "stupid insensibility to the events of human life" (TMS VI.iii.18): the latter violates our natural tendency toward mutual sympathy and, hence, exacerbates the indifference and insensibility potentially characteristic of commercial society.

To review: magnanimity is complex; it begins from the desire to transcend the self but culminates in a pernicious disposition that is yet attractive. So too benevolence, which begins from an admirable solicitude for the well-being of others but culminates in an inefficacious disposition that is yet not unattractive. Each is simultaneously admirable and problematic, and thus incomplete. Smith's second foundation for proper beneficence finds its motivation here. By fusing the virtues of *thymos*, which have recently and conventionally been associated with manliness, with the virtues of care, which have been likewise recently and conventionally associated with femininity, Smith aspires to provide another means of transforming benevolence into active beneficence.[15] His explicit claim is that the excesses of manly self-command require the moderation that only a feminine solicitude for others can provide, just as the weaknesses of compassion can be remedied and benevolence rendered more efficacious only by a recovery of magnanimity.

Smith takes important steps toward developing this synthesis prior to TMS VI. In two previous portraits of "the perfection of human nature" and "the man of the most perfect virtue," he emphasizes that such perfection consists precisely in the capacity to synthesize a superior command of selfish feelings to a superior sensibility to the feelings of others – that is, a capacity to join together both the "awful" virtues and the "amiable" virtues (TMS I.i.5.5; TMS III.3.35; cf. TMS II.iii.3.10). Elsewhere Smith presents this synthesis explicitly in terms of gender – hence, in the first instance, his observation that "humanity is the virtue of a woman, generosity of a man." Humanity accords with the amiable virtues and "consists merely in the exquisite fellow-feeling which the spectator entertains with the sentiments of the persons principally concerned, so as to grieve for their sufferings, to resent their injuries, and to rejoice at their good fortune." Its actions "require no self-denial, no self-command, no great exertion of the sense of

---

[15] The feminine aspects of the ethics of care have been influentially developed by Nel Noddings and Carol Gilligan; see Michael Slote, "Agent-Based Virtue Ethics," in *Virtue Ethics*, ed. Crisp and Slote, 255–58; and Annette Baier, "What Do Women Want in a Moral Theory?" in *Virtue Ethics*, ed. Crisp and Slote, 263–66. On how Smith himself brings together the masculine and the feminine, see Clark, "Conversation and Moderate Virtue," 185, 203–204, 206; and Seigel, *Idea of the Self*, 145, 159; for skeptical views, see Justman's claim that Smith embraces stoic self-command "in part to avert the shaming implications of his own 'feminine paradigm'" (*Autonomous Male*, 4, 14, 26, 81, 150–51); and the emphasis on Smith's debts to the classical republican *vir virtutis* tradition in Montes, *Smith in Context*, 76–78. The gendering of virtue is also an important theme in McCloskey, *Bourgeois Virtues*, esp. 309–11.

propriety." Generosity requires much more: "We never are generous except when in some respect we prefer some other person to ourselves, and sacrifice some great and important interest of our own to an equal interest of a friend or of a superior." In so doing, the generous man seeks "by an effort of magnanimity" to act in accord with the judgments and sentiments of the impartial spectator, and in particular "endeavours to act so as to deserve applause" (TMS IV.2.10). This perfect synthesis of benevolent dispositions rendered active through self-command is further developed in TMS VI in its critique of excessive self-command. Echoing his claim regarding our *telos*, examined earlier, Smith here argues that nature has "formed men for that mutual kindness, so necessary for their happiness" and indeed on these grounds mandates our reciprocity: "Kindness is the parent of kindness; and if to be beloved by our brethren be the great object of our ambition, the surest way of obtaining it is, by our conduct to show that we really love them" (TMS VI.ii.1.19). Put differently, the animating principle of TMS VI shifts from a masculine love of esteem to a possibly feminine love of love itself. At the same time, Smith illustrates the insufficiencies of both a purely feminine ethics and a purely masculine ethics. Indifference to masculine virtues is a great failing: "The want of proper indignation is a most essential defect in the manly character" (TMS VI.iii.16). Reminding us that "we esteem the man who supports pain and even torture with manhood and firmness," Smith notes that "we can have little regard for him who sinks under them, and abandons himself to useless outcries and womanish lamentations" (TMS VI.iii.17). Thus "the man of too much sensibility" or "too exquisite sensibility" is incapacitated from functioning in the world and is advised to avoid those situations "for which he is not perfectly fitted" (TMS VI.iii.19). And thus Smith reaffirms his fundamental lesson: that the deficiencies of the virtues characteristic of one gender can be remediated only by the perfections characteristic of the other – itself another manifestation of Smith's commitments not only to ethical and psychological moderation but also to a dialectic that encourages transcendence of partial or particular views and attempts to understand problems in their totality (cf. TMS VI.i.15; TMS VII.ii.4.2–3; TMS VII.i.1).

Smith's propensity to synthesis of this type is evident in several of his models of actual human greatness, each of which emphasizes the synthesis of moral categories that seem irreconcilable. Smith famously regarded Hume "as approaching as nearly to the idea of a perfectly wise and virtuous man, as perhaps the nature of human frailty will permit." Hume's perfection lay precisely in his capacity to balance "magnanimity" free of "parade" or "affect" with "cheerfulness." Smith reiterates the point in noting that his friend exhibited not only the "steadiness" characteristic of self-command but also the "gentleness" characteristic of benevolence – a combination that prompted Hume's "acts both of charity and generosity" (CAS 178).[16] Another of Smith's eulogies makes the same point. In 1758 Smith was commissioned to compose a largely forgotten dedication to an edition of William Hamilton's *Poems on Several Occasions*. In celebrating the character of Mr. William Craufurd, "merchant in Glasgow," Smith represents his friend's friend as an ideal synthesis of the commercial, classical, and Christian virtues, joining an "exact frugality" and "downright probity and plainness of manners," to "a magnanimity" that supported a "cheerfulness of temper" amidst death's pains, to an "openness of hand and a generosity of heart that was free both from vanity and from weakness" (EPS, p. 262).[17]

Smith's synthesis may also be understood in another way. In addition to calling us to rethink the division of labor between the masculine and the feminine virtues, Smith calls us to rethink love itself – particularly the sort of love that is most necessary for a flourishing social order. Smith's name of course is hardly synonymous with love; indeed his critique of erotic love is sufficient to render him one of the least erotic philosophers to have written. His claims that eros is "ludicrous" (LJA iii.21), "ridiculous" (TMS I.ii.2.1), "partly loathsome, partly ridiculous" (LJB 103), and characterized by "grossness" (TMS I.ii.2.2), coupled with his insistence that strong expressions of it are "upon every occasion indecent" (TMS I.ii.1.2), are evidence of Smith's departure from Platonic conceptions in particular.[18] To some degree, he is more friendly to the classical ideal of friendship in the form of *philia*; his

---

[16] Schliesser's comprehensive study of the letter ("Obituary of a Vain Philosopher") helpfully demonstrates how Smith's portrait of Hume reflects its author's attachments to heroism and magnanimity (345–47) and to a propensity to regard philosophy as an extension of generosity or benefaction (328, 336–37, 343–44). The latter point is further developed in Schliesser's discussion of WN as "a work of political philosophy, in service of the working poor" which "presupposes a commitment to a certain kind of public benevolence and humanity" ("Smith's Conception of Philosophy," in *New Voices*, ed. Montes and Schliesser, 342–43). For reasons discussed later, I think WN is better understood as the work of a wise and virtuous man rather than a "philosopher," but I fully agree with Schliesser that WN is best regarded as an expression of beneficence.

[17] McCloskey nicely treats this dedication in "Adam Smith, the Last of the Former Virtue Ethicists," 54.

[18] On Smith's critique of eros as evidence of his distance from the ancients, see esp. Den Uyl and Griswold, "Smith on Friendship and Love," 628, 633; Griswold, *Smith and the Virtues of Enlightenment*, 147–53; and Nussbaum, *Upheavals of Thought: The Intelligence of Emotions* (Cambridge: Cambridge University Press, 2001), 463–70. In response, see Brubaker's useful reminder that Smith "is neither for nor against *eros* in the abstract" ("'Particular Turn or Habit'," in *Love and Friendship*, ed. Velásquez, 240).

denigration of the false friendships of the young founded on fleeting affections, his distinction of genuine friendships from business partnerships, and his celebration of the sort of friendships that are "founded upon the love of virtue" and "can exist only among men of virtue" who consider each other "the natural and proper objects of esteem and approbation" are reminiscent of Aristotle's concept of friendship (TMS VI.ii.1.16–18). Yet Smith's reconceptualization of love is more complex than a mere trade of Plato for Aristotle. To some degree this is suggested in his reiterations that individual happiness depends on – and even, perhaps, is one with – the consciousness that one is loved (TMS I.ii.4.1–2; TMS I.ii.5.1). Yet love plays a crucial, if underappreciated, role in Smith's vision of the flourishing social order as well as the flourishing life. This view is most clearly presented in a crucial passage in TMS II:

It is thus that man, who can subsist only in society, was fitted by nature to that situation for which he was made. All the members of human society stand in need of each others assistance, and are likewise exposed to mutual injuries. Where the necessary assistance is reciprocally afforded from love, from gratitude, from friendship, and esteem, the society flourishes and is happy. All the different members of it are bound together by the agreeable bands of love and affection, and are, as it were, drawn to one common centre of mutual good offices. (TMS II.ii.3.1)

Studies of Smith have tended to focus on the argument that follows this claim, namely the insistence that, in a society "without any mutual love or affection," a stable "though less happy and agreeable" social order "may still be upheld by a mercenary exchange of good offices according to an agreed valuation" (TMS II.ii.3.2), and for obvious reason. The society of mutual dependence described there is clearly the civilized society in which we each stand "at all times in need of the cooperation and assistance of great multitudes" that is described at length in the *Wealth of Nations*, and which of course rests precisely on the reciprocal exchange of goods and services mediated by price-signals (WN I.ii.2). Yet in taking up Smith's invitation to compare these two societies, it is clear that he sees the latter as decidedly second-best; however stable, it hardly "flourishes and is happy" in the robust sense indicated here. Smith of course is sincere in his devotion to the second-best society as the best possible, and he never suggests that a society built on reciprocal love and esteem has existed or could exist. Yet what makes Smith helpful is his capacity to explain what is at stake in choosing this path, and precisely what its citizens might stand to lose. His delineation of the best society from the best possible society, coupled with his identification of the loving society as the flourishing society, is sufficient to suggest both that the conditions of life in a society that despises love must be inimical to genuine human flourishing, and that a society that hopes to preserve the hope of flourishing must recover some degree of love. Smith's vision of the wise and virtuous man's role in commercial society suggests a means by which some modicum of this love might be recovered, thereby forestalling the corruption, or degradation, of such a society.

Smith describes this role in two separate accounts of the wise and virtuous man's excellence. The first lies at the heart of TMS VI.iii and is perhaps best regarded as a synthesis of three discrete claims which to this point have been largely treated separately: first, that appreciation of the divine is necessary for an appreciation of perfection; second, that an appreciation of perfection induces a healthy humility; and third, that the practical effect of such humility is active beneficence. The first claim is introduced by a repetition of Smith's familiar claim that in judging merit we can take recourse to either or both of two standards: first, "the idea of exact propriety and perfection," and second, "that degree of approximation to this idea which is commonly attained in the world" (TMS VI.iii.23). This conception, of course, merely repeats the central claim of his discussion of the art critic: namely that, in judging human productions, we may evaluate them either by "the common degree of excellence which is usually attained in this particular art," or by "an idea of perfection" which "neither that nor any other human work will ever come up to" (TMS I.i.5.9–10). In both cases, the aim of attending to the two standards is the same: namely to induce a humbling recognition of the limits of human endeavor in the light of perfection. Yet the methods of apprehending such perfection, as well as its implications for ethical activity, deserve close scrutiny. Smith's very decision to speak of "perfection" is itself perhaps surprising; at first glance, the language of perfection seems to sit uneasily next to his seeming skepticism. Yet the route he describes to pursue the idea of perfection is uniquely faithful to both the empirical epistemology he elsewhere professes and the longing for nobility and perfection in which he is equally invested:

The wise and virtuous man directs his principal attention to the first standard; the idea of exact propriety and perfection. There exists in the mind of every man, an idea of this kind, gradually formed from his observations upon the character and conduct both of himself and of other people. It is the slow, gradual, and progressive work of the great demigod within the breast, the great judge and arbiter of conduct. This idea is in every man more or less accurately drawn, its colouring is more or less just, its outlines are more or less exactly designed, according to the delicacy and acuteness of that sensibility, with which those observations were made, and according to the care and attention employed in making them. In the wise and virtuous man they have been made with the most acute and delicate sensibility, and the utmost care and attention have been employed in making them. Every day some feature is improved; every day some blemish is corrected. He has studied this idea more than other people, he comprehends it more distinctly, he has formed a much more correct image of it, and is much more deeply enamoured of its exquisite and divine beauty. (TMS VI.iii.25)

Several elements of this account are striking. The first is that apprehension of perfection is hardly the province of a philosophical elite; this idea rather exists, as Smith twice says, in "every man."[19] Second, although this idea is rendered clearer by a certain type of intellectual activity, that activity is much different from the activities of those who aspire to apprehend the forms. Philosophical contemplation is here replaced by an earnest and sustained observation of everyday life. Put differently, consistent with the epistemology developed elsewhere, the account sketched here teaches that perfection is only perceived through the empirical study of the ordinary.[20] The confluence of the two positions is a deeply hopeful and optimistic conception of our capacity to "see" greatness, for not only is this idea "in" each of us from the beginning, but its development depends neither on a revelation nor a refined reason that belongs only to the few; apprehension of "exquisite and divine beauty" is, on Smith's account, within the grasp of all whose love of such beauty is sufficiently strong to sustain them in their quest.[21]

The wise and virtuous man's study of the idea of perfection is, furthermore, not an idle one; his researches shape his actions. In particular these researches prompt a specific self-conception that in turn prompts a specific type of action. So, far from being satisfied with the contemplation of perfection, the wise and virtuous man chiefly values the study of perfection insofar as it provides him a standard against which to evaluate himself. In so doing, the wise and virtuous man undertakes the central challenge of virtue: namely the struggle to achieve a proper estimation of one's self and one's own value, unalloyed by the distortions characteristic of self-love. In this respect, his

---

[19] Cf. Plato, *Republic*, 518c.

[20] And thus a development of Smith's claim, expressed elsewhere, that morality has its origin in "those more vague and indeterminate ideas of what is prudent, of what is decent, of what is generous or noble, which we carry constantly about with us," and which are refined to the level of the "general maxims of morality" via "experience and induction" (TMS VII.iii.2.6). Hence, Smith's account of the origins of our understanding of beauty and morality is consistent with his accounts of empirical observation and experience as a departure point for inquiry (see, e.g., HAP 2; Senses 69).

[21] Smith's claim that this quest requires fortitude and perseverance suggests that prudence and magnanimous self-command are themselves indispensable to the aspirant to wisdom and virtue.

researches into the nature of perfection are specifically meant to transcend the destructive arrogance and "complete self-satisfaction" characteristic of the magnanimous man (TMS III.3.27):

He endeavours as well as he can, to assimilate his own character to this archetype of perfection. But he imitates the work of a divine artist, which can never be equalled. He feels the imperfect success of all his best endeavours, and sees, with grief and affliction, in how many different features the mortal copy falls short of the immortal original. He remembers, with concern and humiliation, how often, from want of attention, from want of judgment, from want of temper, he has, both in words and actions, both in conduct and conversation, violated the exact rules of perfect propriety; and has so far departed from that model, according to which he wished to fashion his own character and conduct. When he directs his attention towards the second standard, indeed, that degree of excellence which his friends and acquaintances have commonly arrived at, he may be sensible of his own superiority. But, as his principal attention is always directed towards the first standard, he is necessarily much more humbled by the one comparison, than he ever can be elevated by the other. (TMS VI.iii.25)

The idea of perfection thus serves, on some basic level, to induce humility. Yet his is a certain kind of humility. It is not the humility of "idiotism," marked by a propensity to undervalue merit, and thus tending to abasement (TMS VI.iii.49); the wise and virtuous man is always "sensible of his own superiority." What is distinctive about his humility is rather that it is the product of a recognition of his limits – a recognition that is itself the product of his profound consciousness not only of the limits of human pride but also of the difference, more fundamentally, between God and man.

The significance of this recognition cannot be underestimated. In the first place it tempers the propensity to excessive self-estimation to which the man of superior talents is prone. It also reiterates the central danger posed by the tendency to "worship" wealth in commercial societies: such worship flattens our horizons, and by placing the objects of our worship within easy reach, obviates both the salutary check on certain passions and the salutary stimulus of others that a concept of a transcendent excellence provides (TMS I.iii.3.1–2); rendering the other-worldly this-worldly, that is, obviates any possibility of transcendence, and thus greatness, itself.[22] Even this fails to

---

[22] A further relevance of TMS VI.iii.25 must also be noted. One of the most vexing questions in Smith scholarship concerns his religious beliefs. While not the subject of this book, TMS VI.iii.25 bears centrally on the question of whether and how much these can be said to have changed over time. One time-honored claim is that Smith's decision to modify in the sixth edition the passage at TMS II.ii.3.12 concerning Christ's Atonement is evidence of his increasing skepticism toward revealed religion (see, e.g., Raphael and Macfie's "Introduction" to the Glasgow edition of TMS, 19; Raphael, *Impartial Spectator*,

touch on the most important aspect of his recognition, however. So, far from leading a wise and virtuous man to either resentment or resignation,

96–100). This may be true (though it should also be noted that Smith's substituted statement, insofar as it merely presents a version of the argument from universal consent, may just as soon attest to Smith's appreciation of the anthropological necessity of religion). More importantly, though, one would want to note that it is not, strictly speaking, true to say that the passage on the Atonement is dropped from the sixth edition. TMS VI.iii.24–25 is itself a reworking of the "dropped" material from TMS II.ii.3.12. This is signaled in part in textual details: TMS VI.iii.24–25 preserves intact several idiosyncratic locutions (including "weakness and imperfection" and "still greater imperfection") present in the original TMS II.ii.3.12, but not, so far as I have been able to discover, used elsewhere in any other edition of TMS. But what is far more important, TMS VI.iii.25 takes up, in the passage quoted, the central theme of the deleted passage, and in particular the following claim:

Man, when about to appear before a being of infinite perfection, can feel but little confidence in his own merit, or in the imperfect propriety of his own conduct. In the presence of his fellow-creatures, he may often justly elevate himself, and may often have reason to think highly of his own character and conduct, compared to the still greater imperfection of theirs. But the case is quite different when about to appear before his infinite Creator. To such a being, he can scarce imagine, that his littleness and weakness should ever seem to be the proper object, either of esteem or of reward. But he can easily conceive, how the numberless violations of duty, of which he has been guilty, should render him the proper object of aversion and punishment; neither can he see any reason why the divine indignation should not be let loose without any restraint, upon so vile an insect, as he is sensible that he himself must appear to be. (TMS, pp. 92)

Smith's central claim in TMS VI.iii.25 is merely a reiteration of the original claim that pride before men cannot be sustained before the divine. The sixth edition passage of course makes an important change. In the original passage, the weakness of man is taken as evidence of our dependence on the mercy of God and the recognition of our need for atonement in light of the weakness of human endeavor, where the final version emphasizes less the submission to and acceptance of mercy but rather a need for active beneficence toward inferiors. But so far from indicative of a loss of faith, it would seem that the reconsideration of the themes of TMS II.ii.3.12 reflects rather an abandonment of the quietism or fatalism of the earlier position, and a greater emphasis on active beneficence. This is further suggested in another passage newly added to the sixth edition, TMS II.iii.3.4–5, itself distinguished as the second major revision on which Smith was silent in the sixth edition's "Advertisement." In the sixth edition, on the heels of his account of the human *telos* at TMS II.iii.3.3, Smith inserts an additional passage (TMS II.iii.3.4–5) that glosses his account of how man has been taught by nature "to reverence the happiness of his brethren." Here he claims that "the wisdom of Nature" has rendered the happiness of all innocent men "holy" and "consecrated" and that all violations of the innocent require "some atonement in proportion to the greatness of such undesigned violation." In this case, atonement is the product of beneficent performance of "every good office" possible – the remission of sin thus comes from good works rather than divine forgiveness, "the mercy of God" (TMS, p. 92). This is of course an important shift, but the persistence of Smith's interests in violation, forgiveness, beneficence, and atonement here mitigates the more thoroughgoing conclusions that one may be tempted to reach on the basis of Smith's reworking of TMS II.ii.3.12 alone (though cf. Minowitz, *Profits, Priests, and Princes*, 194–95).

despair, or defiance, his reevaluation of his self-worth in light of the divine determines his orientation and actions toward others. A wise and virtuous man who can "discover no ground for arrogance and presumption, but a great deal for humility, regret and repentance" is hardly condemned to the misery and despair that have been associated with "moral saints" (TMS VI.iii.24).[23] On the contrary, his humility is itself a motive for a specific sort of action. The reevaluation of his worth via comparison to the divine affords him not only a profound appreciation of the distance between God and man but also a recognition of his essential equality with other men. The recognition of this equality, in turn, leads him to act toward others in a manner characterized by a certain type of beneficence. Such beneficence is free, first of all, of the sentimentalism of compassion and pity.[24] It is also free from the condescension inevitable in benefactions in which either a self-consciousness of superiority or a desire to claim nobility enables benefactors to reap goods greater than the merely useful goods that they distribute. The wise and virtuous man is a benefactor, to be sure, but one of a very different sort:

He is never so elated as to look down with insolence even upon those who are really below him. He feels so well his own imperfection, he knows so well the difficulty with which he attained his own distant approximation to rectitude, that he cannot regard with contempt the still greater imperfection of other people. Far from insulting over their inferiority, he views it with the most indulgent commiseration, and, by his advice as well as example, is at all times willing to promote their further advancement. If, in any particular qualification, they happen to be superior to him (for who is so perfect as not to have many superiors in many different qualifications?), far from envying their superiority, he, who knows how difficult it is to excel, esteems and honours their excellence, and never fails to bestow upon it the full measure of applause which it deserves. His whole mind, in short, is deeply impressed, his whole behaviour and deportment are distinctly stamped with the character of real modesty; with that of a very moderate estimation of his own merit, and, at the same time, of a full sense of the merit of other people. (TMS VI.iii.25)

In this portrait – the peak of his account of human excellence – Smith brings together several of the fundamental categories of our inquiry. First,

[23] For a study of unhealthy pretensions to perfectionism and the unhappiness they produce, see Wolf, "Moral Saints," in *Virtue Ethics*, ed. Crisp and Slote, 79.

[24] Although it seems correct to say that Smith thinks "the perfection of a human being is ultimately intelligible in terms of doing good to others," his efforts to ground the wise and virtuous man's benefaction in a form of commitment more substantial than sentimentality suggests his goodness was hardly "'goodness' in its homeliest sense" (Cropsey, *Polity and Economy*, 10, 63). Bullard helpfully locates this aspect of the wise and virtuous man in a tradition of reflection on modesty in the conclusion to "'Physiognomy of the Mind'."

his portrait offers a glimpse of how a single inquirer might combine both descriptive and prescriptive modes of inquiry; the wise and virtuous man, moving serially from empirical observation, to norm derivation, to practical action, replicates in his own inquiry the discrete stages of inquiry that define the trajectory of Smith's inquiry. On the level of substantive ethical categories, the transcendence of the distortions of self-love enables the wise and virtuous man to recognize the merit and excellence of others free from envy, and convinces him of his status as one of the multitude. At the same time, this recognition inspires him with the actuating principle of charity in which the recognition of others' value sustains his dedication to practical betterment of their conditions.[25] In so doing, the wise and virtuous man transcends both the inefficacious sentimentalism of the pitier and the arrogance and indifference of the magnanimous man. His charity distinguishes his beneficence as "proper" (TMS III.6.11–12), just as his dedication to promoting the advancement of others fulfills our duty to promote the betterment of others' "external circumstances" (TMS II.iii.3.3).

Herein also lies, it must be noted, the reason why Smith's concept of beneficence, and indeed his concept of the wise and virtuous man, can properly be said to be Christian. Transcending self-preference, or vulgar self-love, is only half of this excellence; the other half lies in his appreciation of a "full sense of the merit of other people." But what exactly does this mean? It is easy to hear certain familiar concepts in this locution. On the one hand, it resonates with ears accustomed to a contemporary, secular conception of "equality" and "human dignity." On the other hand, some may hear in it a celebration of "common" or "ordinary" life. Yet neither of these familiar conceptions captures what is distinctive in his orientation. The wise and virtuous man is not merely tolerant of or respectful toward others. To have a "full sense" of the "excellence" and "merit" and even "superiority" of others is to recognize that no human being can properly be called "ordinary," and indeed to recognize that nothing about human life or any human being can properly be said to be "common."[26] Those who aspire to appreciate the "full sense of the merit" of others necessarily regard such perspectives as condescending. So too, from this perspective, a community

---

[25] I am grateful to the reviewer who pointed out that Smith's comments on commiseration (some of which were quoted earlier) are frequently qualified; see, e.g., his qualification "scarce ever" (rather than "never") at TMS III.3.18, and his qualifications of "not commonly" and "seldom" at TMS IV.1.11. Such locutions naturally prompt one to wonder what exceptions to this rule Smith may have had in mind. It may be that the wise and virtuous man is himself the principal exception to the general rule of "pure sympathy."

[26] Pieper, *Faith, Hope, Love*, 279.

built on the mere negative respect for laws or rights seems wanting. The Platonic tradition, with its image of Socrates' willingness to obey the death sentence of the Athenians; the Stoic tradition, with its injunction to each to appreciate his relative significance in the cosmos; the modern liberal tradition, with its emphasis on the preservation of the equal rights of others: each of these contributes to the cultivation of an appreciation of the necessity of restraining self-preference. Yet it is difficult to see where, other than the religious tradition of his society – and specifically its claim, examined earlier, that God has, in creating man, "created him after his own image" (TMS III.2.31) – Smith could have derived the idea that the cultivation of an appreciation of the "full sense of the merit" of others is a goal to which those ambitious for the best possible life might properly aspire.[27]

A final fact of the wise and virtuous man deserves recognition. The orientation to praise has proven to be a key ground for discriminating the vain from the magnanimous, but it is no less so a key means of distinguishing the magnanimous from the wise and the virtuous. Indeed one of the defining features of the wise and virtuous man is exactly the transcendence of the love of recognition that unites both the esteem-loving vain and the nobility-loving magnanimous men. In sharp contrast, to be confirmed in "wisdom and real philosophy" is precisely to have cultivated an indifference to recognition, deserved or not (see, e.g., TMS I.iii.2.8; TMS I.iii.3.2). Such a confirmation in the first instance enables the wise and virtuous man to

[27] Two caveats are necessary: first, to say that Smith's conception of beneficence is properly regarded as a Christian conception is not to say that Smith was a Christian. Second, while I have sought to emphasize the theological commitments implicit in Smith's idea of the wise and virtuous man, I see nothing incompatible in this vision with a position common to other Western and non-Western religious or spiritual traditions, including Judaism and Confucianism (on which see the studies cited in this chapter, Note 5). The crucial point has been stated in more general terms by Lovejoy in his largely overlooked remark that Smith follows Milton in believing that "the moral consciousness finds its completion in the religious consciousness" (*Reflections on Human Nature*, 264; cf. Berns, "Aristotle and Smith on Justice," 86n17). Dickey is among the few commentators to develop this point; see his excellent discussion of how TMS VI.iii.25 is grounded in an "ethico-teleological argument" that suggests the influence of Protestant theology ("Historicizing the 'Adam Smith Problem'," 604–9; Alvey helpfully contrasts the Lovejoy-Dickey reading with the dominant view in "The 'New View' of Adam Smith," 78–79). Dickey's interpretation has been lambasted as "ludicrous" (Raphael, "Adam Smith 1790," 115) and dismissed for having gone "far astray" (Minowitz, *Profits, Priests, and Princes*, 310n2); but quibbles over the particular provenance of Smith's theological commitments aside, Dickey's intuitions regarding Smith's commitments to teleology and transcendence strike me as accurate and insightful. For an introduction to Smith's theological context that illuminates some aspects of this provenance, see Pete Clarke, "Adam Smith, Religion, and the Scottish Enlightenment," in *New Perspectives*, ed. Cockfield et al., 47–65.

persevere in the face of the indifference and lack of gratitude that he knows are the likely recompense he can expect from his benefactions. Thus, "to act with cool deliberation in the midst of the greatest dangers and difficulties; to observe religiously the sacred rules of justice in spite both of the greatest interests which might tempt, and the greatest injuries which might provoke us to violate them; never to suffer the benevolence of our temper to be damped or discouraged by the malignity and ingratitude of the individuals towards whom it may have been exercised; is the character of the most exalted wisdom and virtue" (TMS VI.iii.11). Such a disposition not only enables the wise and virtuous man to act for higher motives than immediate reward; it also enables him to see another happiness beyond that available to the men of excessive self-admiration. "The excessive self-admiration of those great men is well understood, perhaps, and even seen through, with some degree of derision, by those wise men who are much in their familiarity, and who secretly smile at those lofty pretensions, which, by people at a distance, are often regarded with reverence, and almost with adoration" (TMS VI.iii.27). Wisdom and virtue thus hold out the best prospects for promoting not only the happiness of others but also the happiness of its possessor. And from this we might take away one lesson above all. The activities characteristic of wisdom and virtue have as little to do with the pursuit of honor or glory as they do with the pursuit of knowledge abstracted from human affairs. Put differently, both virtue and wisdom, taken separately, are insufficient; in their synthesis lies their perfection.[28]

WISDOM AND VIRTUE AND ADAM SMITH'S APOLOGY

The central claim of the portrait of the wise and virtuous man in TMS is that his contemplation culminates in action. In accord with this claim, Smith's practical writings offer a glimpse of the wise and virtuous man at work. These portraits themselves testify to the fact that the account of the wise and virtuous man, so far from an eccentric moment of hyperbole of the aged Smith, represents an ideal that is central to his political economy as well as to his moral philosophy. His most developed such portrait is to be found in the *Lectures on Jurisprudence*, and specifically in its treatment of interdependence and division of labor at LJA vi.19–24. As this passage would in time form the basis of WN I.i–ii, it should be noted that Smith here introduces the peak

---

[28] See also Brubaker, "'Particular Turn or Habit'," in *Love and Friendship*, ed. Velásquez, 251, 257. My view is closest to that of Brubaker when he writes that "there is little if anything in [Smith's] discussion of the virtues that requires wisdom in the sense of philosophy" (245).

ideal of his ethics concurrent with his introduction to the central claims of his economics. The main economic claim made in the LJ passage is that all elements of society, high and low alike, are bound together in an interdependence that unites their efforts to provide themselves with the necessaries on which the sustenance of life depends. Such efforts, Smith notes, we often "look upon as the objects of the labour of the vulgar alone" (LJA vi.18). Yet they are hardly ignoble; thus, he reminds us that "law and government have these as their final end and ultimate object." His striking redefinition of the ends of political life here is itself superseded by the even more striking redefinition of excellence that follows: "Even wisdom and virtue in all its branches derive their lustre and beauty with regard to utility merely from their tendency to provide for the security of mankind in these conveniencies" (LJA vi.18–19; cf. LJB 210–11). Smith then reiterates the point:

In a certain view of things all the arts, the sciences, law and government, wisdom, and even virtue itself tend all to this one thing, the providing meat, drink, raiment, and lodging for men, which are commonly reckoned the meanest of employments and fit for the pursuit of none but the lowest and meanest of the people. (LJA vi.20–21)

Here Smith provides his most direct illustration of what it means for a wise and virtuous man to better the external circumstances of others and thereby "promote their further advancement" (TMS VI.iii.25). Put simply: the duty of the greatest is service to the least. At the same time, the manner in which this is done, the great are called to realize, is as much an aspect of excellence as the very act of bestowing such services. Smith is profoundly aware that the sort of services that the great frequently render to the least – what both in his day and our own fall under the category of "charity" – are often more condescending than loving. Appropriating an insight common to the Aristotelian and the Christian and the Maimonidean conceptions of philanthropy, Smith is aware that "to receive a present is a sign of dependence and inferiority, as it brings the receiver under an obligation to the donor" (LJA iv.32–33). He knows too that a philanthropist's distribution of useful goods is often motivated by a love of honor and a love of superiority; thus his contrast between a "proud minister of an ostentatious court" who "may frequently take pleasure in executing a work of splendour and magnificence," and a much more admirable sort of benefaction, the sort characteristic of those who "execute a great number of little works, in which nothing that can be done can make any great appearance, or excite the smallest degree of admiration in any traveler" – the sort of work, that is, which the more grandiose benefactor is likely to consider "in every respect too mean and paltry to merit the attention" of the great and influential (WN V.i.d.16). Thus the challenge of the wise and virtuous man and any other aspirant to proper beneficence: to discover means of providing others with useful goods while ensuring that such philanthropic benefactions remain free of both condescension and a desire for recognition.

But where is such a benefactor to be found? And one might also ask: how does Smith's own life compare to that of his wise and virtuous man? Put differently, how can Smith justify the life he led in the light of the best life that he describes? Any answer to this question is complicated by Smith's death-bed destruction of his work, as well as his reticence in correspondence. But in the few glimpses we have of his life, we can see not merely "humanity" but a dedication to several discrete elements of the wise and virtuous man's excellence.[29] The aged author of the sixth edition clearly aspired to transcend censure and applause, evident in a letter to his publisher insisting that he was "almost perfectly indifferent both as to praise and as to abuse" (CAS 294; cf. CAS 31; CAS 88; CAS, p. 414). Of his humility we have several examples as well – from his insistence to his publisher that his name be given plainly on a title page, without associations or affiliations (CAS 100); to his indifference to the gossip of the literary journals (LRBL, p. 230); to his insistence that his gravestone, in contrast to Hume's, contain only the titles of his books; to his reticence in correspondence to dwell long on "the worst of all subjects, ones self" (CAS 158). Of his dedication to others we also have testimony from both his students and his own insistence that he came "under no engagements which I look upon as so sacred as those by which I am bound as a member of this University to do everything in my power to serve the young people who are sent here to study, such especially as are particularly recommended to my care" (CAS 37; cf. CAS 35 and CAS 43). And most importantly, Smith's philanthropy was of a sort that a wise and virtuous man could approve; an apparently frequent and generous giver, he took considerable care to make his benefactions anonymously.[30]

[29] A critical account of Smith's failure to live up to the duties of beneficence and justice characteristic of the wise and virtuous man, focusing specifically on his reticence to publish Hume's *Dialogues*, is provided in T. D. Campbell and Ian Ross, "The Theory and Practice of the Wise and Virtuous Man: Reflections on Adam Smith's Response to Hume's Deathbed Wish," *Studies in Eighteenth-Century Culture* 11 (1982): 65–74. Ross and Campbell helpfully note that Smith's portrait of the wise and virtuous man "serve[s] to indicate the direction of his normative ethics in the latter years of his life" (65), but their claim that Smith's "ultimate normative principle is utilitarian" (66–67) leads to an account of Smith's normative commitments substantially different from the one I develop here.

[30] See Ross, *Life of Adam Smith* (Oxford: Oxford University Press, 1992), 407; Rae, *Life of Smith*, 437.

All of these episodes reflect various commitments of the wise and virtuous man, from his preference for self-approbation over external recognition, to his consciousness of the sacredness of the duties of those in superior stations. Yet ultimately Smith's claim to wisdom and virtue must be evaluated on the grounds of his life's principal work. Thus our final claim: the authorship of *The Wealth of Nations* entitles Smith to claim the mantle of wisdom and virtue for himself – which is at once to say that his turn from philosophy proper to political economy is itself best understood through the perspective afforded by the example of the wise and virtuous man.[31] This claim is best developed through a more specific claim: namely that the philosopher *in* the WN is also best understood through the lens of the wise and virtuous man. Smith sets forth his vision of the philosopher in WN I.ii, itself an elaboration of the discussion of economic interdependence in LJA vi.18–21, examined earlier. This philosopher is unintelligible through the conventional categories of the philosophical life, or even through the contemporary association of "philosophy" with natural philosophy, or experimental science.[32] So far from seeking either the self-sufficiency characteristic of the classical philosophical life or even the proud power of the modern philosophical life, this philosopher, like the wise and virtuous man, is defined by his acceptance of his equality with others, his recognition of his interdependence with others, and his commitment to helping them meet their needs in a manner commensurate with his excellence and their dignity.

Smith's formal argument here begins with his well-known insistence on natural human equality; like Rousseau, he claims that men are (largely) equal by nature and are rendered unequal by the institutions of civilization: "The difference of natural talents in different men is, in reality, much less than we are aware of," for the obvious inequalities among men are "not upon many occasions so much the cause, as the effect of the division of labour." Of course Smith, unlike Rousseau, insists that moderate inequality is beneficial because it provides the necessary stimulus to ensure that the world's work gets done. But as a moralist, Smith's aim here is quite Rousseauan. Like Rousseau, he seeks to humble the philosopher's pride, reminding readers that "the difference between the most dissimilar characters, between a philosopher and

---

[31] This claim has been strikingly underdeveloped. For rare exceptions, see Raphael's brief account of the normative aspects of the wise and virtuous man (*Impartial Spectator*, 79); and Dickey's brief comment on Smith's "identification" in the sixth edition with the wise man charged to direct vanity ("Historicizing the 'Adam Smith Problem'," 598).

[32] Thus Griswold's helpful claim: "Smitheans are calling into question the Platonic standpoint from which the inadequacy of the Smithean is pronounced" ("Reply to My Critics," *Perspectives on Political Science* 30 (2001): 165).

a common street porter" arises "not so much from nature, as from habit, custom, and education" – even if "the vanity of the philosopher is willing to acknowledge scarce any resemblance" (WN I.ii.4). But for all the vituperation of this rhetoric, Smith is moved here by something other than mere antiphilosophical ire; his goal is to compel philosophers in an age of interdependence to reconsider their orientation to others, and particularly to see that, in complex commercial societies, "the most dissimilar geniuses are of use to one another" (WN I.ii.5).

It is easy to see how a porter may be of use to a philosopher. It is more difficult to imagine the obverse: how exactly is a philosopher of use to a porter? Smith provides an explicit answer in his lectures and in so doing points to a place in commercial society not merely for the mercenary exchange of good offices, but for proper beneficence:

Even the philosopher and the porter are mutually beneficial to each other. The porter assists the philosopher not only by carrying to him what he wants; but by his assistance in packing, carrying, and unpacking the goods which fill the shops and warehouses of the merchants he makes every thing the philosopher buys come so much cheaper than if a less diligent workman had been employed. The philosopher again benefits the porter not only as being occasionally a customer, but by the improvements he makes in the different arts. Every one who burns coals or eats bread is benefited by the philosopher who invented the fire engine or the corn mill; and those who do not invent any engines or improve upon them are beneficial as they preserve the knowledge of the idea for others, or as they form plans of improvement for other sciences. (LJA vi.47–49; cf. LJB 220–21; ED 29–31)

Smith's aim here is twofold. First he means to remind the philosopher, amidst his self-sufficiency, of his debts to the unseen many who perform the labor, once performed by slaves, that enables him to enjoy the leisure and comfort necessary for his life. But even more significantly, Smith means to expose the other half of the equation: namely that true philosophy benefits the nonphilosophical. Its specific benefit lies in the harnessing of the powers of nature for the benefit of the ordinary human life. Thus his portrait of "philosophers or men of speculation, whose trade it is, not to do any thing, but to observe every thing," and "who, upon that account, are often capable of combining together the powers of the most distant and dissimilar objects" (WN I.i.9). Herein lie the two fundamental elements of philosophy, on Smith's account: a synthesis, or "combining together," of observations, and a resulting discovery of new principles of productivity, or "powers." These fundamental elements unite Smith's conceptions of philosophy from his definition of it in the *Astronomy* as "the science of the connecting principles of nature," to his celebration of those philosophers in the "Early Draft" who are "capable of combining together the powers of the most opposite and distant objects" – a celebration that itself comes in a passage that mentions "power" five times (HA II.11–12; ED 19–20).

Each of these conceptions of philosophy emerges from Smith's belief in the superiority of active beneficence to both universal benevolence and to contemplation that aspires to self-sufficiency. Yet some will be tempted to find in such a conception one or both of two other conceptions. On the one hand, to emphasize the utility of philosophy, particularly when combined with Smith's claim that in advanced societies philosophy is rendered a product of specialized labor "in the same manner as any other commodity," will strike some as a denigration of philosophy to sophistry. Yet even in comparing the production and dissemination of philosophy to the processes by which consumer goods are produced and disseminated, Smith recognizes a difference. First, in claiming that it is the philosopher's duty to provide the public "with all the thought and reason possessed by the vast multitudes that labour," he recognizes the superior influence of philosophers in furnishing an individual with "general ideas concerning the great subjects of religion, morals, and government, concerning his own happiness or that of his country" (ED 30–31). The first of these aims comports well with Smith's understanding of religion as presented in *The Wealth of Nations*; befitting the anticlericalism expressed there, his desire that religion be in the hands of philosophers rather than priests is perhaps unsurprising. But another, less familiar aspect of Smith's understanding of religion is also present here. In his lectures he called explicit attention to "the benefit of religion," particularly for laborers and their children, as "a great advantage, not only considered in a pious sense, but as it affords them subject for thought and speculation" (LJB 330). This claim takes on additional significance in light of his comments on the interdependence of the philosopher and the porter. The general ideas provided by philosophy and religion are useful in a different way than that in which either manufactured goods or sophistic wisdom usefully gratify our desires. The use of philosophy, in the first instance, lies in its ability to speak to what Smith considers to be universal natural longings for knowledge on the "great subjects" that concern our truest interests.

The more serious potential critique of Smith's conception of philosophy concerns the implications of its emphasis on the harnessing of latent powers and the discovery and invention of new ones through observation and synthesis; such a conception brings Smith in line, it would seem, with what has come to be known as the "Enlightenment Project," and particularly the Enlightenment's ambition to employ experimental natural science in the relief of man's estate. In one sense, this is precisely Smith's aim – indeed an aim for which he is unapologetic. But does this aim render him merely "modern"? His own reasons for contributing to this project seem to rest on foundations quite different from those of Bacon, Hobbes, and Locke. He is no utopian: knowing the limits of politics, he calls not for the eradication of inequality (which he considers both impossible and undesirable: see LJA iv.23; LJB 20), but the alleviation of poverty. Knowing the limits of philosophy, he seeks not a comprehensive grasp of nature, but a sufficient grasp of the invisible hand that will enable us to achieve those benefits of which we are capable. And knowing both the limits as well as the greatness of the heart, he promotes and embraces a vision of life dedicated to the transcendence of sentimentality through a proper beneficence marked by the benefactor's commitment to the equality and dignity he shares with other human beings. Thus, the aim of the *Wealth of Nations* is to promote the achievement of "that universal opulence which extends itself to the lowest ranks of the people" (WN I.i.10). On these grounds it has been regarded both as an act of justice and by no less a judge than Bentham as a "treatise upon universal benevolence" – a sentiment echoed by the more recent judge who calls it "a charter document of compassion and concern in the development of the social sciences."[33] This is partly right. Yet, crucially, the *Wealth of Nations* is neither merely an expression of universal goodwill nor a work of condescending charity. In describing a method by which universal freedom and independence might be achieved and individuals might thereby have an opportunity to pursue the betterment of their condition, Smith's work stands as a model of how a philosopher might ascend to wisdom and virtue.

---

[33] See E.C. Mossner, *Adam Smith: The Biographical Approach* (Glasgow: University of Glasgow Press, 1969), 18; and Heilbroner, "Paradox of Progress," 539.

EPILOGUE: THE "ECONOMY OF GREATNESS"

The foregoing study sought to develop several propositions with regard to Adam Smith's moral and political philosophy. Stated briefly, these propositions include the claims that Smith was a true friend of capitalism insofar as he not only championed it but also criticized it; that Smith's criticism was fertile rather than sterile insofar as it prompted an extended though unheralded normative remedy; that this normative remedy was founded on a conception of virtue that embraces the greatness and flourishing of the individual in his totality and thus distances Smith from the concerns of classical republicanism and of modern social science; that Smith's conceptions of both the specific vices of commercial society and the specific virtues necessary for its remedy are founded on a reevaluation of self-love; that the dialectical product of this remedy represents a synthesis of commercial and classical and Christian virtues; and that the emulation of the life of the peak of these ethical virtues – that of the wise and virtuous man – was a conscious aim of Smith himself.

In developing these claims, this study has particularly emphasized Smith's propensity to dialectic, or the resolution of seeming opposites through a synthesis that in turn makes possible the realization of new horizons that require our renewed application. This dialectical approach has been evident in Smith's efforts to resolve specific tensions on several levels. As an eighteenth-century moral philosopher, he addresses traditional tensions between egoism and altruism, love of self and love of others, awful virtues and amiable virtues, the masculine and the feminine, and magnanimity and humility. As a student of his civilization, he addresses subtle tensions between ancients and moderns, commerce and Christianity, ethics and economics, and optimism and pessimism. As a philosopher and social scientist, he addresses deep tensions between description and normative advocacy. Some of these tensions, as we have seen, Smith resolves. Others have proven less tractable. Yet here too engagement with his thought is valuable. One of the central aims of Smith's moral philosophy is the harmonization of his competing attachments to excellence and to equality, just as one of the central aims of his political philosophy is the harmonization of his competing attachments to justice and to opulence. In turn, the aim of his philosophical system taken as a whole is not simply the identification of these tensions but the articulation of a hybrid or synthetic system capable of responding to them. His efforts to promote the realization of a true "oeconomy of greatness" (TMS IV.1.10) capable of embracing greatness of both material and moral sorts is best understood as such a response, and Smith thus continues to deserve our attention and esteem for having seen both the intractability and the indispensability of preserving our reverence for opulence and for excellence alike.

Such, I have sought to argue in any case, was Smith's aim. But readers will naturally want to know: was he successful? Is Smith's normative remedy capable of delivering the relief it promises? On the most obvious level, the answer has to be no. Not only are the poor still with us, as they always have been and will be, but we also continue to face the challenges of commercial corruption (evident in our familiar laments of materialism and consumerism) and the misguided love of nobility (evident in our familiar laments of the new religious enthusiasm) so well known to Smith. The fact that we today still grapple with these same ills attests to their persistence, and this will be sufficient to demonstrate to some that, however well intended, his efforts to meet the most pressing practical challenges of politics by authoring a philosophical text were insufficient to obviate such challenges. So too some may object that Smith's assimilation of elements of classical, commercial, and Christian ethical systems, however internally consistent, fails to resolve the deeper tensions that divide these systems. To this objection we reiterate that synthesis is not resolution. Smith's aim was never to demonstrate that the foundational metaphysical tensions that separate the systems with which he engaged might be fully resolved via a final solution. In dedicating himself instead to demonstrating how certain aspects of one system might usefully supplement certain aspects of another, Smith shows himself, as a moral philosopher, rather to have aspired to follow those natural philosophers "capable of combining together the powers of the most opposite and distant objects" for beneficial purposes, thereby illuminating new practical and theoretical horizons that might be further explored by others (ED 19).

The principal scholarly aim of the present work has thus been to illuminate Smith's efforts to achieve such a synthesis, and thereby contribute to what Donald Winch has called "the process of understanding the connections between the overlapping sub-systems that compose Smith's highly ambitious and systematic enterprise."[1] But understanding Smith's intentions on this front is of interest for reasons that go beyond the concerns of specialized scholarship. In particular, those wishing and working for a continued improvement in the conditions of commercial modernity may find at least three reasons to continue to study Smith on this front. First, Smith offers a model for how theory can speak to practice. Whether or not one sympathizes with all aspects of his virtue theory, this theory is distinguished by the fact that it was developed within the context of an appreciation for what is good for human beings absolutely, and yet delivered as an intervention in a specific moral and political debate at a specific historical moment.[2] Insofar as the conditions of contemporary capitalism are in many respects similar to those debated by commercial society's founding fathers, those engaged in the project to ameliorate these conditions stand to gain much from the effort to develop our answers to today's problems in light of their best answers. Second, Smith reminds us of what we might call the non-incompatibility – or, more strongly, the mutual necessity – of normative and descriptive approaches to the study of moral and political phenomena. In both Smith's day and ours these approaches have often been contrasted. Yet Smith's response to commercial corruption suggests a different perspective, one that substitutes for an all-too-common "either/or" approach to political methodology a "both/and" approach – and this for the simple reason that nothing less is required by the nature of the task he set for himself. As argued above, Smith's ambition is never merely the understanding of a problem and the identification of its inherent tensions, but rather the practical solution or amelioration of such a problem to the degree it permits. Such a task compels use of multiple methods; descriptive or scientific analysis is quite as indispensable to the full understanding of the nature and depth of a political problem as normative methods are to subsequent efforts to solve such a problem. The trajectory of Smith's career as a philosopher and author manifests this conviction, and the example of his approach to reform may still prove useful today.

Finally, we do well to continue to study Smith for a substantive reason. Among modern thinkers, Smith may not be alone but he is certainly rare in his commitment to greatness. Many will continue to debate whether his peak of greatness, the wise and virtuous man, is capable of being achieved

---

[1] Winch, "Adam Smith's 'Enduring Particular Result': A Political and Cosmopolitan Perspective," in *Wealth and Virtue*, ed. Hont and Ignatieff, 253.

[2] I am indebted to conversations with Steven Smith for my formulation of this point.

in practice by men like ourselves. But this debate, however important, may well miss the point. Engagement with Smith's account of greatness is not unto itself sufficient to guarantee its realization, but it can reanimate our longing for such – and ultimately it is on our capacity to sustain this longing that the success or failure of commercial society depends.

INDEX

213

virtues (*cont.*)
  feminine, 191 and n, 192, 193, 209
  intellectual, 34–35, 171 and n
  martial, 25, 32, 35
  masculine, 41, 191n, 192, 193, 209
Vivenza, Gloria, 55n, 66n, 75n, 79n, 92n, 115n
von Mises, Ludwig, 24 and n
von Villiez, Carola, 68n

Waszek, Norbert, 75n, 98n
Waterman, A. M. C., 144n
wealth, 2, 12, 18, 22, 27n, 32, 36–37, 41, 47,
  48, 94, 102, 103 and n, 106, 109, 112,
  114–115, 120, 126, 165, 197
Weber, Max, 42
Wellman, Christopher, 53n, 64n
Welsh, Alexander, 145n
Werhane, Patricia H., 31n, 54n, 88n, 101n,
  104n, 148n, 183n
West, Edwin G., 37n, 60n

Winch, Donald, 7n, 15n, 19n, 23n, 27n, 32n,
  33n, 55n, 56n, 58n, 59n, 68n, 95n, 101n,
  108n, 115n, 146n, 210, 211n
wisdom and virtue, 165n, 168, 196n, 202, 203,
  205, 208
wise and virtuous man, 9, 56n, 66, 94, 162n,
  177, 178, 187, 204n, 205n
  character of, 187–202
  Smith as, 202–208
Wodehouse, P. G., 14n
Wokler, Robert, 26n
Wolf, Susan, 150n, 199n
Wolin, Sheldon, 7n

Xenophon, 122

Yankelovich, Daniel, 1n

Zeno, 152–154, 159
Zhang, Wei-Ben, 177n

DATE DUE
